Is Stranged.

LIIAN VARUS

The only thing more depressing
than this book is the fact, you
bought it.

The fuck, Dianna?
Liian Varus

I dedicate this book to my fans, my murder. Without you this book would have never happened. I'm sorry I'm dedicating this piece of shit to you, but I kind of promised my wife and child, I'd dedicate the good book to them. But sincerely, thank you. I'm lucky to have such great friends in my life. Shucks.

"Every myth and legend starts somewhere. For me, it was in the parking lot of a JC Penny's. Kidding. It was in Trenton, Ontario. So, almost as good as a JC Penny's parking lot."

—Liian Varus

I can't believe you bought this fucking book.

Oddities

(WRITE THE PAGE NUMBERS IN YOURSELF)

The Lore...

LIIAN VARUS IS SAD..

  The Whisper Of Flesh...

  Fail To Wave The Anguish.....................................

  Mutant..

  Blood Flux...

  Slash Our Lips Together.......................................

  Drown Me..

  Human Body Swimming Dead................................

  Moth & The Teddy Bear..

  Ripping Skin Symphony...

  Ever-Bloody Doll..

  Regret...

  Dead Script Scroll..

  Necrosis..

  Blood..

Get Back ....

Dead Inside ....

Secluded ....

Blown Echo-Wide ....

Kiss You Forever ....

Scared Child ....

Glass Shards ....

Dark ....

Waste Of Skin ....

Fuck The Angels ....

Nailed ....

Queen Corpse Buried In Snow ....

LIIAN VARUS GOES DARK ....

Next Drop Of Blood ....

Apple Cadavers ....

Hunger & Lust ....

Pieces ....

Goddess That Wept Herself To Destruction ....

Ocean Blue ....

Voices..

Love & Exile...

All For You..

Going Under ....

Casket In A Ruin..

One Beautiful Portrait...

Take Me Back ....

Morning To Paradise (Vampires' Awakening
Serenade)..

Union Underground...

Desperation Of A Lover's Heart..

Lengthening Path Of A Soldier...

Grim Reaper's Persuasion..

Saliva To The Lips...

Filthy Conscience..

Rapture In Paradise...

At The Graveyard..

The Suicidal Fly..

Pretty Girl With Bright Eyes..

Depression for the Grateful....................................

When Zero Comes Thrashing.................................

Mother Serpent...

Lasujah's Decmember...

World Where Everything Dies................................

Circle Of Suicide Goes 'Round..............................

Kill The King And Rape The Queen........................

Paradies...

Silver..

Atlantis...

Vampire Superior...

From Incest To Insects...

Youth Destructed Cold..

Loathed Face...

Filthy Girl...

Red Door, Black Door..

Bloody Mary (The Betraying Whore).....................

Comatose Girl..

Vicious Acts From The Abused.............................

Cupid's Absence Brought Atrocity.................................

Eruptions Of A Serpent Tongue.................................

Wonderland (A Masochist's Well).................................

Paint The World Black.................................

I Promise.................................

KRAKR.................................

Witch Hunt.................................

Julie.................................

Headless Woman In A Coffin.................................

Obsolete.................................

Lambs Tortured Nevermore.................................

Fairytale (Prince Without A Princess).................................

Pack Of Wolves.................................

Put Me Out Of My Misery.................................

Stunning Beyond Misty Falls.................................

S.L.I.T..................................

Listening To The Voice.................................

Hades' Hourglass.................................

Anastasius Lykaios Watches The Sacrificial Fly.................................

Zombie...

Mesmerizing Whore That Wore Bondage Straps...............

The Escape Artist...

Closet Creature..

Elizabeth's Demise..

Slaughtered The Bride To Be.....................................

Overdose On The Poison Rainbow..............................

A Banshee Haunts These Hills...................................

Red As Wine..

I Killed An Angel Today..

LIIAN VARUS LOSES HIS PATHETIC SHELL...........................

Every Guy...

Prescription...

Well Angels...

Blood Pigs...

Lethal STD..

Voodoo Doll Kisses..

Morguetopia...

Lucifer's Thanksgiving Dinner....................................

Sluts Of The Occult..

Ghost Of The Ballet...

The Burning..

Rodents And Insects...

Nightmare..

Accident...

Murder Scene...

Brenna...

Gone...

Violent End To A Peaceful October ....

Pain...

Too Late ....

Mannequin Made...

Safety Pin Butterfly ....

Trust Or Lust?...

Jake Loves Ashley..

Possessed..

Twelve...

Ogre...

Drug Factory..

A Hungry Maggot..

Wounds Of Cupid..

Orchestra Seven...

A Dying Rose That Can't Be Saved...............................

Ms. Macabre..

Diamond In The Dirt...

Black Silk Scarf...

Strangers At First Sight..

Killing Flowers...

Gunshot Ready..

LIIAN VARUS WANTS TO DIE BUT DOESN'T...........................

A Girl And Her Stranger..

My Favourite Gender...

Him..

A Boy Of Bullet Wounds...

LIIAN VARUS MIGHT BE A WRITER AFTER ALL......................

You Live In A Box..

A Girl I've Come To Hate..

Confessional Rot...

Meth Beth...

Self-Destruct Android...

Happy Anniversary (Whore! How Could You?!)...............

Pulse..

Crack Whore Reward...

Actress (Murderer Of Love).....................................

House Of Dead Siblings..

My Pulse For Your Hearse.......................................

Pistols Seem More Attractive....................................

Reanimation..

Haunted...

Dark Flowers...

I Love You And I Hate Myself....................................

Once I Was King..

Ghost Letter..

Without My Prescription..

Far Too Frail..

.44 Calibre Of Mine..

Drowning..

Blue Mercury...

Pinstripes (Dressed To Fuck)...

100mm Cigarette...

Love On All Fours...

I Fell In Love With A Scarecrow...

Boogeyman..

Kiss Me On The Mouth...

New Body Alteration...

Mother..

LIIAN VARUS VERSUS VAGINAS ....

Run (I'm Addicted To You) ....

Holder Of The Zombie Heart...

I Seduce What I Kill...

Corpse Lake...

Autopilot Off...

Groom Kills Bride..

Love Is Absinthe...

Whitechapel Grapes..

Death...

Why Should I Have To Snap Your Neck To Get You To Look At Me?..

As Lovers...

Worms In An Apple..

Mummified...

Secret...

Victims...

Choke Me, Frankenstein......................................

Pack Of Crayons..

Rubik's Cube..

LIIAN VARUS' FOREST..

Lanterns...

A Lobotomy Is A Furnace....................................

Jack-O'-Lantern...

Symbiote (Oh, Love Of Mine)...........................

City Of Desolation...

A Single Kiss To Kill..

Burn Victim..

Identity...

Haunted House..

Felo-De-Se (A Lost Game Of Hangman) ....

Pumpkins & Jack-O'-Lanterns..............................

Cemetery..............................

LIIAN VARUS GRIMM ....

Jill Doesn't Come Tumbling After..............................

Another Android..............................

Black Widow (Along Came A Spider)..............................

The Tower..............................

Glass Impersonator..............................

Three Billy Goats Snuffed..............................

Ringmasters' Sewer Circuses..............................

Red..............................

SeweRat..............................

Let's Kiss..............................

The Relocation Of Necropolis..............................

LIIAN VARUS SURE DOES LOVE HIS REMIXES ....

Medusa (A Gorgon's Last Chance For Love)..............................

Organism..............................

Crows Of Goldilocks..............................

Burial (Proper Funeral Etiquette)..............................

Sirens..

Belle And The Beast...

No Diagnosis...

Hello, Bordello...

Love The Monster...

Infant...

Troll Of All Whores..

Atom And Eve...

Wooden Son...

The Insanity Of John Doe..

Ghost In My Room...

Suffer, Kate Ing...

Bloodlines...

Bleacher ....

LIIAN VARUS TAKES ADVANTAGE OF EVOLUTION ....

Home (Lost Horizon)...

Lust Hunts Me Down Like Feral Dogs...............................

Burrower ....

Deface My Identity (Romance-Scissors).............................

Rabbit Holes ....

LIIAN VARUS TRANSCENDS ....

Debate ....

As We Watch Blood Cascade Into Our Glass Hearts ....

DRAW A PICTURE... ....

The Lore

Originally, Is Stranged. was to be this huge joke. The idea of having a massive book of shitty poetry out there, a book no one in the right mind would ever buy was something I had to do. Too funny not to. This was going to be more than a joke. It was a science experiment. I wondered if a monstrosity as this could gain so many bad reviews and attention, it would gain notoriety as the worst best seller ever published. Then something happened. I saw my chance to help authors and aspiring authors. Writing is hard. It takes practice. Don't think for a second that even the best authors in the world don't have their fair share of garbage hiding around somewhere. You never see it because nobody wants to buy garbage. Fair enough. But it exists. I'm not saying I'm a great author, however, I have come a long way. I want people to see that hard work pays off. So, this is my opportunity to prove that. I had to write a lot of trash before I could write a book, people would love and have respect for. No one is expecting you to write a best seller on your first shot. Remember that. Relax. Breathe. It takes time. For everyone. I compare writing to a clogged drain: You got to get the gunk out before you can tap into your potential, if that makes sense. I must apologize. I'm not one for being prophetic or inspirational. What I can say for sure is, in this book you'll see how I grew as a writer throughout the years, and I hope in some way it helps. I really do. Sincerely. It's also super exciting for me because you get to see how fucking nuts I was. So that'll be fun.

LIIAN VARUS IS SAD

The year was 2002 and I recently discovered the magical world of depression. I was learning to deal with it day by day. Until I met its best friend Anxiety. What a fucking dick. Depression wasn't so bad. Yeah, it was a downer. Kept bitching about its ex-girlfriend Karen. But I could handle it. But then Anxiety would proceed to tell Depression, it's been banging Karen before they even broke up. Depression would intensify. Why it was ever friends with Anxiety I still don't know. Between their toxic bromance, I was trapped. Didn't know what to do so I got a pen and paper and started writing down my feelings, in hopes it would muffle their incessant bickering. Kind of like when you hear your parents having sex so you practically asphyxiate yourself on a pillow, trying to drown out the sounds of how well your mom can take a d... Sorry. I took that too far. Yikes. Anyway... In 2002, I was an angry teenager. You'll see that. That, and obvious issues with women, which probably stemmed from a rocky relationship with my mother. I wrote about a lot of fucked up things, and I couldn't be happier I didn't turn out to be a serial killer.

The Whisper Of Flesh

I heard slitting your wrists in a warm bath is the most soothing way to go. Personally, I'd rather jump out of an airplane without a parachute and hug as many birds as I can on the way down.

She has bloody diamonds printed on her skin: the dripping blood tattooed to her skin. She tells herself she's beautiful. Cut, cut, cut! She yells, "I'm beautiful!" Her slits stacked like pyramids. She's scented by black rose petals: lily pads of sin floating in the blood, caressing against her fragile hurt lines. She zigzags the blade to punish herself. Jaggedly the tiny spear circulates around the dead spots. The blade puncturing inside her like a talon, venturing every inch of her dying body. Dark melody of suicidal obsession, another self-slaughtering session: the whisper of flesh.

The chill of pain: a catalyst to the mind. Her body shakes. Her torn skin twitching in the water, festering in putrid red fluid. It's unfortunate she disguises herself to be unforgiving. She hates herself. She insists that she's ugly. Her self-esteem will be the death of her. The aura around her has cracked. It can't save her anymore.

The razorblade screeching intently. It presses through the outside and in. She tries to suppress the anger: the whisper of flesh. Her will to live is brittle. Her tears are caught in her black-amber eyes. She can't flush out her self-tyranny. Her emotions are jammed together. She can't distinguish what's making her cut.

Everything is moving in slow. She has to let her body go. Maybe the black fields on the other side will be greener. Only one way for her to know.

Unsuspectingly she rapidly cuts herself. The energy leaking. She's sinking. Drowning. Dying. Dead.

Fail To Wave The Anguish

This is a prime example of shitty Gothic poetry.

You're cornered in blind awakenings; fail to wave the anguish. Eat the pain you can't distinguish. Peel down your tear ducts and cry.

Collapse your hope. Lie beautiful within the rope. Fail to wave the anguish. You belong inside a mournful serenity.

Your silhouette of dirt beckons you. Give into dark love. Let darkness dress you with hate and become the goddess of twisted fate.

Ignore the purpose of your cares. They will only bring you lust: a craving that will strap you down and destroy you with mistrust.

Raise your sorrow. Let the blood splatter from your wrist. Drown your existence. Fail to wave the anguish.

Here's your shroud made of the softest black: feathers plucked from a thousand dead ravens. And a coiling crown of three black roses. Please, come rule with me in the world that froze.

I need you by my side. My queen, how I sought for you. And now that I have found you, I beg of you to fail to wave the anguish.

Forget everything and take your place. Hold my hand and embrace this world of lingering souls. Accept this and forever together, we can be damned.

Mutant

Spent a lot of my life feeling like a freakshow. I never expected much but I would have thought under the layers of self-hatred and disgust, I'd have superpowers waiting to be unlocked. Nope. No potential for greatness. It was just misery.

Behind the contamination there is something pure. Through all the lacerations there is a cure. These are my hopes that flood my mind but have yet to find. My dream seems to be empty and replaced by the same old nightmare. I guess I could always pretend, fake that I am okay.

I'm trying frantically to be calm. I need to be soothed. I need this desperately. Being a mutant is not what I wanted. I just wanted to be me. This is not me, but I blend myself in. Can you tell the difference? I can. I can feel I'm a mutant. I can see the deformities within. I notice the demonic presence underneath my skin. When I shudder for no reason, I know that I have been transformed.

Possessed and plaguing from the inside; from this metastasis, I am the mutant, the inner-disfigured creature. I can't hide, can't run, only to bow and obey. To these bounds, I am forced to abide. I want to kill the mutant, leave myself astray. If death means freedom, if death means taking back my kingdom, then death shall take me swiftly. With a sharp shard, I penetrate it into my deep heartache, opening the gates to my kingdom, obliterating the mistake: the mutant that tried to control my life, the disease that took my life.

Blood Flux

This poem is so emo, my laptop tried to slit its power cord.

Dormant from the blood flux; I'm trapped in the scars of a corpse. It smells like death in this scenery: a body fallen from the blood tracks. Little whispers torn on the skin – this is my body. To the elements, my flesh was exposed. It was melancholy, a knife, and no guidance. That sequence led me to ever after, an eternity of living with suicide. Time has wasted to ashes. It can no longer be reversed. I don't give a damn. I'll blow time away.

Life dragged me down. I fell and followed. I tried to grab the sides of the hole, but it just got wider. Wave goodbye to my soul – it was all I could do when I got swallowed. I didn't have the strength to fight. I was dumb from the counselling. I was too numb from the medication. Life had no purpose to keep me living, so I started falling. Now I'm at the bottom, dead in the hole that no one seemed to see. I dripped red to black from the blood flux. Death came so easily to me. The sound of droplets spiraling down, it was the sweet lullaby that put my tortured body to sleep.

I'll be gone missing. The last time you will see me is in the paper, my picture beside my obituary. You can cry and soak my face, but it doesn't change what happened. I died from the blood flux. My soul entombed inside a silhouette chamber. My soul frantically pacing in this hellish palace. I'm searching for the exit, but I can't find its entrance. Suicide didn't set me free. I can't seep through the skin I perforated. My soul will dim to nothing, rot to nothing, vanishing right behind the body that I tried and failed to escape.

I'm awake in this perdition, dealing with a reoccurring thought. It's floating right here beside me. It echoes to me, "No matter how many times you shatter a mirror, it will always reflect." It didn't matter how many times I changed. You can't hide the soul inside. From the blood flux, I got an answer – death wasn't the answer. But it's too late now. I'm dead in the cicatrices of a serpent. Burn the corpse and eat the glass, then you can set my soul free at last.

Slash Our Lips Together

Dated this girl who always tried to rip my bottom lip off when we kissed. After a while I hid my lip inside my mouth likes a reclusive turtle, waiting 'til the coast was clear. She'd go bonkers and accuse me of not loving her anymore whenever I did that, truth was – I was just fucking terrified of her. This poem has nothing to do with her.

Ashes to ashes, dust to dust – these words hold my goddess. Her beauty is entombed away from me and all I have left of her are impaired visions. It shouldn't be this way. The body of my love shouldn't be grey. It's unfair to leave love stranded.

It was up to her to bleed out her soul, to follow the lead of a suicidal role. Did I do something wrong? Why would she leave me? We were unbreakable, but she shattered away from me. Inside my heart is breaking. It's broken. I'm kneeling in a puddle of polluted tears. Fears are racing. Strength is depleting. Nothing matters anymore. My life is expendable. Without her, breathing is like swallowing razor blades. It kills me with every breath, but I just bleed. Still breathing. I'm all covered in blood and I have nothing to hold onto. My angel has rotted away from me.

I'm going insane. I can't help but embrace the pain. I'm always cutting myself even though it never seems deep enough. The paths I make aren't wide enough to die after her. I can't get her out of my head. The way her green emerald eyes glistened, her blood-red lips, pale-shaded skin, the way her silk gown seemed to make her translucent, the smell of her flesh, and her raven black hair. Why did she sacrifice herself? Didn't she know how much I loved her? I can't go on like this. Melancholy traced by lethargy – both daggers are stabbing into my mind. I'm being swarmed by a welcoming depression. My god how I remember her body. The way it danced like a leaf being carried by the wind, it was beauty in its purest form.

I take comfort in sadness; all around me is darkness. I am the wings my angel left behind. I just bleed without purpose, then decay from the inside and outside. How my soul aches without her presence, her essence. How I miss her. I remember how we used to slash our lips together and kiss. We loved how our blood concatenated, how our lip flesh separated. I remember how we bled hollow inside each other, the way it tasted, the way the blood fluxed. I swear I must have died and gone to Heaven a billion times, but she's dead away from me now. Remnants: an abundant amount of her blood-stained to my lips, my tongue, my throat. It's the only evidence I have to show of her existence.

I would like to think we will be as one again, but if she left me once it might happen again. I'm scared that I have lost her for good. The only feeling I have left of her is how we used to slash our lips together.

Drown Me

Her: "Tie your heart around your ankle like an anchor and drown yourself in a lake."
*Me: *enthusiastic as fuck* "Okay!"*

Blind my grasp so my claws miss your flesh. Love me so I become confused and sever my own. Drown me with regret so my suicidal thoughts can save me, away from this world, and the hurt I gave. I am hating the tears you kneel in. It's sin — the way you circle in despair. Every rotation adds a cut to my wrist. Turn after turn after turn.

You act like your heart has been destroyed, but why do I see a smile underneath that frown? Drown me in the emotions that reached the surface. I need a sign of purpose. I need to know if my self-inflicted wounds are meaningful. If it's right for me to stare at all this blood.

When you close your eyes at me is that your love gone black? I have become lost. My burning heart has withered to tears of frost. Why are you being this way? Why won't you tell me if it's love or hate that you feel? I beg you to tell me which one is real. We were lovers that fought the odds. Now, look at me. I'm battered and bruised from them, but you still soar high. Above me you are free. Drown me in jealousy and sadness-filled envy.

Did you really care for me at all? Voices tell me, "No." as I fall. It gets blacker and blacker. My innards are turning into stone. I am so cold.

I clench my heart as my soul screams. Time freezes. Life seizes. I was my own disease.

I look back and I know now I deserved this.

Human Body Swimming Dead

Before you read this, I want you to picture the boy wearing a pair of Alf water wings. Trust me. It will make the poem funnier.

Broken skull. Cold blood retreating from the head. Skin running pale white. Deadweight in the water. Body spoiling. Necrosis devouring the body. And in it, parasites are vacationing. From it, fish are feasting. The skull is smashed apart: head trauma shown by shattered fragments. Human body swimming dead.

Eyes are empty-glazed, forsaken behind the dead stare. Lips are frost blue: a tragic smile. These are the aspects of a rotting boy floating still in black waters: pale skin peeling away to bone, in the water floating silently, body decaying, flesh from bones separating – human body swimming dead. Buoy of soft flesh, a macerated corpse so infatuating, a true sight of beauty – Mother Nature eating it into extinction.

Facedown in the liquid deathbed; the head perforated from anger. Human body swimming dead. Tunnels of rot make the body transparent. Circulating decomposition insulates the corpse: human body swimming dead. Drama keeps it afloat. Another artistic masterpiece by the hands of cruelty.

Moth & The Teddy Bear

Bruce Banner transforms into The Incredible Hulk when he's mad. I have the same superpower except I transform when I'm sad. You can call me – The Incredible Sulk.

When I was young I was like a teddy bear: cute, soft and loved. I had no worries, not the simplest of cares. But in the midst of happiness, my life took a wrong turn and I became ruined. Like an eclipse, my life's light was swallowed whole. The teddy bear I used to be died into a moth. I'm ugly, hard, hated, sadistic, malicious and callous. I'm always with misery, always angry. This transformation has killed me inside.

I ran trying to escape problems, but I can no longer hide. There's nowhere else for me to go. I've run everywhere else. I'm stuck at my last stronghold and if it falls to ruins, I will die in the snow.

I want my life the way it was, but I won't do anything about it. I'm too pessimistic, too weak. It's just much easier to give up, to enter the cold and freeze into a statue of death. I'm fighting, but I'm tired of losing. I want past tense. The word "died" by my picture in the paper, to be tragic, the forsaken, to be the winter corpse.

Moth and the teddy bear – I am the same person made worse. When the stitching broke, I leaked into a pile of suicidal welcoming. Repulsive and scabbed with wings, I am the moth soaring on cruise control, directing myself by suicidal flight. This is the creature I have become: no soul and living in fright. My death is inevitable. Soon it will find me, kidnap me. And in the scenery of a winter night, the teddy bear, the moth... whatever I was, whatever I am, frostbitten skin will be my cerement.

Ripping Skin Symphony

Note to self: You can't create music by cutting your wrists. It just hurts. And bleeds. It bleeds a lot. Should have answered that Kijiji ad for free violin lessons. Yes, it was fucking shady that it was in the back of some homeless guy's van. I'm assuming that's how he was able to pass the savings on to me. #AnotherMissedOpportunity

Mended wounds broken open. The blood spilling in an erotic dance, putting my mind in a trance. My razorblade cushioned within my wrist; in a funnel rotation, I twist. The faster, the deeper I go, the blood and pain join in harmony – a ripping skin symphony. Like a violin I slide the blade across my wrist; a nothing sound echoes throughout my body. The blade holding sturdy as blood runs down staining my arm, my clothes, the floor. My wrist torn and bloody like one of Jack the Ripper's whores – a ripping skin symphony. My razorblade enslaved to my wrist. I cough up blood like mist. My eyes hypnotized by the feeling and sight. This is my sick room, my dying room. I carve "damned" in thick letters across my throat. The blood floating until it hits the ground. The slits pounding as a waterfall of red streams down my chest. Now I'm a bloody fucking mess, listening to chimes of an awaiting death – a ripping skin symphony. My eyes closing. My mind draped by a black haze. I'm passing out. The blood loss still surfacing out my cuts. My hand releasing the hold of the blade. I won't retreat myself. I grasp the blade tightly. I strike down on my untouched wrist. The vein pierces open. I fall like concrete. The blood secreting. My corpse lying in the dead room.

Ever-Bloody Doll

I showed this to a friend when I first wrote it. She told me it was the best poem she ever read. I hate liars. Although, she was only being nice to me because she wanted to sleep with me. Probably. I mean it's not too farfetched to think I'm attractive, is it? Shh... no more words.

I watch you closely, dancing the blade in your flesh, your eyes closed with anguish. I can feel the blood running fresh, staining the tips of my fingers as I drag them across the floor. With scarce emotion, I streak the floor. You are my friend. I love you dearly. My ever-bloody doll, I am here for you.

I can hear your faith of life burning. You cut with the rhythm of your teardrops, soaking the ashes left of your soul, creating a lake of blasphemy, a puddle of sacrilege. You've been scorched, bled and torched. Ever-bloody doll, my soul bleeds for you. Unlock the gates to your paradise; bleed yourself into a corpse. I want you to have a Cheshire smile when you die. I want you to be happy. I just wish I could have made life better for you, so instead, I'll make death easier for you.

We've been friends since we were little. The memories, the days we laughed and cried, our heart-made and broken stories – we could never be torn apart. Our lives were as one. Now everything is coming undone. Your suicidal strokes sadden me, but as your friend, I comfort you as you bleed. I see your hands trembling, shaking with my slow-beating heart, your head tilted down, your pale face draped with your dark, wavy hair, I can tell the blood loss is killing you. My ever-bloody doll, I love you. I'll miss you. I want to come with you.

All the times I'll have to cry alone, laugh alone; when I need you, you will never be there. I can't live when half of me is dead. I can't live knowing you're gone, so I'm coming with you. My ever-bloody doll, when you bleed your last drop, everything will stop. My life will crumble in your still presence and with a whirlwind of sorrow, the blade that stole your life will embed into me, erasing the sour feeling of your disappearance. I'll die by your side as our blood joins in a spewing frenzy, but until then I will wait for your death. My ever-bloody doll, I will see you on the other side.

I feel the vibration of your collapsed body, the blood rushing like an angelic riptide, the smell of death rising, circling and growing, a tiny grin with empty eyes showing. Ever-bloody doll, die peacefully, decay beautifully, and I will weep at your marble skin until I die. We're wretched, a love line eternally stretched. I reach for the blade drenched in blood. It drips as I bring it close and with desperate purpose, I recreate self-destruction. Pasting pernicious red lines on my body, I become weak into the hands of Death. Nothing can keep us apart. Ever-bloody doll, I'm bleeding after you, dying behind you, retracing your steps so we can laugh and cry together like we once did. Ever-bloody doll, I love you. We are friends always, forever, and together never apart.

Regret

And this is why I don't kill people anymore.

Wind whistling around my body, I fall to my knees, cowering myself into a ball of flesh, kneeling from eerie voices. The fog rising for the occasion, inhaling my body, insulating the screaming: biting chimes that haunt me. My victims are stalking me. Their spirits hunting. Waiting. Revenge is carved in their souls. The weak have become the immortal. They whisper my name loud enough to echo the pain, cracking my sanity into tiny fragments. I tried killing myself, but they won't allow it. For eternity, I am damned. Chained by them, I am condemned. I want to die. I can take no more. I've already drowned in my tears that poured, that wrote the sorrow on my hands that killed. I do regret, but it won't make them go away. For all the innocence that wept, they deserve to stay. I sit against a tree. My fingernails peeling my face. I am cursed, poisoned from a hundred broken families. The moon frowning upon me as the clouds blanket its soft light. I hang my head in acceptance. I give in to the ghostly faces. Flowers will blossom and wither with the months of sun and snow, followed by the people that will come and go — that is the portrait I will watch forever.

Dead Script Scroll

I suck at being a Secret Santa.

This is the end. This is not a suicide letter, just an explanation and a reason, an exclamation mark on what went wrong, on how I failed to be strong, how things came to be. This is my dead script scroll. My list that dug the hole, hollowed the soil and put me to rest.

Dead from a bloody crest, the coat of arms on my chest, I took the knife and carved myself vividly. I left all of you, the loved ones I hated and ran from the life that was complicated. In the end, I was the coward.

Here inside of me, I was dead. By myself, I was decomposing. My sanity was being eaten away, but you all laughed like I was telling a joke. So now, will you still laugh when maggots eat my decay? Will you laugh when you choke on the flashbacks of my corpse? Or will you all just forget about me, acting like I was never born?

I was neglected. I fought for everything I wanted and all I wanted was your love and acceptance, but instead, I got ignorance and solitude. What did I do to deserve this? I hope you all laugh when you read my dead script scroll. I want to know that I was right. So please show your true colours. Show me that I was a burden, and now that I'm gone your lives are better. I never felt like I belonged, like an outcast taken in: looked after but no one really gave a fuck. But it's okay now, I'm free.

Glass soul child - that is who I was. Shattered in a fragile state of suicide, I wrote this dead script scroll. With red tears and a plastic smile, I wrote this dead script scroll. I broke away, fell apart. I bloomed into a corpse and became just a soul, a transparent being but not too far from whole. My death was my gift to you.

When I seen your protruding eyes when you opened my door, I relished at your shaking. When you unwrapped your gift and seen the end of our war, I laughed. When you read the note, when you read the words printed in blood "Merry Christmas." I cried.

Necrosis

Trust issues? *pulls knife out of back and slits wrists with it* Whatever would give you that idea?

Am I dead? The secrets on my body are visible. Are people blind? My body torn asunder and bloody, and people still can't see my pain? The knife's velocity, the marks left behind on my skin – those wounds call for help, crying thick red tears, but no one seems to hear. No one seems to see the dripping. Someone needs to save me from myself. I'm my own predator. Dead to the core. Necrosis palpitates deep within. The knife across my skin slipping, leaving lines of hurt, a sense of euthanasia. I'm my worst enemy, a losing battle. Can't anyone see what is happening to me?

I don't want to die. My words are muted so I put myself through destruction: a neon sign of fury. I don't understand why people don't see the absence of unscathed skin. Am I already dead? Am I an unconscious ghost? My body decorated with necrosis, to people I'm just a corpse, a shadow gone inside the light. I need strength, not the blade's sharp length. Every day is like night: cold and hard to see. Must this be me? I try to stand out by leaking liquid red rubies: a fluid that resembles a fiery scarlet. I bleed to get attention. I put myself through this mutilation because it's the only way to get people to notice, but it's not working.

I've become eccentric, static. I want to push through this world of plastic, but when I get close, it melts and becomes harder. Death has me underlined. I'm on the top of his list. Is this the life I was supposed to have? To have this necrosis? To fail? This life isn't celestial. My screams, the waves of wailing, they are all real because people are distracted to themselves.

The way I'm treated has affected me. I'm all mixed up. I'm made to shut up. The words won't come out. I'm turning into one of them: broken-hearted and insane.

I hate reality. I'm nothing in its society. I'm love-starved. I show my hunger for it with my body always recently carved. I have no scabs. I won't let myself heal. I'm tenacious with cutting. I'm loved by necrosis – my drug, it hugs me. Tightly I wrap myself in it, set away from life, the void I have with people. I'm coloured red, closer to being dead, but living for as long as time allows me. I'll cut, crawl in my suicidal sickness and finally realize this is my scarred shell.

Blood

I'm not invited to family reunions anymore.

Definite killer. Knife-swinging maniac. Hybrid insomniac. Bloodthirsty painkiller, writing a story of death on the walls. Blood-dripping blade: a spring of pain from stab wounds that bled over and over again.

Cold steel insulated by blood, reflecting screams of despair. I am words that were cursed, emotions bled dry, taste buds of sweet vengeance held strong by an alliance. Coiled together with loving darkness, I am immortal.

Their bodies jig-sawed together, outlined by a moat of sour blood. Their ignorance brought them this: my knife-wielding bliss. My eyes are black, shaded by the colour of my heart. Toward them, I'm kissed with hatred. They're not sacred. My being is. My fragile soul is.

Look at all the silence I found, not a sound, only a slight whisper that soothes my anger. They brought this upon themselves. No matter what I do they should love me, but their beliefs hesitated that caring. They just treated me as an outcast, a judgement that lasted until this day. I never wanted this to happen.

Get Back

You know you have mommy issues when you go out of your way to write a poem about stuff that never happened.

Get back! One more step. A little further. I fucking hate you! Get back!

So, you knew all the answers. When I was little you made me believe, but I grew up and now I'm free. I realized my whole life I was deceived. Fuck you! I'm on the rage! Loose from my cage! Fuck you! Get back!

You said that you loved me but when I got a mind of my own, you abandoned me. You said I was wrong and that I'm not your child. Now with swinging fists, I've gone wild. My eyes are red with revenge. My life has become a threatening challenge. It's hard to stay alive, to survive. You drove us apart!

I'm a gutter baby, a living abortion. My head is filled with distortion: suicide always walking by but failing to see me. No matter how deep the cut, my eyes won't shut. You fucking bitch! I fucking hate you! Get back! Do you even notice what you wove? Look at you and your millions and me in the diseases. Do you notice? Have you ever grieved for me? Do you care I'm on the steppingstones of death? Do you see my deteriorating health?

Years passed and not a word from you. Then you grew old and senile. You came out from your denial, realizing you were wrong. You've grown weak and through all your selfish shit, I stand strong. You're pathetic.

Don't reach for me with your wrinkled, arthritic hand. If you touch me, I'll cut it off. Fuck off, bitch! What didn't you understand?! I said get back! Leave me be! I don't and never had a mother! Because of you, I never knew my father! You set me facing in the corner, but I've turned around and seen the monster that was cloaked. I see the reason why every day I wanted you to choke on your cancer-filled smoke. I see why I am this way. Mother, I only have one thing left to say – When this war between us is over, it will be me, hanging over your body when you're six feet under. Not the child you disowned and tried to forget. It won't be me, mother! It won't!

Dead Inside

Yet, I can still achieve an erection. YOLO!

I'm dead inside. My heart has stopped beating. I'm bleeding. I'm dead inside. I have no emotions to hide. I'm dead inside. I let myself slide. Everything inside me died. And look at my face, does it look like I care? I don't. Why should I bother? If I cared, guilt would infest me, regret would play the role of suicide so I stay dead inside. Why do I need to feel? This is my attitude. Without it, I would be dead already. I would have fallen into the depths of negativity, wanting to kill myself would blossom, so why would I want to deal with that? It makes no sense to put myself through it. I'm dead inside. Decayed inside. Not a smile or frown to spare, not a tear to cry. My emotions have bled dry. I like the way I'm distant. It barricades me. I feel free. I love the feeling of open wings: emotions that would infect me, affect me. Closing my wings would only bring me death. I'm dead inside. I don't mind. I let myself go. This is what I want to be – a zombie.

Secluded

This poem is about the aftermath of an awkward hug that went on for way too long.

Everything is distant, so far, so cold. I can't grab hold. I'm surrounded by emptiness. I feel so fucking worthless. I'm losing my head over this. How I fucking hate this. Day after day, night after night, I'm secluded, diluted. I tighten my fists with rage. I want out of this cage. This mistake – I want it to break. Let me free, step back and you will see what this is fucking doing to me. I feel like I'm in a straitjacket, in a silhouette casket: no room to move, no room to breathe. Every blink and it gets smaller; I grow taller. I can't get out. There's barely room to shout. I cuss and fight, but I'm being cornered. I try to bust through, but it's too late. I've been secluded. There's nothing I can do, but accept this fate, the one thing I hate – the haunting thought of you. You left me, ran from. You had to take everything. You had to leave me with nothing. Is this the way it has to be? I'll stay secluded, but I am taking you with me and we'll be together. Together as broken lovers, together we will suffer.

Blown Echo-Wide

I've read this poem so many times and I still have no idea what the fuck I was talking about. Guess it has something to do with sadness. Definitely a prime example of trying too hard to be prophetical. You know what? I don't think I like myself very much.

'm screaming, crying for attention. I'm drowning in the waves of my fears. My spirit is dying in the seclusion of misery. Sepulchral thoughts aesthetically whole: fragments of malicious cruelty. I interlock myself into an outline of dying. Voices are whispering; from their drones, I'm blown echo-wide. I'm so sincere. I'm happy like you, but I smile from the inside. Can't you tell by my window of apocalyptic lacerations? The synthetic tones feel it. I hear their perverse wailing. My skin reaped from the flesh; from its silence, I'm blown echo-wide. My body shakes from the blade's erratic motions, opening up red cracks on my skin. My eyes teardrop away the pain, masking the emotionally-disemboweled creature, the terror I'm fused to, the cynical sadist that is me.

My body is sheltered from the waterfall of blood I dripped and scarred from heartbeats that skipped. I'm blown echo-wide from the blood that spelled my perdition. I'm dead-hollow within. I planted the seed. Now watch me grow into a desolate sin, a crossbreed of grotesque emotions. I am a reincarnated soul of porcelain. I'm fragile to the core. Cold. Stiff. Undead. Awake with my marble skin corpse. I've foreshadowed my future. Blurry images sail in my mind. Death is flying around me like a vulture, waiting for that last puncture, to pull my soul down into the undertow. It patiently waits for me to bust through the fleshy texture. This could last a lifetime or a perennial lifespan. All I know is that I'm blown echo-wide from this world. I look outside from the outside. My mind is frostbitten from the winter.

There was so much I had to filter. I needed to be cleansed, but Death found me first.

The last thing I saw was the snow shadowing my eyes. The last thing I felt was a blistering freeze. The next thing I knew, my flesh was being torn by ravens.

Kiss You Forever

Careful of what flavour Chapstick you wear. It could really make or break a relationship. Raisin was her undoing.

I am not going to kiss you forever. I won't do that to you. After this last kiss, I'll disappear. I'll be gone forever, away from your embrace. I'll sink deep away from your presence, breaking your threshold to my heart. I'm leaving you, pulling us apart, because I won't drag you down with me. You're too fragile for me. I can't stay with you. I won't kiss you forever. I'll set you free from myself. I do this to save you. I'm not true love. I'm repulsive inside. You being with me will make you ugly like me, that's why I can't kiss you forever. I tried to stay distant from you. I tried to stay far from close, but obsession grows. Like poison ivy, it came to you. I couldn't control myself. Your beauty became my appendage. I just had to be with you all the time. But I know who I am, what I am like, so this is why we can't kiss forever. My love for you is ever, but a demon lurks inside it. No one will love you as much as I do, but my love isn't pure. It's contaminated and contagious. I won't be the bacteria that will infect you. I won't kiss you forever – my lips are too tainted. I don't want to manipulate you. You're too angelic for me to do that to you. My love, listen to me. I do love you dearly so and that is why I can't kiss you forever. I'm dying just thinking of this. When I leave your sight, I'll die in the place inside my heart where it is always dark. My nymph, I love you. I wish I could kiss you forever, but it wouldn't be fair. I refuse to bring you despair, so that is why I must leave you, but only for a knight to sweep you off your feet. Someone that is not me. We were lovers, together made broken. I'm sorry I tried when I knew I would do this. I'd kiss you forever, but I love you too much. Farewell, and forget the creature. Farewell, I will never forget you.

Scared Child

Me, as a motivational speaker.

Here I stand in a puddle of bloody suicide. With a bullet left astray in fragments of my brain, I stand. I had nothing to lose and nothing to gain; everything around me was grey. All the hurtful things never went away; my strength depleted. I started to suffocate. I started to lacerate. I tried separating my skin to let out the pain, but all it brought me was a bleeding strain. I crawled to the light but it kicked me down. It bruised my hope. My will to live evacuated, left me behind. The knife across my wrists began to grind. I prayed my suicidal tendencies would help, but darkness came rising, killing my soul.

I was a freak of nature, a masochistic creature, a plague tainting the very life I breathed. I was just a monster that I feared, a scared child. My paranoia macerated my mind. The blade tried cutting it out, but the attempt for bravery failed. I knew my time was up when the blood wouldn't dry, when voices in my head told me to die. So, I loaded a gun, snuggled the bullet in the chamber, aimed the lead, the sleeping pill to my head and hoping for an eternal slumber, I pulled the trigger.

Warm soul capsule bewildered – it went the wrong way, landed in decay. I became cold. I died. My brains splattered the ceiling; my ghost stared at the corpse. It was darker on the other side. Nothing changed. I wanted out but it never happened. My punishment was for everything to stay the same.

Glass Shards

If you hate people but don't want to be alone when cutting yourself, then I suggest using a piece of glass, like a mirror. I believe your reflection still counts as an audience.

I lie beneath the scabs, eating the blood that hardened, causing the healing to itch, getting myself into your head, to be dwelling in your emotions again. My dormancy under your wounds makes you scratch. Pieces falling off, dead particles crumbling apart. Your violent soothing causes you to bleed; from this, I'm released back into your head again. I knew you would give in. I am your contamination. My toxins are too drastic for you to handle. You will obey back to mutilation and listen to my heartless demands.

It was your life that brought me to you, that one bad relationship took me to your welcome mat, so I entered and became your disaster. When you shattered your mirror, I made you pick up those glass shards that you created, the glass shards that manipulate. Their silence tells you they will erase the hurt, every memory of the girl you love, every hurtful thing she did to you. I am the clarity that made you realize it's because of me you massaged your skin apart. And the blood which crawled out your cuts trickled into my golden chalice. From a full cup I drank you; I tasted your blood and the glass shards. Your taste was heavenly. I could taste the hint of death. A few more cuts would bring its flavor, but you had to stop. You tried to scar me over, to regain your health. You tried to do things differently and all of it was for nothing. I knew you would let me in again. You are just too weak.

So, because of your insolence, I will possess you to cut deeper, to sever yourself faster. I will make you create a river of blood: wild rapids to bring Death downstream to greet you at your bloody shores. And when you feel a needlepoint pain behind you, you will notice an extra weight on your shoulders, but you'll feel lighter and you will forget all about her. That's when you'll look behind you and there will be me, knitting your black wings of suicide.

Dark

I'm terrible at Hide 'N Seek. My incessant crying always gives me away.

I scratch the surface to see if there's light at the end of the tunnel. It's just dark. I'm stuck in the void, this gaping hole. I close my eyes so it's not so dark. I'm paranoid, frightened that I will never see myself. I hear voices but I see no one. My heart is charred. I cry unnoticeable tears. My body is scarred, devastated from an unseen blade. I'm stigmatized. The evidence is written on my skin: a bleeding scroll of a nefarious reincarnation, poetic schemes of self-mutilation. Inside I'm grotesque, ugly from sinking in life's mutation. It's contagious. I'm rocketing under its quicksand. I'm reaching for a hand, but I get nothing. Swept under from the undertow, I shell myself tightly. It's so dark down here. I'm gasping to exhale the woe, but my lungs won't ventilate. They just retaliate, closing off the path.

Negativity smudged together: a burning ball of suicide and sorrow. I pray I won't see tomorrow - for my demolished life is overflowing with razor cuts. It's feeding the need, the hunger for my suicide's growing seed. Its blooming is killing light to dark. I feel the tension. My lifeline is fraying as it gets tighter and tighter. I can hear the threads snapping. I need to make a decision: life or death. Time is caving. I can't concentrate. Thoughts are rushing too fast to grab. Grains of sand are falling scarce; the hourglass is empty. I'm dead in the dark. I'll run my soul from existence until I fade into nothing. This is what I died for – to cower myself from the living.

Waste Of Skin

Am I self-loathing right?

Disfigured creature. Waste of skin. A worthless being. I'm just a burden. A jar filled with sin. I have no desire for believing, no emotions, no sense of morality. I'm a waste of skin. Animosity – the only aspect I carry. I was born to feel death; fuck immortality. Reap my body asunder and bury the entrails; cover the waste of skin. I'm a waste of skin. Don't hesitate. Let's begin. Peel back the skin, reveal the flesh, tear apart the flesh, break the bones, set me down six feet under and take my soul. Who cares what I feel? I don't. Accidents happen, so take your hand and erase the mistake; delete me from the face of this disheartened world. Soil the waste of skin, steal me away, kill me to where I belong, to the land of decay. Suffer me gone, feed the maggots, save my parents, send me to the burning fires of Hell. Show me no remorse. Annihilate me dead. Mould this waste of skin; my life is in your hands. Bleed me to a corpse. Make me into ashes, to bone dust. Destroy every trace of my living, blank me from the memories of all, except for the agony I went through when I was dying. It will make them smile – knowing that the pain I gave came back to me. Leave nothing left, devour the maggots that hold pieces of me inside. I want it to be like I never existed, I never had a breath, I was never here. Make it so that I only knew death. I'm a waste of skin; give me what I deserve. Rot everything away. Leave nothing to preserve. I don't want to be remembered, just dismembered, amputated into thin air, into nothing. That is what I want, so give me what I want.

Fuck The Angels

Needless to say, the Vatican has denounced my version of the Bible. Don't worry. I'll get 'em next time, kids. Shucks!

'm oppressive. Fuck the angels. Slaughter them until their wings moult from their backs. Strangle them with their golden halos. Suffocate them until they're decapitated. Fuck the angels. Colour the world black. Masquerade love with hate. Fuck the angels. We all know they're disguised demons. At least I show the red pigmentation on my skin, the horns that protrude from my skull. I hide nothing. I accept the dead poltergeist festering inside me. I'm ominous. Hate-enraged courageous. Don't get inside my head; it's poisonous. Your soul will turn gangrene and the next thing you know you're dead.

I heard it's a sin when an angel cries so I'll watch them die. Is it a sin to laugh when an angel dies? Fuck the angels. Tear their wings off and replace them with concrete blocks. Cut off their white robes and stitch them with a darkened shroud. Kill away their purity. Hang it violently with barbed wire. Fuck the angels.

I'm stuck down here. I'm holding a grudge. I hate everything but literally love nothing. This is my circuit. Deviously I praise in my ways. I'm plotting against the glow. Fuck the angels. I'll be piling blood-starving angels into a pyramid of genocide. Fuck the angels. I want them dead – their faces out of my head. If I have to eat every angels' heart so be it. When I'm done I will have persuaded them all into a grave – a chamber deep within the gates of Hell. I'm cold-hearted. I'm merciless. Fuck the angels. I'm better than them.

I'm drastic. I take their deaths to another level. I fuck their corpses: an orgy of necrophilia lust. Their slain bodies are subtle so delicately I fuck away their existence until they are all fossils in my pocket. I am the manifestations of Lucifer. I manipulated the angels to the fold. A new page flipped. This is my chapter, their manifold. This is my world. I'm in solitude – just me and my neurotic half-life. Who knew I would be sitting on the throne?

I chained God. Dead angels my slaves. For eternity they'll rot enslaved. In the end, I fucked the angels. I smashed the chalice of the Heavens. It exploded like glass, reflecting its own destruction. I am the darkness that seeped in and drowned out the light. I was Heaven's downfall, the angels' outbreak virus introduction, the black plague that wiped out the white demons.

Nailed

Tried to turn the Bible into a romantic comedy, but the Vatican also turned it down. They're a tough cookie to crack, but I'll get them.

Nailed. Crucified like Jesus. My goddess in deep sleep. She lies corpsed on a cross, cushioned on my bed. My decaying princess - she is my trophy of undying love.

I know she smiles at me. Even with her frightful eyes, tear-stained face, I know she smiles at me. The flickering candles light up your lifeless body. Its light dancing around the room. You are so perfect, my gangrene queen. Just look at you – so seducing with nailed hands, so desirable with nailed feet. Who could not love such a magnificent thing?

Your hair tangled on your face masking a portion of your pretty face. Your hair follicles breaking down, your hair falling out, still beautiful, nailed. You're crucified and blood-starved, dead and framed, you're nailed. You're my portrait of necrophilia love. A smell your soul released: the feeling of your body deceased, filled with sexual disease. I lick your lips – sweet taste of death. I lick my lips – bitter taste of lust. You are my angel in a jar.

I snatched you from the Heavens; you are my Amazon. Though you lie in frozen motion, you give me light even when you're gone. You are in the decay cycle, but your skin is still soft and silky, your skin still white and milky. Nailed. Limb-impaled. My little porcelain doll, how I reach for you to rise from the ashes. I miss you so. Making love to you isn't the same when you're not breathing. I loved inhaling the air you exhaled, your voice that ran throughout my body. The way your blue sapphire eyes blinked, it was more exuberant than a newborn horizon, but they're stiff, your eyelids sealed shut. You're nailed. Life isn't the same without you. My bedsheets are never clean. You're decaying too fast; the sex is getting worse. You're nailed in the missionary position, but it's disappearing from decomposition. I keep hitting bone. No flesh for padding, but I love you still.

Beautiful, when Grim finally finds me, I'll be armed beside you with a bouquet of roses and a gun. I'll hand you the roses; you'll kiss me and smile. And when you sniff the thick scent of flowers, my blood will polka dot your face. For in shame, I will kill myself twice. I'll leave you because I should've never kept you.

Queen Corpse Buried In Snow

Grade four was around the time I stopped writing Valentines for classmates. Kept getting suspended. I guess they were just too real for them.

Queen Corpse buried in snow, dead flesh touched by ice, a body decaying from malice, a decomposing cicatrice, my frozen beauty layered in a blanket of cold; in the icy winds, I watch her mould, blending with the winter months as the frost over her body rolls.

Frostbitten statue fallen – Queen Corpse buried in snow. Motionless wounds swollen. Blood insulated but solid as cold stone. She is my corpsed raven, beautifully dead in her blood-soaked gown stitched to her body by ice. Her cause of death laminated for eternity to her corpse, clothed in the wear she died in. Her death was sin. Her beauty printed those gashes on her skin. My envy of her, my agitation of not having her gave me magic to surprise her with murder.

I was faceless to her but grotesque enough for her to shackle me away from her light. It wasn't fair how I rushed to be at her side, to feel her inside, to create life and die holding hands. She would have nothing of it, so in psychotic jealousy, hatred lit. I mutilated her, captured her screams in my head, tasted the blood that ran wild, watched her die ever so slow, my Queen Corpse buried in snow.

LIIAN VARUS GOES DARK

t's 2003. By that time, I've joined the Dark Side. The Sith of society if you will. I've gone full-blown Goth. My eye makeup was thick, my skin was pale like I took tips from a Morticia Addams beauty tutorial. My clothing had also changed. It went from active lifestyle to what I can only describe as Medieval cosplay but gave up halfway through the transition. I've embraced every aspect of my new lifestyle. Disconnecting from people, perhaps even myself - that was how I dealt with my depression, my anxiety. I did a really good job pretending I had self-confidence in this new state. There was a sense of power when I walked down the sidewalk and people got the hell out of my way like I was zombie Moses parting the Red Sea. The scarier I looked the safer I felt. Of course, I would get picked on a lot. Mostly from jocks, normies, but it didn't bother me. I felt superior to them. That. And I also was dealing with a sex god complex where I felt like everyone wanted to fuck me. I laugh now thinking about it. It was my go-to burn when dealing with bullies – "Yeah, a faggot that could steal your girlfriend." I got into a lot of fights. Making friends was hard. But I digress. My writing was different too. Yes, it was still terrible, but my imagination started to spark. My poetry became more horror-based, fear-driven, bloodier... Death was my main muse. In every sense of the word, I was your stereotypical Goth.

Next Drop Of Blood

Seems like a lot of work for a simple blow job.

Squeeze the blood from your wrist. Stare at past scars that were kissed, touched tenderly by the rusty knife. Glare at your wounds that failed to take your life. Be strong. Be patient. I could be hiding behind the next drop of blood. So, to you, I say keep the healing minimal. Be the rabid animal; wildly swing the knife into the blood tunnels. Constant penetration is key; be the suicidal machine. The next drop of blood could be your long-anticipated dawn. The next drop of blood can give you dying, so bleed until the blood is gone. One drop can take you where you want to be. Just wait and see. Believe me.

Pour yourself dry. Fill yourself with space. Leave not a trace. Not a single drop of blood. I promise you. I swear that I could be in the next drop of blood. I'm waiting in one of the ruby droplets; with my life-shrivelling touch, I am waiting. Find the right capsule and you will see me there. When goosebumps flourish on your skin, when the hair on your arms stands vertical, then know I exist in the next drop of blood. Just don't stop writing your cause of death, keep the ink flowing, the blood loss growing and you will see me as you're falling. I'm a blurry vision when you're dying, but when you die I come in clear, so keep the blood rushing. Feel no fear. I'm coming to save you, to take you away, to sweep you away to a beautiful paradise. I swear. I promise this to you.

Apple Cadavers

When I first wrote this poem, I honestly thought it was the best poem ever written by anyone in the last ten years. Which is a hilarious statement to make since I don't read, so it's not like I'd know if it were true or not. Not even kidding. I was that stupid, that naïve. I'm such a piece of shit.

I cut the apple in two. Unfurl your hand and I'll share with you. Open your mouth and chew; taste the poisonous centre and swallow. Burn your woe to ash that grew; kill yourself like new. Enter the newborn season without reason. Devour the red-tainted fruit until it's gone; savour the flavour until your lungs are shot and done. Descend heavily from the coursing venom. Then when you're struggling on the foliage blanket on the dying leaves of a fresh autumn, I'll bite through the other half and decay by your side. I'll be your Romeo if you'll be my Juliet, and we'll die together as our last sunrise sets.

Hunger & Lust

It's painfully obvious I watched a lot of vampires and porno back in my Gothic days. Unfortunately, Twilight ruined vampire movies for me forever. Porn has yet to let me down. Great. Now I'm hard.

In the circumference of darkness, in the shadow of night, two vampires are dancing. With teeth fused into each other's throats, they're spinning, circling round and round up above the ground, feeding and drinking, drowning one another whole, exchanging souls. Tightly held together they're rotating out of control. Scattering drool is being chased by blood as their mouths flood. Overflowing with a liquid scarlet that's painting their white robes red, resembling the mark of the love rose. They bite harder and harder, deeper and deeper as hunger and lust grows. As they tear away from their Gothic clothes with pale skin showing white as snow, these two ancient creatures refuse to release their hold.

Naked as the skin can get, both bodies are traced by wandering hands - fingers descending, splitting apart hair, fingertips dragging down chests and underneath breasts, down sides and between thighs with nail scratches left bleeding behind, their bodies reflect hunger and lust. Quite the spectacle this erotic ritual: two vampires of the female species in delight, embracing together by molestation and perversion, caressing milky skin. From the skin to the flesh, it feels like silk. Just ask the nails that dig in deep.

Low tone moans, blood circulating in and out, bodies of marble stone, odd sexual habits and tendencies: hunger and lust from a mythical species. A morbid fairy tale I yearn to be a part of. Just once I want to be bitten twice and have four puncture holes bleeding slowly. I want to be tender as porcelain and have my bare skin connected to theirs. I want to taste as they taste, touch as they touch, bleed and moan at once. If fate ever gave me the chance, I would join in their bloodsucking dance.

Pieces

Can you imagine calling a suicide hotline and having me answer the phone? You would be fucked.

My life is crashing down before me. Pieces are falling. My whole world is dying. I can't fit the pieces back together; there's too many. Everything is breaking apart. I'm getting swallowed. I'm drowning in my sea of broken pieces. Nothing is making sense. It all seems hopeless, all pointless. There's no point in running. I don't know what to do. My life is deteriorating, like an avalanche, it's consuming me. The pieces are tightly wedging against me. I can't move. I feel so heavy; pieces are weighing me down. I can't help myself. I'm getting buried alive. I fear I won't survive. The pieces stacking over me are circling the darkness around me. My life has been devastated into a nothingness. I feel weightless. It's blank. It's dark in here. I'm blind. I can't even see my hands in front of me. I'm not even breathing. Now I know what happened. It's perfectly clear. As the pieces fell like shooting stars, suicide followed and inhaled me to the side of dead light. This continuous carousel of black scenery, this merry-go-round I ride is the death that comes with a coward's way out. It's what the other side becomes when you commit suicide.

Goddess That Wept Herself To Destruction

Women love it when a guy grabs a guitar and sings them a song, they wrote for them. They do not like it when you read them a poem about them killing themselves because of self-esteem issues. I know that now.

People tell her she's beautiful. She tells herself they're lies, only sympathetic words said because she's ugly. Her self-esteem is out the window; inside her sadness grows. Compliments to her are empty. They're just words said for pity. She feels hated. She hates herself. She is so gorgeous, but when she looks into the mirror, she believes she's hideous. She relates herself to Medusa: So grotesque. One look and you're stone. She blanks her face with thick, black makeup. It's confusing why her mind thinks this way. Maybe she's insane. Maybe she's too self-conscience for her own good. If she keeps it up, she'll find herself alone. She'll find herself dead.

All her negative thoughts have led her to this moment...

Wind blowing to the subtle drop of her tears, the breeze lifting her silky, white dress; she smears her black makeup across her face, her hands coated black. And as the inevitability of suicide elevates as it rises with the cold night's moonlight, she takes that one step, that forward step where it's too late to go backward. Off the cliffside, she walks. Death has her in cruise control, tumbling her to a horrid ending. With a last breath, a last tragic twinkle in her eyes, her body crashes against the jagged rocks, and in tragedy, her starry eyes still shine. Though her blood is spilled from the fall, she will always be eternal. In people's hearts and in spirits, she will always live on.

People will never know why, they'll never figure out why she killed herself, but for the rest of their lives, every breathtaking scenery they see, they will think of her – the goddess that wept herself to destruction.

Ocean Blue

I was also hoping we would bang.

Darkness rising, killing the sun. All the stars glowing white, highlighting this already perfect night. It's almost time to give my gift to you. I spent all day searching, trying to find the perfect one, and there I found it, standing beautifully in the middle of the dark wood, shining like daylight will never return, like the world has sacrificed everything but spared this for you – my gift to you.

The silent bells of time set off. I can't wait to see you, to indulge in your surprised eyes of ocean blue. Anticipation has set my heart on fire. The high notes of time's muted choir, the melodic symphony that makes no sound rings throughout my body, the messenger telling me it's time. So, with gift-in-hand and a body full of adrenalin of the love I have for you, in a rush to see you, I go to you.

It's midnight, the climax of night. All is black except the love that burns brightly: the bursting flame that burns eternally. Goddess of my heart, you keep it burning. Through the darkness I find myself standing under your window with stars staring down at me. I look above to see a branch from your tree scratching your window, swaying against it so carelessly. Your lightbulb on makes me smile – you're up. I feel like I've melted into vapour. With a sense of weightlessness, I climb the tree, the only obstacle that stands in my way. I've reached the top and there I see you sitting, reading the note I gave you in class today. You're so enchanting. Every time I see you my jaw drops. It never stops. You are the ticking of my clock, my reason for living. My Gothic beauty, I am forever yours.

Slowly I crawl across the tree's wooden tentacle, the branch, the bridge that leads me to you. You're smiling, reading as I tap on your window. You turn and there I sit with a locked gaze on you. You let the note go. It falls like an autumn leaf. You run to me and there I go, getting lost in your irises of ocean blue. You open your window and ask why I'm here. I can't respond. I'm lost in your orbs of ocean blue. But you know I'm here just to see you. You call me a silly boy and we lean in, to kiss. Short distance away from ecstasy fades into Hell. The branch breaks before our lips touch. I fall heavy like a collapsing cliffside with my gift falling slowly behind me. And as I look at the fright that devours your ocean blues, I hear your screaming. Then it all goes quiet, it all goes black as my neck breaks. I never got the chance to give you what I found. I'm a corpse on your lawn, a corpse on the ground, but a soul that will be waiting for you with another rose on the other side.

Voices

Not lyrics to Randy Orton's entrance music.

Screaming around like banshees, voices circulate in horrid overture. Invasion of squeals and screeches terrorize my mind. My sanity is in a violent portrayal of haunting rapture, faltering from the vibrations I failed to capture. Where did these voices come from? They're out of control. Their waves of percussions are taking hold. I'm not myself. I can't help but let this torture roll. What did I do to deserve this?

My head is exploding. A feeling that is jammed on repeat. One vocal spear after another. I'm paralyzed from the neurotic beats that drum against my brain. I'm drained, weak as a sick kitten. These voices have designed me insane. My clarity of thought has been bitten, infected by these parasites. My sanity has become their eatery. I'm a lost cause. I can't defend against their thievery. Life has been etched in the state of pause. Movement only exists in my head. Everything stops as the voices maul. The world around me is dead.

I brace my hands against my head, trying to subdue the pain. Inside I hear, I feel, I holler from the pounding: disturbing melodic chords that ripple across within. Logic has become paper-thin. Voices dance about and shout, celebrating the new host they found. Their harmonic wailing is so excruciating that my eyes are bulging from their sockets and for dear life, my hands are gripping my pockets. I'm trying to hold onto the last of my composure, trying to keep myself sustained from the voices: blasting rockets that eat away at my posture, my mind's health. Inside I'm a mess, a fucking mess.

I've developed a mental illness. I'm mentally diseased. Pills now fill my mouth's darkness. I swallow the mouthful of suicide seeds. I gulp hard as I taste the bitterness drag down my throat. After a moment of quick silence, hell unleashes. My stomach starts churning, things start spinning, I can feel my body hardening, white-tinted vomit gushes out, I hear the voices popping. Like a holocaust, the overdose eradicates the voices. Extinction crashed right into them. All the failing voices are nothing but broken stems. Nothing more than faded whispers that can't be heard. My mind is finally free from the sounds. I would love to indulge in my new quietness, my new sense of tranquility, but unfortunately, I got caught in the blast.

Love & Exile

Never underestimate the power of a vagina. Don't fucking kid yourselves. Emotions constantly get mixed up with hormones, to the point you can't differentiate between the two. Make sure before you tear yourself apart, you're thinking with your head and not your pelvarian sausage. You can listen to your heart I guess, but that asshole just wants to hug and cry all the time. It's not a reliable source of logic.

I don't want them. I just need them: drugs to make the pain go away, pills and needles to push me through, toxins to make me whole again, to dilute apart the hurt, the thoughts, all the times we fought. I'm trying to get rid of you, but you stick like glue. You just won't go away. I can't get you out of my head. I'm lost in the pendulum's sway, engraved in the void of a choice: keep thinking of you or move on. I don't know what to do. You are forever with me it seems. Like a bad dream, you stalk me. In my mind, through sleep, through wake, you're always there. An erasable mistake but I still love you. This feeling that still decorates my every emotion puts my body in an awkward stimulation, but I have come to accept it. This visceral journey of two, this torn heart odyssey, we inflicted upon each other is a concatenation of memories paved, of all the times we never forgave. We should have walked it hand-in-hand, but we sifted away like a fistful of sand. Our love drowned in the grains: the dreary remnants of what we used to be. And that is why we can never be.

All For You

I know. I know. I have severe issues with women. It's a problem. I get it. Just be thankful I don't write movie scripts for the Hallmark Channel. I'd be ruining a lot of holidays.

I want to cut out your laughter and fill the void with screams, to use the nightmares you gave me, and haunt your dreams. Every day your face is in my head, very much alive, far from dead. I loved you but you played possum. You waited and waited, then tore my heart from my chest. That day everything stopped. I never thought you could do this. I thought wrong.

The only thing I have of you is this wound, this scar that won't heal. Its pounding waves of hurt is all I can feel. This pain is unbearable. I want to slit your throat, but I love you too much. I fucking hate you not enough. I'm trying to be tough, but my mind is dying to a fragile waste, a bitterness I can only taste by the agile, silver blade that releases the bait: the blood loss that my sorrow will follow. And that's where I'll find myself: sleeping in the casket built by suicide when silver and I collide.

I tried for us but you had something else, something up your sleeve, something I couldn't believe. You just wanted a heart to break so you could feel better, and you did without any remorse. That blow pushed me backward into a wall of fire. Everything good about you went up in flames, so I blew away the ashes which left my body creviced with gashes. I have no words that could describe what I feel for you now; besides, I hope I am the crash test dummy you wanted, the wreck you wanted me to be. I'm glad I make you smile. I just wish I could cut it off and carve it upside-down. How I want you to regret what you did, but I'm pathetic and I know that will never happen. I'm just a hopeless romantic with no brain and a murdered heart. How could I be so blind? You destroyed everything; I walked right into a trap. Now it's too late to restart because I have nothing left. I never knew love could be so deadly.

Before I take my role in the black valley, there is one thing I want you to know: Everything I said and everything I feel, good or bad, it's true. It's real. It comes right out of what you left of my heart. And even after what you did to me, I would still take you back. That is how much I love you, how superior it is to the hate I have to force towards you, but I'll unite with death before that chance comes. Just know what I said and what I feel, it was all for you.

Going Under

On today's episode of I Can't Build Anything Right – I try to retrofit a casket into a functional submarine so I can dive deep into the ocean and tell weird-looking fish all about my fucking problems.

Every moment that passes by I breakdown and cry. Wanting to open the casket and fall inside, I count the amount of time I've died. Deaths from broken hearts and horrible parents have given me the strength to give up. Tragic is all my life has ever been. I'm torn at the seams; from the side, I'm leaking into a puddle of weakness, into a lake of loneliness, where my hopes and dreams sift past my fingers and rot into failures and nightmares. My existence is a ruthless ocean and I'm drowning right down the centre. I'm sinking fast with nothing to hold onto. With a mouthful of caged words, I'm afraid to say, I float downwards to the darkness. I'm going under the hard way, like a rock I'm shooting down like a meteor. Everything is beginning to make sense. It's all coming in clearer. I'm going under to a different state, turning into something else. I'm not quite sure what it is, but it doesn't feel right. Definitely not tonight. The air I breathe is strong and thick. It's making me sick. I'm feeling ill like I just swallowed a vial of pills. I'm being taunted by terrifying voices and screams. I'm seeing illusions of terrible things. I'm going under and I can't help but sink, down deep where it's too far to think. I'm helpless and growing tired. So, I think I shall pray for my soul to keep, close my eyes and sleep. And maybe when I revive if I'm still alive, I'll wake to whatever I am becoming.

Casket In A Ruin

NICE! I've always wanted a coroner office.

My self-esteem is all I've been: low and out of control, searching for a soul I've never known, to only find emotions that have been blown.

Pieces of me are all over the place, scattered behind my face. I'm all mixed up. I try to let it out, but I shut myself up. For I am afraid of what people might say. It isn't fair that my life's a nightmare. I scream to try and scare it away, but it's still the same old, fucked up dream – always there to murder my day. I'm a casket in a ruin.

I try to be a good person. I give and give, but people just take and take. I need a break. Why does everything I do seem to be a mistake? Is there anybody out there that can relate – wanting to be loved but all they get is hate? I'm scared to think I'm alone, frightened that my fate is a name etched in stone. I fear I'm accident-prone: a malfunctioning catalyst heading for disaster, raging down a dark hole until I'm gone, gone, gone.

The blackness of the night sky is my life. People are the stars and I'm the moon. And sure, I might be bigger, but in numbers they kill. Like a pack of hyenas attacking a lion cub. I'm torn into tiny pieces for wandering scavengers to finish what's left, until the corpses of my emotions are still, bled empty to the point where I feel nothing. I'm a casket in a ruin. And with these razor cuts slashed to my wrists, I know my time is coming to an end, coming soon, to be a ruin in a casket.

One Beautiful Portrait

In case you were wondering what a prelude to a restraining order looks like.

'm bleeding red and blue because I can't stop feeling you. After all the breaks, one beautiful portrait falls into place. Your worth must be significantly precious if so many crumbled before you because I never felt a love like this. I only wish you were stronger than my subliminal urge for loneliness.

The way your painted skin was torn from the frame – the forceful impulse shattered my heart. When your paper flesh hit the floor, I fell apart. I miss you so, like autumn trees that lost their dying leaves to the cold days that lead to winter. But like the rotation of seasons, I'm hoping that a new spring will arrive so I can come alive. I'm praying that a new chance will come forth so I can embrace your worth.

I can't believe rapture was standing right in front of me. Ignorance is bliss and now I know why I failed to capture. How could I have been so blind? Since your seam tore away from me, I've been a vulture closely stalking you but not to devour, but for you to eat me alive. I want you to scream. I want you to cry. Abuse me until I die from the inside. Just try. Then maybe I can drown my dream, my hallucination of having back what we used to be, what we should have been.

One beautiful portrait: the girl I degraded. Never have I felt so stupid. I stripped away the most ravishing gem, saw right through her heart for me, and treated her like a filthy harlot. I never knew she'd be different, that she was the one. I whored her until she was gone. My first true love accident, my first picture that I coloured over the lines and wanted to fix, my first Sleeping Beauty I let sleep, my only jewel I ruined to keep.

The day we stopped was the day I grew an impaled dot. That's when I realized I made a mistake. Since her departure I just wanted to give myself to her, reveal my pathetic state to her, show her how much I love her, beg her to stitch into me once more, just be forgiven by my beloved and hang her on the nail that's lodged in my heart.

Take Me Back

She didn't take me back.

Take. Take me. Take me back. This broken heart is killing me. Take my hand and set me free. Let's go back to the way things used to be. I'm sorry I yelled. I apologize for your black eyes that swelled. I love you. I do. I didn't mean to strangle you. Sometimes I get lost in emotions I can't handle. I know it's been a battle. Just trust me. One more time is all I ask. Please, one more round? I've taken off the mask. Everything you see now is everything I was meant to be. I stabbed you one time, but you didn't die. Your flesh and skin healed fine. Now please say you'll be mine.

I'm holding on by a thread; don't let it break. I don't want to make another mistake. Erase all the black I painted on your heart. Love me again once more. A new start. I will be everything you wanted me to be, but if you say *no*, you better go, run as fast as you can, because this knife in my hand is in position, ready for mutilation. I take back everything I've done wrong. I really changed but without you, my life is a nothingness. I'm asking for your forgiveness and you at my side. Take my love back inside. Trust me. Take. Take me. Take me back and I promise... I promise I won't make you scream.

Morning To Paradise (Vampires' Awakening Serenade)

This is the worst thing that's happened to vampires since Twilight.

Morning, it came without warning like night died suddenly. It caught me off guard, found me feasting, drinking blood from humanity, enjoying my thirst and my hunger, staining my lips red as my victim suffered, but from the sun's spears of light, I fled. I ran away as fast as I could to escape the day. Higher and higher, the burning ball of fire, rose. Quickly and violently my cold flesh was scorching; my marble skin was mutating into a bed of hot coals. Desperation was setting in; paradise seemed to be a millennium away. The cemetery was a lengthening distance. It was vast but I could find darkness there. Tiny pieces of me were fading to ashes. I was becoming scared, but haven was coming into sight. A few long breaths and I'd be safe, free from morning's cage and into paradise's arms, into my artificial starlight.

Which seemed like forever I beat the wave of heat. Into the chamber that holds my coffin, I made it to darkness, but it wasn't flawless. Grotesquely I was burned, torched and disfigured, but by nighttime, I will be rejuvenated, fully replenished. My black-burnt skin will again be polished back to its cold temperature and pale white texture. Once again, I will be beautiful. From now on I just have to be more careful, because next time I might not be so lucky. Today was close; I was almost engulfed and viciously decomposed. From this night forth the sun will no longer stalk me.

The night is arising. Charring red ambers on my body are gone, gone with the sun. My icy blue eyes have broken through the scabs: boils that bubbled on the surface. They glow fiercely and wild again, absolutely haunting. Like an unreal miracle, I'm fully healed like an immortal, to the tragic spectacle I am. I can hear the day's lullaby orchestrating the midnight star parade — the vampires' awakening serenade. It's hunting time; time to feed. I'm starving. Killing is racing through my veins. May the brutal line of slain begin: all the people I will devour dry, the sheep I shall drain to ease my bloodthirsty pain.

With one eye open, I'll always be gone before morning wakes. This vampire will not die in the daylight trap. I'll puncture and wade, basking my mouth in the blood cascades. I do not fear the bright glow, though I am cautious. I'll drink until dehydration is done. And before the illuminating fist of morning seeps up past the horizon I will already be slumbering in paradise, sleeping until the sun drowns and blackness drapes like wet curtains, poisoning the cure to infect itself with stars — the vampires' awakening serenade.

Union Underground

Joining a secret club sounded glamorous. I did give it some thought but declined their offer. Figured I'd have more fun alienating myself from society and becoming a chain-smoking alcoholic. I wasn't wrong.

Cut deep until the blood weeps. Inject silver to bring out the red. Every lifeline ends in death. Time will eventually catch you, so stab the knife through and through. You're hated. Why take it? Steal a second. Concentrate. Why deal with this pain? You can end it all today. Death can silence their vile words. Lie in the hands of decay. Set yourself free. It's meant to be. Steal a second. Think back and see – you belong underneath a dirt mound with the union underground, six feet down and beyond from Hell. Be the boy who fell down the well.

All the hands that reach for you are gripped fists: flailing knuckles that bruise your skin. Stay away from the firewall, run from the abuse, fuck all the cold words they use, fuck everything about them and fall to the union underground. We'll protect you, suffocate you away from it all. So, stab the knife through and through, begin the blood crawl, crashland and we'll take your hand. We'll save you from this place. One more blood spill will give you our hands, so stab the knife through and through.

Sure, I'm just a voice inside your head, but you're sane enough to hear me. And sure, I could be a figment of your imagination, but I am no liar; my words are true. Join the union underground and we promise, we will always be there for you. Down here we are all family. In the union underground, there are no such things as gripped fists, hateful words from loved ones, or tears of pain. Be with us and we will give you everything you wanted. We are here for you, so finish what you started and stab the knife through and through.

Desperation Of A Lover's Heart

Women love men who practice good hygiene. I feel like that is something she could have just told me instead of making me play two years of Breakup Charades.

I f I knew what this was about, if I knew why you are doing this, then I could figure it out because I know you hate me, but I want to know when you get closer to him, why do you get farther away from me? In your eyes, I don't know what you see, or what you want me to be. I'm lost but I'm trying. I'm dying but not giving up. You won't tell me anything, so if we slip and fall it's your fault. I'm forcing out all that I got and you're not. All I hear from you is this parasite and it's not right - how great and perfect he is. I could probably scream into your face, grab you by the neck, and chase... following your tears with my eyes and you still wouldn't tell me anything. Why? Why him over me? What did I do wrong? What have I done? Is loving you not enough? The tattoo of you across my heart – is that not enough? The letters and poems I wrote to you, weren't they enough? I'm losing grip! I can't take it! I'm slipping! I'm falling! I'm dying! I HATE YOU! I HATE YOU! I FUCKING HATE YOU! I died without you.

Lengthening Path
Of A Soldier

I take Call of Duty way too seriously.

Bullets flying. Bodies falling. Horrific sounds of thunder crashing. Friends fighting at your side. One blink and they're all gone. They all died. You have to fight back, but fear and sorrow hold your bravery and trigger-finger still. The sight of gushing blood makes you ill. Tears and vomit stain your colours of pride; you just died inside. You wish you were home, in the living room with your wife and kids. Instead, you're playing this deadly game of dodgeball. Allies and fellow troops by your side, fighting, crawling, dying. Their corpses blanketing the landscape into a rotting Hell, and just a few hours ago you were smiling to their smiles. Now you're losing it from their screams and yells: fatal blow chimes and gasps of suffering. You pray for this all to stop: the killing and blood spilling. But into the flesh of comrades, bullets keep drilling. With tightly closed fists and a feeling of deepened anger, you clench your tool of destruction, inhale what could be your last breaths, and rise from the trenches, hollering your patriot war cry. You start running against the hail of gunfire. You shoot rapidly and aimlessly, and somehow you've made it arms-reach of the enemy, then uninvitingly you take two in the chest. You bend from searing agony, collapsing to your knees. Your helmet retreats from your head and in a last-second, life goes into freeze-frame. Time thaws and a bullet rushes into your skull; everything goes black. You died like the rest, decorating this valley of dead.

Grim Reaper's Persuasion

I hate pushy salesmen. They only care about commission.

Cemetery gates rusted from centuries of rain – with the wing expansion of a great stone wall, this is the border separating the dead from the living. A world broken in two – two different worlds of their own. One is ugly, the other is unknown, but I know which one is beautiful. You just have to see past the corpses and eerie statues, past the haunting sounds and myths. Behind it all is the utopia, people are looking for. You shouldn't be frightened. Commit suicide and create your passage, then I can take you to your dirty carriage. Bliss waits for you in a brighter light than this, so take my black lips and kiss, absorb their dusty texture and I will take you there. Allow me to cut you in half with my scythe and take your soul where people fear. Go weak and give in to my words. They are the camouflaged bravery, the password to get you in. I won't repeat myself again. Just think about it. Know how much happier you will be if you let me be your tour guide. So, commit suicide, take me inside and as your dark horse, I will take you there.

Saliva To The Lips

Why my mortician's license was revoked is none of your damn business.

I kiss your shaded pink lips where saliva slightly drips. Smell of loving affection, a contagious temptation, a feeling that makes the heart skip, pounding so fast it misses a beat. I notice the change in temperature. The elevation of heat causing sweat once in a while to slowly revive from their pores, appearing, giving our faces a dim glow. Love is the reins that control us and it shows because we are so close, so close that how we do it nobody knows. They can't figure it out, but all that I care about is this embrace and how we don't let a second of time go to waste. You're perfect and that's why I'm paralyzed, kissing you as I get lost in your shining eyes. The world could crumble around us and I'd never stop to say goodbye, not while our bodies are bound and tied.

Wrinkles in the tender flesh cause my pupils to widen and darken. Attractive they are. Like tiny, little stars, vertical they lay. Each one filled with flavour: saliva beds where together lips savour. Sanctioned. Saliva to the lips from the collisions of two blinking eclipses: mouths opening and closing, playful gestures of vivid pleasure, an articulate leisure where every feeling is too far to measure.

Reacting to the pressing of lips moving is a dream where every kiss is redeemed, every kiss is better than the last. Sense of ecstasy that reaches vast, sensitivity stretching so far it overlaps, lapping a fragile state of bliss: an orgasmic enigma so extreme that I wish it stopped. But I don't stop, so these fervent emotions can last on, continuing until breaths come in pill-like doses, sizes of shrivelled petals from withered roses, kissing until every breath is gone.

Short crevices engraved on the soft devices: gullies for when the tongue slips. Saliva to the lips: the lubricant for when we kiss that softens and moistens. Saliva to the lips: lip water from our fountain tongues, the mouth stems that are long. Protruding simultaneously, they hug together; the momentum of them together is spellbinding. Twisting and winding, flicking and dancing, absolutely enchanting.

Saliva to the lips makes the massaging of our face pillows soothing, relaxing and moving. I could do this forever. As long as our lips stay soft and tender, I could taste you over and over. When our lips synchronize, everything inside me dies - strangled from the exerted rush when our lips touch from the hypnotic push. Peculiar it is when we kiss. It seems like we're trying to find shelter inside one another and this makes me want more, a complex feeling that's hard to define. But what I am more hypnotized by is that you and me, you and I, I am yours and you are mine.

Filthy Conscience

Now seems like a good time as any to reassure you that I have the utmost respect for women. I wouldn't lay a finger on them. The last thing I need is, there to be a serial killer dressing up as a crow, going around and murdering women, then someone informing the cops, and they read this shitty poetry book that was written by a crow who talked about killing women a lot. You heard it here first. It's not me.

Rip the screams from her lungs; pull them out strong. Sever your wrist flesh, until the body rot is fresh. Murder her and kill yourself. Rewrite Romeo and Juliet with every morbid aspect. Ruin this love tale sadistic and dramatic. Be the psychotic lover. Be insane, crazy, unsane. Break yourself from logic's frame. Take the blade to her torso; gut her like a fish. Let the liquid spectrum of colours flow. Make a wish. Put yourself to shame but give her the blame. She's the villain of this game, but two deaths equal a right. So when she dies, turn on yourself and bleed pungent waterfalls while your maggot buffet of a love feeds the baby fly horde.

I see you kissing her tenderly. I can feel your red hearts beating softly. Your two doves in love, but can't you hear me screaming? Don't you hear my cries that are bursting your eardrums? Don't you hear that hypnotic, pulsating hum? I'm your conscience, a ruptured valve. I'm out of control and flying blindly and I want you to rid of her. She's yours to dispose so make her decompose, then hear me again and enjoy suicide. Then you can decay and be the crop: another harvest for the insects to eat.

I see you sleeping at her side. I can hear the sound of light breathing. I invade your dreams and nightmares, but you don't seem to care. You still touch her gently and talk to her every day like those are your last words.

I'm trying to crash your world. I'm doing all I can, but you still ignore me. By now your head must be starting to swell, building up every time I yell. All I want is for you to burn in Hell. Is that too much to ask?

I've used every tactic I can think of. I tried everything to get you to hate, but you seem to be impossible. If I could only be visible, I know I can turn you into something terrible, but you're not registering my compulsive screeching. All I wanted was for you to sin and fall. I suppose I'll leave you be; you're too strong for me. So, I guess this is goodbye.

Wait… What is this? What… is… this?! To my astonishment I see your hand grip her wrist tightly. I can smell the hatred spew from your iron fist. And I tell myself, and it shows, that there just might be hope after all.

Rapture In Paradise

How the fuck am I still alive? Hey, Professor Xavier – if you're interested in recruiting a mutant whose superpower is botching suicide attempts… I'm you're failed draft pick.

Quick as lightning, blood from my veins come out bursting. The pain is a surging catalyst to elevate the falling of tears. So excruciating the pain that my screams stimulate, massing so loud that it tears away the stars, masking this beautiful night ugly beyond revolting. I always wondered what the perfect life would be like, but as I stand in the shape of a cross, dying, howling at the night sky, a life that could make Hell disappear doesn't exist. It's just a thought, a dream that's no thicker than mist.

From devastation and blood starvation, my memory drains; euphoria fills in the space. It feels good. It feels so good: the bloody cascades from piercing blades. I don't think I would stop it if I could. I'm the mutilation whore with a pretty face, dressed by dancing spade imprints and a masochistic wellbeing. I'm the suicidal king with no kingdom. I've given up the search for my castle. By the subliminal messages from cutting, you can read that I gave up on everything. I'm the lost cause never found, that dug his grave nineteen feet down – a foot for every year he couldn't find his way.

I'm done with dreaming; fuck Eden. I can see clearly – to rot was God's plot. I was God's guinea pig that couldn't stop. I couldn't stop myself from splitting skin. The bleeding dried up everything within. I couldn't stop, that's how my name became engraved in stone.

So much for rapture in paradise.

At The Graveyard

Most young adults fantasize about getting laid. But nope. Not me. Sometimes I think back on how much time I wasted feeling sorry for myself and letting depression consistently blindside me. I owe my sex life the biggest apology.

At the graveyard, I let my solitary wounds heal. I hated feeling alone. Why was this the only place I felt I belonged? Surrounded by bones and broken stones – this place adorned my eyes. It was picture perfect inside my head; maybe that is why I longed to die. I sat under this weeping willow many times, on a spot untouched where I felt in solace, where no frown glowed, no tears fell. Not in this place. At the graveyard, I reeled in bliss.

My life was so empty. No one cared when I was bleeding. No one was listening. The only ones that did were the ones that weren't breathing. At the graveyard, I found comfort. Pain didn't live here. Into Mother Nature's womb, I yearned to be, to be happy with the rest, with the ones who took off my heavy-hearted vest. At the graveyard, I wasn't alone. At the graveyard, I'm someone.

My fate was clear – underneath me, Heaven was near. With my ticket to go, decorated with a noose, I stood on the willow's branch. I decided to let my life go. So as the sky wept, I tried to forget all the things I kept. I fell with the rain, forever escaping the pain of loneliness. The noose tightened and I slept into darkness. When the sun killed starlight and the moon died with the burning night shards, there I was seen hanging at the graveyard.

The Suicidal Fly

This has nothing to do with the poem, but I would love to see a three-hour Spider-Man movie where Peter Parker does a lot of meth and attempts to do chores around the house. That would be neat.

Spider, spider, ravenous little spider, my ruthless predator, where are you? I'm stuck in your cocoon, strangled within your web. Crawl to me and chew; drink my blood until I'm dry. Drink my red liquid, all my fluids. Taste me. Don't waste me. Sink your daggers in deep and be carnivorous, spill your poison inside me, paralyze me, hold me still and I'll be yours at will.

Spider, spider, ravenous little spider, you caught me fair and square. Kill me, the suicidal fly. I double dare, triple dare you to feast upon me. Punish me for flying so carelessly and I promise when you devour me, I won't stare.

Spider, spider, ravenous little spider, I'm begging, pleading for you to quench your thirst. Forget the rest and drain me first. I am yours for the taking. Broken wings and exhaustion strangle me still, so pierce me violently. Make me empty like an old century well and I swear I won't tell.

Spider, spider, ravenous little spider – vicious, deadly arachnid, you are the carrier of my release. Stop hesitating and stab your fangs into me. Intoxicate me. Inhale me right past the last drop and I will be forever grateful. Eight-legged reaper, murder me this day so I can finally feel everything beautiful.

Pretty Girl With Bright Eyes

She still killed herself. Guess I wasn't as attractive as I thought. Well, that was a fucking waste of time. Shucks, you guys!

Pretty girl with bright eyes, why do you frown? Pretty girl with bright eyes, who let you down? Who gave you that knife? Please don't take your life. There is something I need to tell you, words that need to be said, thoughts that have been swimming in my head, all these feelings I've felt since we were kids. Since the day I first saw you... Pretty girl with bright eyes, listen. I know your life has been a rollercoaster with more downs than ups, but I've been always there for you. My hand was there for you to grasp, my shoulder for you to cry on. When the world became cold, I was your warmth. When people fucked with your heart and tore it apart, I was there for you to hold, to comfort you back to a whole. I was always there for you. Pretty girl with bright eyes, I know suicide seems to be the answer, but wait before you sever. Just hear what I have to say before you end this day. Pretty girl with bright eyes, you are my world, my everything. Without you I'm nothing. I never attempted to cross the line, never asked if you would be mine, but if you end yourself that will be it. I'll set my heart on the shelf and let dust and cobwebs bind to it. Pretty girl with bright eyes, you are the only heart I seek. Pretty girl with bright eyes, what I am trying to say is... I love you.

Depression for the Grateful

BDSM - is probably the best way to describe my relationship with mental illness. I'm a Bottom. I would be a Top, but I'm too lethargic to put in any amount of effort. For anything.

Depression, burn fiercely. Set my sanity ablaze. Bring back my dark days. I miss your torment. Come back and treat me like vermin; fill my head with suicidal thoughts like you once did. I'm done living fantasy; I fell back to reality. I was born to be sad, but I want more than that; make me your casualty. I crawled back to you. Now take me in. Embrace this surrender. Inhale my mind until it's soft and tender, then give me my veins to sever, pull back the lever, open my mouth, send white pills down south. Please, finish what you started.

Depression, increase your decibels and your voltage, levitate the dosage, make me more suicidal than I used to be, program me so I am out of control. When the blade is in death's reach, let the blade absorb its potency and cut me down with its cruelty. I don't want to stop it this time so make me weak. Let the knife against my wrists creak, causing friction against the skin until the blood erupts, until every blood droplet drops. Depression, show no mercy; lay your malice upon me. Depression, bloom into suicide. Do that for me and I will be eternally grateful.

When Zero Comes Thrashing

You think you're emotionally unstable? This poem was about a hamster I had to flush down the toilet. What else you got?

Underneath the silence I can see the signs fading. I can feel the hurt pacing. Complete meltdown has already started counting down. This relationship is unstable. I fear it is coming to a violent end. And when zero comes thrashing, one of us will die from the blast. I thought forever we would last but it seems not. Between the crossfire of two fates, we were caught and made to go separate ways. But I need you. I love you. There is no way I can live without you.

Below the hush sounds, the whispering, cracking of tragedy, a fairytale-like love disintegrating rots my mind. I will lose my nymph, my goddess, to open whatever is left of my heart to darkness. When zero comes thrashing, I'll shield you and let the flames crash into me. Our love is going to be destroyed. This apocalyptic event is going to be merciless. I can feel the rage already swarming inside the gap between us. The signs are fading of our love going on. The jury of inevitability has given their verdict: devastation will break us apart and in anger, our love we made will explode. And it kills so much that I know this isn't a dream, and that soon I will hear the painful sounds of our screams. How I wish this was a dream.

In my head, as the countdown finishes off, I finish off the last of my preparations. I am now prepared for the fatal onslaught. I am ready to take myself where my casket is waiting, to hate myself for the amount of eternities for every tear you cry...

ZERO...

Mother Serpent

I made this all up. I was created in a lab. And by that I mean my mother was a black lab, a bitch if you will. What I'm trying to say is that I'm not a crow. I'm a dog. Mom, if you're reading this, I don't think you're a bitch. This is a fictional poem. I love you. Please don't hit me again. That was also a joke. Congratulations on getting your forklift ticket!

What's wrong with being free? What's wrong with being me? Please, stop lecturing me. Stop yelling at me. I don't care so don't stare. Don't stare! Don't stare! STOP FUCKING STARING AT ME!

So, darkness dresses me but the inside is still the same. I didn't change. I just evolved. Stop trying to find me. Stop trying to save me. It's useless. I'm a puzzle that can't be solved.

You slay me with misunderstanding. It hurts. Your words fill my heart with dirt. I can't believe the things you say. You want me to stay but you're pushing me away. Stop your serpent tongue from salivating. Stop before I forget how to breathe. Stop. Let's talk. It's not too late to go back to the days of yesterday.

Maybe I'm not the kid you chose, but I'm yours. You took the risk. I'm sorry I was your mistake. I guess you should have kept your legs closed. Why can't you see through the shades? Underneath the black drapes, there's red: the love from a son to a mother. Tragic you pierced it with your verbal daggers, though, because we could have been perfect, but that can't be if I'm a defect. Mother, why can't you love me?

I love you. Hate you. Almost time for the final goodbye. Shadows disappear in the night and the sun is sinking fast.

Lasujah's Decmember

Lasombra and Brujah are two vampire clans. That's where the name Lasujah came from. I'm so fucking dark and mysterious.

Lasujah the Winter Beast, by many mortals named and feared. His coming was told to us in a dream. This hunter is the reason for the Red December: the month where bodies of the town's people were found severed. Every morning a frostbitten corpse appeared, mutilated and amputated limb from limb, with their heart torn out and placed in their left hand. Definitely a symbiotic pose of damnation. A total of thirty-one dead were calculated by the month's end. These terrifying images scarred in many heads, causing a string of suicides from sanities that bled. If there was one word for this town, it would be *tragic* – a place of sadistic, murderous magic.

Lasujah, a plague from the depths of Hell, and he let everyone know it by the red, cursive *L* glided into the snow, beside the sword-painted flesh abandoned under the streetlamp's glow. For so long he has never been seen, until the wake of fog on the thirty-first morning. I was walking, catching some fresh air, and as I turned the corner of the old sawmill, there he was, standing by his innocent with his blood-soaked sword dripping from the slaughter. I have never witnessed such a being in all my time. He wore a black top hat impaled by a grey rose. A long, black velvet coat that tickled the ground, held together by silver buttons, and dark leather boots hugged by broad, brass buckles. But the one feature I will not forget is his demonic eyes. Black and silver hair peeked out the front of his hat, which highlighted these fierce blue eyes. They were haunting, yet, mesmerizing. In them, I saw a coldness, a coldness colder than winter: all my friends and family that died by his hands. Yet, I did nothing. I just let him grin his pale lips, fade into the fog, allowing him to leave his scent of a past presence behind. That was the last day of the killings. And from what I saw I hope, I pray he never comes back. They call Lasujah's term of events "Red December" – a month that will always be remembered.

World Where Everything Dies

Just about there.

Plagues and diseases dancing by, stalked by siren-weeping cries, bodies dropping like flies – this is the world where everything dies.

Plantations that bloom the scenery are blight, withered and in the state of rotting. Every day is night; the air is bitter and stars barely glitter. Not even creatures come out to kill. Death overlaps, pausing life to hold still – this is the world where everything dies.

Friday the thirteenth is abused, on the calendar overused. Accidents and mishaps, cruel tricks and traps, all misfortunes assisting humanity to their demise. This place is run by sadistic temptation, the infection wiping out the population – this is the world where everything dies.

Weather is relentless. Frostbiting winds adorn the darkness: the sheet of black that hangs like a corpse. Breezes are malicious, penetrating the skin like barbed-wire pellets. When they enter, the flesh splinters, dividing unstably like a chain reaction Kamikaze, shredding your insides and you can't stop it no matter how hard you try – this is the world where everything dies.

Life expectancy here is slim; everyone born here is starving thin. Anyone still alive is cadaverous, fucking ravenous. There's nothing to eat but their own kind. They've all hungered into cannibals. They're ruthless animals tearing and biting into each other. Blood and betrayal stains behind, outlining everybody torn by canines, sharp human teeth, porcelain-like razors hugged by gangrene gums, once white statues that stood above the jaw, thorns that cut like a dull, jagged saw – this is the world where everything dies.

Species of sorts dying to extinction from malnutrition and dehydration. Carrion and corpses lying amongst empty watering holes, where the only liquids they found were blood and saliva: bodies of grey resting where trees were fruitful, where great meadows were once beautiful. Tragedy swept through here like a disaster; faster and faster it drowned out life. Nothing and no one had a chance. All they could do was panic and fear, for they knew death was near, soon to appear because this is the world where everything dies.

When the animal kingdom perished and plant life fell to sand, when surely humanity was the next to end, humans transformed into sheep and begged their god to have mercy, hoping he would vanquish this unforgiving misery. To pray to a god who abandoned them, that was desperation. When their god did not answer their pleas, that was suffocation. When they found themselves choking with curled fingers and with heartbeats beginning to linger, when they realized they were falling into aisles, they knew they lived in a world where everything dies.

Circle Of Suicide Goes 'Round

Yup. I see it now. My wife is right. This is totally an unacceptable lullaby to sing to our child. Oops.

We climb further just to fall farther. We try but fail. Ladders always seem to break and derail, launching us in a net of betrayal. Soaring vertical from love gone stale, there's no one calling, no one to stop us from falling. We're all alone in this world of sons and daughters.

"Abandonment equals hatred" – we've been shackled by that phrase for too long, past a length of time where we can no longer hold on. Strength is not amongst any of us; our minds are completely out of focus. People try to separate us with lies, but we know better. Only the words and actions that bleed from us is trust. We rely on each other. We survive by sticking together. Why did our loved ones turn their backs? They left us as rogues, but we still have hands. From blood to dust, we engage in the sense of touch, as one by one our hearts combust.

Lately, there has been something growing, something ominous crawling up our spines and into our minds. We search but cannot find. Every day that inches by, weakness strikes. Nefarious images and thoughts are developing and retracting into logic, melting the walls of plastic: armour we built to protect us. Lately, our empty fists have been filling, masquerading with poisons, knives and guns. Hopeless we stand, silently screaming for help; no one answers. Mouths open, wrists split, brains shut down – like dominoes we die to the ground as the circle of suicide goes 'round.

Kill The King
And Rape The Queen

Turned out I was daydreaming. I'm still dancing around like a fucking idiot in front of a bunch assholes. Being a eunuch sucks. Yes. I'm also a eunuch.

Because my rank in this kingdom is near bottom, doesn't mean you can treat me like trash, doesn't mean I'm your slave. I'm the court jester. My job is to make you laugh, to relieve any stress you have by crazy antics and silly jokes, but this lack of respect is getting to me; it's making me choke. Lately, my head has been twitching, my makeup eyes have been blinking, voices in my mind are telling me awful things. I don't know how much longer I can hold back. Every day they say,

"Kill the king and rape the queen.
Kill the king and rape the queen.
Kill the king and rape the queen."

I don't appreciate food being thrown at me for your comic relief or sympathetic grief, because you think my life is sad and pathetic. All this sadism floating around inside my aura is making me psychotic, fucking nauseous. I've been mentally damaged, and I don't think there's much left to salvage. It's all your fault. Why do you laugh at me? Why can't you laugh with me? These voices are getting to me. Every day they tell me,

"Kill the king and rape the queen.
Kill the king and rape the queen.
Kill the king and rape the queen."

I'm possessed by their hypnotic chanting; sanity has crawled away from me. With my wooden staff, I lunge for the king but his prestigious, silver guards block my assassination attempt. With all my hatred and might, I kill all those that stand in my way. Behind me, in front of the king, his precious, silver soldier horde lie dead – dead with bloody, broken faces and loose-gripped maces. His mighty four became the dead quartet. So, with black lips smiling, I raise the murder weapon high as the voices cry,

"Kill the king and rape the queen.
Kill the king and rape the queen.
Kill the king and rape the queen."

With eight severe swings, I crack open his skull. Beating it to a repulsive pulp, I batter him as he gulps a last mouthful of blood. Hail the death of the king! Praise the golden corpse on the throne! From compulsive loud screams, my attention is diverted to his beautiful side. There is nowhere for her to run in this great hall. All the doors are locked. She is mine to fall. In a corner, I tear her from her red robe and dainty clothes. I strip her naked. I quiver from the touch of her skin. A slight feeling of numbness, a vague feeling of being sedated runs throughout my body. In ecstasy I fuck beauty. As the army bangs on all the doors, I leave a piece of me inside her. Through the window, I escape. In the end, I got the last laugh. I killed the king and raped the queen. And as for this dungeon, may ashes become of this kingdom. May everyone burn with it. May their deaths be slow and excruciating. May this whole godforsaken place blaze to dust.

Paradies

Vacationing with Pinhead like...

can't make it go away – the dark picture embedded inside my head. This frozen oasis feels so fucking real. I think clearly and constantly but the same image just stays the same. It won't go away.

My mind is a holocaust, a desert wasteland, grey skies and black clouds accompanied by cracking thunder that pounds, and white lightning that scorches the ground. The water is black with acid, the air is putrid, immense thorns span across the ground, and I've gone too far to turn it all back. So, this is what I have to deal with every day. This is what I see, this paradies, this imaginary world created by poisoned eyes from all the dreadful things I have been exposed to. I waited too long for help and now there's nothing I can do, but to slowly wither apart into my paradies – the place far from my heart.

I have been growing a slight immunity to this nothing community, but there is one thing that frightens me: There's this one spot right in the middle of the thorns' eye that haunts me. It's my dead body. And there I am sprawled out with bloody wrists, curled beside an open grave with a tombstone that says, "Not too much longer now." I don't like the sight or the sound of that. My paradies is going to be a reality. Soon I'm going to be a casualty, a corpse by fatality. My fate is going to trace this imagery. Soon I will blend in with the scenery, dead as dead can be.

From my paradies, I cry clear rains that darken red: tears that drip razors close to my veins. I'm a fighter but this strain is a god; losing is the point of this battle. It seems the image in my mind will be picture-perfect, the hand that will squish me like an insect because I think a razor got carried away and tunnelled too far, down deep enough to leave a scar. It fell vast and sliced apart the vein. Now ruptured, it's giving out blood to the floor. I can't stop the flow. I can see paradies stitching to my eyes. Blood drops. I drop. Breathing stops. A nightmare come true.

Silver

Get over yourself. He's not actually going to kill himself over you. He's just too sad to get an erection. He'll be fine. I'll... Er... He'll find someone else. I mean he found someone else and is SUPER thrilled about her. I'm n... He's not sad at all.

Silver through the flesh; red drapes collapse. A few more cuts. I hate you less and less. Love disabled. Fragile heart shaking – the decibels quaking too far. Images of your river-eyed face: my weeping scar embalming me. You are my dying star.

Silver in my hands; green liquid inhabits the chalice. Swampy fluid tilted slightly downward, many sips past the lips. My mouth is viral, infection spirals. Poison spews its gangrene colour around my insides. From the inside, I drown. Your face still stitched to me; together we fall down.

Silver to silver: the knife leaning against the chalice. Emblematic for a suicidal cause – my body in forever pause. Breaths to a corpse: silence from failure conquering love. I killed myself out of spite. I could no longer get lost in your eyes. I always found my way out, so dying was my fatal exercise. I bled for you, poisoned myself because of you. And it might not have been your fault but like it or not, with gashes and toxicity my cadaver will rot.

Atlantis

New drinking game: Take a drink every time you read a poem that's about me killing myself over a girl.

Struck by a wave of emotions, a passionate light inhaling; love that drowned in my dark seas of cold, broke from its concrete and began soaring. That is the glow that forms around my heart. I thought I tore it apart into pieces of unfixable shaping, but the sight of you fused them together. I thought I put it in the cycle of forgotten, into the deep shades of lost, but like a phoenix rising from the ashes it came rocketing out of its cerement, the memorial bog I damned it to, and flew into my heart that's been dead for years.

But then like Atlantis everything sunk heavy, disappeared and forever unreachable. I told you how you made me feel and like a blade to the heart, your laughter fed the thrust, giving it the hurt to stab it through. Your words with the background laughing killed everything. It all froze as it turned back to stone, hardening and falling even farther than before. From the aching sore, the rejection you highlighted for me, I left without an expression on my face, went to my room in zombie-like fashion, grabbed a razor, leaked myself into a fright of dying, and all because of a girl.

Vampire Superior

Depression may have taken a lot of things away from me in my lifetime, but it can never have my shitty vampire poetry. That. That is mine. Hey, also... Is my sex drive showing? Cool. Cool. Cool. Cool. Cool. Cool.

I bathe in a casket of blood, absorbing the energy of another fallen, cloaking my pale flesh an illuminating red, gathering energy for another slaughter. I am the Nosferatu Father, Vampire Superior, the leviathan of my kind. Down here I am time; I decide when things begin and end. I am the Nurturer, the Reaper, the Vampire Superior.

During high moon I unleash destruction, casting out my children to feast. They kill in violent spurts, killing unseen, drinking innocence until their teeth hurt. Every action they make is flawless because I am their trainer, the most vicious warrior, their leader. I am perfection beyond perfection. I am the Vampire Superior.

We live under an old cemetery and every night we're multiplying. Welcome to the shadow of Utopia. A world where I watch the spectacle of humans dying, the transformation of innocence writhing into sinners: specimens chosen to join the clan. And by the pace we're populating at, in days I will hold this universe in the palm of my hand. I will be the universal ruler, the iron fist dictator. I will be Jesus and humanity will be my flock. It is just a matter of the ticking of the clock; inevitability is on my side. I will be the virus, the plague, the reason why humanity died. I will be their destroyer, for I am the Vampire Superior.

Blood, sex and power: the trio of things my black heart desires. Perversion for orgies with sweet-made virgins and the last graven kiss I bestow to them, indulging in the reddest of blood during vampire mass. When the thirst is quenched, my lips blood-drenched, I lock each one in a casket of glass. Losing my winter-reflection's stare at decay, I taste my lips while the flesh from their bones rots away. I am the Murderer of the Inferior, too much to endeavor, the Vampire Superior.

It is simple. From the catacomb castle, life all around me will wither and die, then when silence is all that is left, I'll sing and dance while angels kneel and cry. From the movement of a finger, I'll create a wasteland; grains of sand will sift through my fingers from my cold, ruthless hand. Nothing and nobody can prepare for what I have in store, the image I will portray. Men will crumble like ancient walls, women will be fucked like whores, then drained into the pose of a corpse. Oceans will boil and dry. From grass to forests, everything will burn. Skies will be scorched to an eternal night; when I am finished not a creature will stir. I cannot be stopped. I am the Executioner, the Holocaust Carrier, the Damned Martyr, I am forever, the Vampire Superior.

From Incest To Insects

Incest isn't best but sometimes it's all we have. Don't quote me.

Humanity: a species built from two, all made from the same cloth. It's sick how we are all brothers and sisters. We are all related. This world is an orgy of incest. We're all fucking insects. We are mindless rabbits. To breed seems to be the only point of living and it's sad how not enough of us are dying. Somehow the process needs to be quickened, a plot of vast annihilation needs to be thickened. People are so blind. Why can't they see that they're the pests? Why do they think they're better than the rest? Because of them, we're surrounded by problems. But I know how to solve them. Just give me a gun, infinite ammo, and watch me go. By the crack of dawn, half a country's population will be gone. I'll take the duty, the privilege of being Death, the new holocaust to humanity's health, a resurrected plague to wipe away the disease, to cool down people with a bullet's breeze. We went from incest to insects. We fucked our brothers and sisters. Then after the wave of disgusted lust, we became tragic and began digging our extinction. Fuck mercy - it seems we don't want it, so stuff us with misery. Our culture consists of murder, rape and greed. I have my hatred and that's all I need, the fire I need to succeed. I'll get by and watch the population die. I'll laugh until it's my time to say goodbye. We went from incest to insects; this world is what we project.

Youth Destructed Cold

Totally made this up.

He says I need discipline. He says I'm trash. He says I'm not his little boy. He hits me. He throws me around. He pounds me to the ground. Bruises are coloured to my body; blood is stained to the carpet. Where's my mommy? Oh, there she is. She's drunk on the couch, passing out her days, leaving me to play with daddy, but he's too rough. He batters my face. He beats me, his own kid. And mommy just lies there without a care, smelling like booze as I bruise. He's already broken my arm, but he still causes me more harm. I'd cry if I wasn't overwhelmed with so much hate and confusion. I'd cry if I wasn't filled with so much love and frustration. If I live through this bad treatment the tables will turn; when I'm older the tables will explode and burn. I'll take my parents down the same road, except their ending will be different. Their last chapter will end in a ditch. Goodbye, asshole! Goodbye, bitch! So mother, keep drinking your alcohol. Father, keep the wrath coming, lay me on the borderline of dying. Just don't change a thing because I have my revenge already plotted. And when time gives me strength, I'll put my plan into effect. I'll have you two begging for mercy. You'll be screaming for forgiveness as you grab my pant legs. A pant leg for both of you. Something for you two to brace yourselves against. Then in a silent pause, two gunshots will break the muted barrier. Two parents – BANG! BANG! One corpse! Two corpses! A problem cured by two bullets. But for now, for the time being, I'll just take these scissors and jab it into my father's hand, call my mom a fucking whore, and run out the door.

Loathed Face

A simple "No" would have sufficed.

Look at your face. It's so grotesque. Keep it away. Keep it away. The sight of it makes me sick. Here's a mask; cover it and turn the other way, the other way.

What were you thinking? Look at yourself. Did you really expect me to smile back? Are you that fucking stupid? You lost your chance with me before you even thought about me, so get out of my face by removing yours. Cry like a baby for all I care, because you know you're worthless and ugly. Just get out of my face, out of my space.

Why are you standing there? Remove yourself from my sight; your face is more than I can bear. It's so fucking disturbing. I can't help but stare. I don't care that you love me. I could care less that you're crying, dying without me. I want nothing to do with you. I'm not yours, never will be. Now make yourself useful - go home, look into the mirror, peer at something awful, and realize why I loathe you.

Filthy Girl

Don't lie. This poem made you hard, didn't it?

Decrepit girl dying in the attic; lunacy has power of the controls. She's not all there, or not there at all. I can tell by the soiled mattress that reeks on the floor, and how she lies on it like an over-diseased whore. This cesspool has consumed every bit of her. There must be a reason why she acts this way, a cause for her grotesque behaviour because I have never seen something so innocent, something so beautiful to enslave oneself in such filth.

Petting her cat, she killed with an old rusted wrench, she breathes in the stench of its decomposition and exhales the smell by vomiting. She inhales so she can savour the taste of regurgitation because her feline is her favourite flavour. Disturbed; she's everything absurd. I swear she'd frown if she ripped those staples out of her smile, but if she wants to play pretend that's fine with me. I'll just pray until she finds her end.

Filthy girl, filthy girl; she's dirty without a piece of soul left to sell. Filthy girl, filthy girl; I will be waving my hand when she falls down the well.

She has no friends only predatory arachnids: spiders that decorate her kingdom with cobwebs and dead flies. Drained insects floating in her teacups full of rainwater: miniature oceans that seeped through the crack in her roof. Her surroundings are sickening. Her health is threatening. Maybe she should take that blade and carve the ace of diamonds, bleed that suit straight from the wrists because I don't see a sign of consciousness anywhere. She just doesn't care.

Her white, gorgeous dress slain to murky shades by constant defecation and never-ending streams of urination. There are old and new signs of orgasm all around her: female secretion from vigorous masturbation. Even through human waste, she gives herself pleasure. It's revolting but for some reason, I'm mystified by it all, slightly aroused by it all. And I guess that makes me as sick as her if I have these vivid thoughts of romancing her, making love to her, fucking her.

Filthy girl, filthy girl; she's dirty without a piece of soul left to sell. Filthy girl, filthy girl; I will be waving my hand when she falls down the well.

Is she a sinner or victim? I can't tell. This catatonic is a mixed breed. I know only one thing and that's inevitability: the kisses for suicide that are glowing on her wrists. She possessed by something. I can't figure it out. But as the window is pelted with winter rain, she continues to drain, leaving no time to solve the mystery. She dies in the scenery of misery with her rotten cat still cradled in her arms. Filthy girl lost. Young corpse cold as December. Frozen as the window stabbed with frost. A delicious treat for the maggots to eat.

Red Door, Black Door

I would make a terrible game show contestant.

In my mind a path breaks in two: To the left stands a red door, to the right casts a black door. Each one shaded transparent. I can see what waits behind them. If I pick the red door, a life of bloodshed lies before me. If I choose the black door, a life of loneliness grows before me.

Bloodshed or loneliness: flesh cutting from too many problems or abandonment from family and friends. This all seems unfair. Life must have another door to bare. If not, can't I live life between the doors? Must I choose? I have everything to lose. I refuse to pick a one-sided fate, but it's become harder to fight. Every day the doors move closer. It's come to the point that I'm wedged against their rusty knobs. Rusted from the tears I cried. Rusted from every time I struggled inside.

I can feel being ripped apart from this game of tug-o-war. I can't take it anymore, but they keep pulling for more emotional gore. Both yearn for me. Their desire is thick in the same, dangerous like predators untamed. Both doors are grotesque in their own way; none is better than the other. Live my life alone or sever – these options are unfit. Just more of fate's propaganda bullshit showing it has a darker side. I already knew about this and I don't want to be a part of this. Isn't knowing good enough? Why must I experience it? I won't let this happen. I have one last move of desperation to give the doors desolation, one chance to escape, to steer away from solitude and mutilation. Without hesitation, I deceive fate and run away from Hell.

Red door, black door, go away. I am no good to you anymore; leave me be. Can't you see I have found another way? Stop being resistant and fade distant. Red door, black door, I can't open you and walk inside. Can't you see I'm transparent like you? Notice how I'm smiling? Notice I'm no longer crying? Red door, black door, I found the swirled door. Red door, black door, I found suicide.

Bloody Mary
(The Betraying Whore)

Yeah... if you're religious you might want to skip this poem entirely. You won't be able to unsee it. If you decide to read it, let me be clear - I'm not a Satanist. I just think religion is a joke. Hope we can still be friends after. Consider this a test. You've been warned. Shucks!

God is dead. Joseph is still and drenched with red. There's a bullet wedged in Jesus' head, and the Virgin Mary is sprawled across my bed. Dead creator, passed away father, brain-collapsed messiah, and a slut lying bare, licking her lips as she stares, curling her finger at me, calling me over, impatiently signaling me to violate her. I can smell the sexual innocence in the air: the lust surging past her cunt hair. An expression of a curious whore burns on her face. Her delicate hands gripping violently to the satin sheets, opening her legs wider and wider, obeying my fierce heartbeats. She whips her hair away from her urging face and moans in a low tone, "Fuck me. Fuck me now." In a hormonal daze, I hesitate. In awe I watch her fingers slide. In awe I gaze as she vigorously masturbates, daring me to feel her inside, luring me in with her juices that drip. And I can't help but bite my bottom lip, imagining it's her tantalizing clit. I want to suck her dry, rape her until I make her cry, but through the looking glass of sadism, I see right past the chance for an orgasm and decide that I'd rather her die. So, instead of playful actions of passion, I choose my weapon of eradication. Aiming it high to her stomach, with a grin of sin I fire six shots. Her eyes burst with surprise and fear. Her naked, perforated body jumps as her mouth dresses it with red vomit. Her lust bleeds to dust. Bloody Mary, the betraying whore is dead: the manipulated doll so breathless and lifeless in my room, slowly rotting to the speed of time. A quartet of corpses now waits to bloom, waiting to ripen into succulent meals, into four buffets of decay for carnivorous insects. This is the Bible inside my head.

Comatose Girl

Boy, I sure do know how to pick them.

Blade-holding hand flailing, controlled by a mind thirteen shades darker than midnight. White dress seeing the effects, bleeding red, covering the satin pearl: actions made by a comatose girl. She's a rare beauty made up of a mangled, thin body, a masochistic smile, hair that dangles like dying leaves and tiny, black pupils silhouetted by irises that resemble a fresh puddle of bile. She smells like rotting flesh and lilacs - a stench so peculiar, to corpses so familiar. The girl is a disaster; the girl is comatose.

Comatose girl, sick tattoo artist – milky skin scathed. Now it bleeds crimson waterfalls: a feature that drips with silence, descending murals of violence. Comatose girl unleashed, screaming banshee that flies on mutilation, always yearning pain and suffering, and anything odd to add to her collection of deformities. Her imagination is compiled of coloured pills that arouse her body to a selection of ecstasies. Organs that inhabit her body are choking, but she pops to keep her insanity soaring. Comatose girl so beautiful – a tale ended by fluent blood loss and bitter Skittles. Comatose girl so awful – you weren't meant for this world.

Vicious Acts From The Abused

Eerie how I'm married and have a daughter now. That's unsettling. Life is funny. Oh yeah, don't call the cops. This is fiction. I love my family and my parents aren't fucking assholes. Well, to each other they are, but that's their problem. Ah, divorce... lingers longer than herpes. Gross.

Dragging the corpse; tracks playing Follow the Leader. I went too far; with fists, I beat her. I beat her until she had blue skin, pulverized her until inside she was black. There's no going back. I crossed that line that I shouldn't, from doing something I told her I wouldn't. I promised. I lied. She died.

Her perfume is spoiled from death. The smell is so bad I'm afraid to take a breath but to take her to her hole, her new home, I breathe. Gagging and stumbling from the stench, I breathe a scent procreated from anger-directed flailing fists. It won't be paradise but for the maggots, it will be Heaven: a meal to feed all of them. Vicious acts from the abused gave them this; it gave her this.

Her face reminds me of when our daughter finger-painted it. All the colours are present from the past, except these ones are made to last, there to stay until she decomposes into bones. I destroyed the perfect family portrait. I ruined the gift life gave me. Will my daughter suffer the same fate? I don't know. I just know that I love her, and she loves me. And if I repeat this with her, if I drag her through the dirt, I pray she knows, that she won't forget I still love her and her mother.

I lay the blame on my parents. I copied and perfected what they did to me. The hurt they gave me killed my world, my wife and I hope not my daughter too. I'm insane – that's the diagnosis of my brain. My mind is draped with an evil I can't comprehend. I'm the flawless reflection of the way I was raised: lost and blindly sadistic. The death of my wife has become quite sardonic, but it makes me sad. This should've never happened, but it did, and there is nothing I can do to bring her back. Vicious acts from the abused – I was the only one that could have stopped this, but I was persuaded by the excuse of having bad parents. Are you ready maggots? Here she comes.

Through the thinking process, I slide her into the hole I dug for her, her palace of soil. In the filthy cradle, I will lay the corpse to rest. This is where slimy vermin wait for her, ready to devour her as the body spoils. The mere thought of this cannibalism is gruesome. It will be my new nightmare, my brand new, dark reverie. With these added hauntings, I fear my daughter will be the next contestant of my wicked game. Death better find me first and save my daughter. I don't want her to be a victim of mine, an innocence targeted by vicious acts from the abused. So, as I bury my wife, my daughter's mother, my love, I whisper softly for death to find me fast before another day does surpass because I don't want this shovel digging for two.

Cupid's Absence
Brought Atrocity

For being an adorable cherub, Cupid is kind of a dick.

You remind me of my faults and everything I'm not. Around you I feel like a failure, so fucking insecure, yet I stay at your side. Maybe I'm stupid or just waiting for Cupid, hoping he'll shoot his arrow right through you, puncturing your heart so we can have a clean start, to poison you whole so you can open your eyes and stop filling my head with lies. Wishful thinking perhaps. Is this sane thinking? I don't know anymore. My sanity is about to snap. I think I'm okay even though my life has died grey, three times thicker, five times darker than yesterday... But I keep hope lit, praying that this missing puzzle piece will fit.

I love you more than I should. I'm at the point that I would take it all back if I could. I just want you to be like me, to love me as I do you. Is it really that hard to see we're meant to be? Why am I the only one that sees this? You said you loved me once, so how come you won't say it twice? Please don't say our love was a hit or miss because I think it missed. You unplugged and became disconnected. Why do you have to be so complicated? It makes me so frustrated; you won't even talk to me. Is this the way things are truly meant to be? I guess nightmares come true too. Cupid's absence brought atrocity; it set you free, caged me up and threw away the key. From a broken heart, I fell apart.

You're fascinating, completely intriguing, in every way beautiful. I thought you were something special; perhaps you still are. But when I read this scar, this gash slashed to my heart, I realize how much I love you, how much I will put my heart on the line, how hard I will try to make you mine. But in clarity, I see no matter what there's nothing I can do. Cupid's absence brought atrocity; already I miss his arrow's velocity. You weren't struck – bad luck and old news. Time to move on and accept you're gone, still in sight but out of reach. Cupid's absence brought atrocity, broke a lovers' tale, painted a goddess' heart pale – Cupid's absence left me to a world of ashes.

Eruptions Of
A Serpent Tongue

Can you hear me now?

Cursing words blast from my serpent tongue. Heated with anger, burning with a malevolent rage, my poetic speech of cruelty stabs within. With drowning eyes and a melting smile, I can see my Kamikaze words devouring, ravenously tearing apart your faith, deconstructing you as they wraith. They're eating away at the core and I admit I'm lusting over your face. Your pathetic, sad posture I want to trace. It's beautiful. Your mental breakdown makes me feel so sadistic, so fucking alive. Your weakness is my strength, so you keep crying and I'll keep yelling, and I will strangle your hand, pierce my fingernails into you, and scream about how much I hate you. Maybe then you'll understand. Maybe then you will finally realize how much I love you.

Wonderland
(A Masochist's Well)

This is my ten-point plan on how I plan to take over a Chuck E. Cheese. Notice how completely insane I am.

Walls closing in, clocks erupting, blades in the skin, veins rupturing – welcome to my Wonderland. Pills, inhalants and liquid poison, unseen whispers and shadow-curtain skies – welcome to my haven. My world that took the black from the raven. I built this cage to keep me in, to keep people out. This is my place, my realm imprinted with bloody palms, a docile place that's calm. You can always find me here in my little globe of imagination and loneliness. Here I am free. This is where my happiness lies. Through my tiny window, you can see, see what I mean. This is my capsule, my guardian. I am protected in my dark and twisted stadium. It's somewhere I belong, a place that's meant for me. It knows no destruction. I built it with eternity. When I die, it follows. If I die, it won't become hollow. When I die, it's made to follow. I won't leave my paradise. It can't leave me. It is my Utopia. I saw it in my mind and built it with my eyes. I stitched it to my soul. When I die, it will be my Heaven, my Hell, my castle, a masochist's well.

Paint The World Black

Thank you for coming to my TED Talk.

This rage inside is burning malevolently. I can't control it, so step away from me. Just get the fuck away from me. Close your eyes and make me disappear, then you can see the colour of my heart come in clear.

Twisting and shooting, spinning and spurting, dancing and exploding, violent urges giving me sadistic flames, wildfires to hate the world, to grab it by the throat and torch it into wind-scattered ashes – payback for all the pretty razor slashes it gave me. What goes around comes around. Scorching coals: the world blanketed on the ground. I'm going to paint it black. I'm never turning back. I'm going to heal and paint the world black.

Sanity crept away from me, left me distant and unprotected. Insanity came knocking and look at me – I'm dangerously infected. Kill people; murder everyone that done me wrong. I'm going to paint the world black with a malicious mind that pulsates and a heart that hates. I'm going to attack; corpses and silence will circle me. And don't judge me so negatively, because you would agree if you felt my pain.

Hate me if you will. I'll just feed off the energy. You don't understand. I can't stand this constant chill that kisses my spine. I'm going to paint the world black; revenge in time will be mine. No cure can save me. Only when the last body falls, the last eyes that saw, then I can be soft, raw and die feeling whole. When humanity is a desert wasteland, my void will be filled, and I will no longer be a hole.

I Promise

And you thought your wedding vows were bad.

I can change. I can change for you; shed my skin and replenish myself like new. I'll make it so you'll want to reframe those pictures of us you smashed and let wrists heal over that you slashed. I want to be your shoulder to cry on and make it like I was never gone. I realize I was wrong. It took me awhile I admit but I miss your skin, your smell, your eyes, your lips. Your absence has been my eclipse. No lies, no tricks. I just want to hold you like I once did.

I know you miss me too. I can hear your heart. I know it's blue. I see past stains on your face from tears that dripped, that catapulted from your faucet eyes. I know you get goosebumps when you think of me. I just don't understand why you won't take my hand. Deep inside we both know we're supposed to be. Maybe you're scared to get hurt again, but I promise I'm a new man. Just believe me so we can be together. I have so much to offer now. There was a lot of shit I didn't realize, but I've opened my eyes. I know now how to be the prince you wanted me to be. One more chance is all I ask, and I promise I'll take you to a paradise where we can bask and leave all our problems behind. I'll make life perfect for you. I'll do anything for you. Accept my apology, trust me, love me, and I promise I'll always be there for you.

The distance between us is drowning me.
It makes me breathless. It's so unnerving.
The distance between us is plaguing me.
It makes me vomit. It's so painful.
The distance between us is haunting me.

130

It makes me scream. It's so frightening.
The distance between us is killing me,
and it makes, and it makes me, and it makes me,
it makes me feel so fucking insane.

I know I should've never broken up with you. I thought it was the right thing to do but when I left, like a phenomenal force it hit me - that I did love you after all. And I am sorry I never saw it before. I promise this time I'm here to stay. I'll never leave you again. Let me show you how much I need you, how much I love you. Please take me back into your heart, into the place I want to be. I'll give you my tears, my smile, these flowers I picked for hours and my heart. I'll give you everything you wanted from me. Just take my hand and I promise... I promise, together our heartbeats will synchronize, and never again will the sight of me leave your eyes.

KRAKR

Would this be considered a red flag? Trying to get into a fancy art program. Not sure if this cover letter is alarming, or if the Board will appreciate my honesty. Thoughts?

'm a kidnapper, a rapist, an artist, a killer, a radical. The blood from women smeared across the pavement - I'm painting what's inside my head: blood-splattered streets sprinkled with chunks of flesh. Isn't it beautiful? It takes innocence to make a masterpiece. Sure, my heart is hollow and heavy as lead, but look at my critique, look at my work; tell me that doesn't take skill, that there is no talent involved. Sure, I find it fun to kill, but does that make me a serial killer? To kill again when the blood dissolves, does that make me a monster? I see it as I'm an inspiring artist, King Kong on the rampage, here to bring carnage and the artistry of a genius.

The blood from men will surely follow the women because the show must go on. The killing won't stop. I have to plaster down ideas before they unfurl, and I forget. It would be an atrocity if that happened, that's why I constantly spread murder on the concrete.

You read this letter, now you know what's afloat. Though you don't know who I am, you do know what I am. So, I hope I put your minds at ease with this letter. I have to go now. The screams of people are calling me. Their blood needs to be transformed into a beautiful portrait. So have a nice day and thank you for your time.

Yours truly,
KRAKR

Witch Hunt

Yes. This is about my stepmother.

Guts from arachnids and withered orchids, spices to enhance the flavour of her meal: the flesh of children that's cooking in her cauldron. Fresh meat is implanted in her eyes. She licks her wrinkled lips as the scent flows up her nasal passage, a stench that's heaven-sent, a meal of the century. She will dine well tonight.

In a jagged cave that sits in the middle of the dark wood, that is where she lives, that is where she sleeps, that is where she eats. In the forest's deep, she indulges on children meat. She is horrid, quite morbid, not very beautiful at all. Just look at all the blood-spattered on the wall; so many have fallen. When will the killing stop? The witch must be burned.

Dozens of bodies hanging from the cave's ceiling, bleeding dry so they can be cooked. The count has been lost on how many children have died, but look into her beady, green eyes – no trace of remorse can be found; she's empty like a corpse. Fierce action needs to be taken to arms. The villagers must kill the beast, to stop her ravenous feast: the slaughter of everyone's child. They must burn the witch.

Sitting at her wooden table all alone, she's tearing children meat apart from their bones, humming with joy with every mouthful, but then she hears something awful and fright runs to her face. It's the sound of an angry mob on a witch hunt. Frantically she gathers her things. She runs out to escape, to hide, but in a twist of fate, the angry mob is just outside. She never had a chance. They grab her, beat her and tie her. It's over; her day of reckoning is due. On the stake she's hoisted, perfectly vertical; this torching will be fatal. What goes around comes around; the first flame is set.

In seconds she writhes in flames, moaning and crying out ancient verses so demonically that the crowd stands back in fear, as the witch sears. By sunrise, she falls to ashes. The people rave and cheer; they got their revenge. They've accomplished their dream, but not everything is what it seems.

While the villagers were smiling and laughing, the witch was hexing and cursing. After her perverse verses, she died; the inhaling fire was too much for her. When her torched remains hung there, everyone thought the horror was over, that they could go back to their lives. The next day when they woke, their village was scattered with newborn corpses.

Julie

I'm sure she's fine.

Her hair hangs over her face, absorbing the tears she sheds. Surrounded by the blade of a knife, she tries to conceal the wounds on her wrists, trying to stay clear from death's embrace: the suicidal circling that tries to seduce her in, that causes her sight to spin, blurry movements caused by blood loss.

Suicide calls her by the bloody lettering on the wall. Suicide screams for her by the masochistic mural of the name *Julie*, that runs to a vertical dripping. She doesn't know who she is anymore even with the carousel of her name stained. She needs to be wakened; life has got her down. Being hated and beaten has pasted her with a heavy frown. And with the carving of a magnificent crown, the vicious blood lines cut into her forehead, she pretends she's a princess. But as reality hits, she breaks down and begins to whisper the words for disaster:

"Sweet death, take me away; take me far away.
Sweet death, take me away; take me far away.
Sweet death, take me away; take me far away."

And as the words seep out her lips, the blood erupts from her veins - more ink made to spell her name, the tortured name of *Julie*. It's too bad she let the ink run dry; the drought to her body has disturbed the silence. From the violence, death awakes with the purpose to take, to take Julie away, far away.

Headless Woman In A Coffin

During the Salem Witch Trials, this was also known as "Tuesday".

Neck of tender porcelain in the path of a guillotine. Why is she there? I don't know. Just sit back and watch the show.

Notice the different expressions on the crowd's faces? Some are happy. Some are sad. Some are petrified. But the case has been juried and tried. Nothing you can do. Nothing you can do for her, but to cringe as her head severs, as her head is cut from her neck.

There goes the guillotine blade as a suspenseful silence plays as background music. The blade crashes into its dead, and there goes her separated head. See the pretty patterns from her blood that spattered. Look at her face in the basket so emotionless, so breathless, so lifeless. Hear her body being thrown inside the long box. See the headless woman in a coffin; watch her disappear. With the last pounding of a single nail, watch her disappear.

She was so frail, but few cared, few took notice. Everyone could see the fear and terror in her eyes. She drowned herself in tears and echoed fierce screams into the air, and most of them just laughed. Only a few cried when she was executed. Angels must have been on vacation because not the smallest interruption was there to postpone her decapitation. Not even a simple miracle was present. And she became a headless woman in a coffin.

She had such innocence to her. What could have she done wrong? What such crime could she have committed? Her death was supposed to be justice, but it looked like a blood-hungry sacrifice, a sheep tossed to the wolves. And if you don't believe the words I say, then just ask the recently born corpse. I have never felt so sick in all my life. I am not sure about a lot of things, but one thing is for certain – society has lost all touch with humanity.

Obsolete

Where in the world is Carmen Sandiego?

Disengage my heart, cut it down to nothing, pull it apart, mutilate the beating, break it from the stitching, take it and be the shredder, tear it like paper, then glue it back together. Make a collage from the fragile pieces of my heart. Show its true shape: distorted and ugly like me. I give you my heart to take, to repair the mistake. Dispose of it, rip it right out of my chest, throw it against the wall. And as it slides down into the trash, leaving its pattern of a vertical stain, set it on fire, let it burn, leave it until it's ashes, then place it in an urn and sink it to the bottom of the ocean. My heart is a parasite. It needs to be terminated. It has to be destroyed. The parasite is a plague. You don't understand the pain it's made, the pain it has taken in, so take the sharp spade, inject the blade, and as the blood secretes, my body will harden like concrete because my heart is obsolete.

Lambs Tortured Nevermore

Parenting is hard. However, you're in luck. Just do the opposite of this poem and you should do relatively okay. No guarantees because you may or may not be a completely inept human being. At least my advice might give you a fighting chance. Not sure? Practice safe sex. I'm helpful.

A distant voice coming from the basement: tiny whispers of someone dying, faint sounds of a little girl suffering. Bound to the cold floor by chains, shaking from the reaction of her pains, she's been kept alive by a bowl of food and water. In the dark, she whimpers, "Mommy. Daddy. Someone, help." Repeating the chant over and over. She cloned those words for days. For days and still no result.

She's weak as a kitten, left as forgotten, left behind to her brother's decaying corpse. He never had a chance. He was four years too young. Her crying echoes throughout her surroundings: the cell she's dying in. She's praying that somebody will find them, but as days go on, hope fades. Everyone is gone. No one is coming back to save her. There's going to be two dead children. That is what will happen if no one comes.

Their parents abandoned them, left them for dead. They treated them like caged animals, deserted them in this tomb with only dog food and dirty water for rations, but now there's nothing left. She's starving; malnutrition is caving in. "Why would mommy and daddy do this to us?" She cries this to herself over and over. Still… no result.

Heaviness is growing inside her; the strength of her limbs are depleting. She tries to keep balance on her hands and knees; the attempt failed as her arms give out. Her head crashes down like a shooting star, and like a tribal sacrifice the blood splatters violently, erupting as her head collapses against the basement floor. Whatever lights were on, whatever strength she had, they've been blown out from the charging blood loss. Her hand falls upon her brother's – two lambs tortured nevermore.

Fairytale
(Prince Without A Princess)

This is the fourth princess who has died this week. Wow. I'm a terrible prince. I really should learn how to be more in touch with women's feelings. Next one. Next one.

Kneeling in the snow by your gravestone, I've been mourning here since the burial. A part of me won't let you go. I can't move on, not without you by my side. Why did Death take you away? How come he couldn't let you stay? It kills knowing you're underneath this tombstone and how it reminds me that I am alone. I want you and only you; you were the only one for me. My long-sought soulmate, you were the stitching that kept me together, but your absence loosened the hold. Without you, I fell apart.

Why did you take those vitamins that made you ill? All I have left of you is this empty bottle, this container where you fed yourself pills. Why did you engage Death's throttle? I don't understand. Why did you speed up the calling of your number? I love you so much. Every day I ask myself if it was my fault, if I was the reason, you're in that wooden vault but I'll never know, not while you're lying underneath this shield of snow.

If I could take your place,
revive your face,
in a blink of an eye, I would.
I would if I could,
but I'm powerless, fragile and helpless.

I hate this fairytale, this story of a prince without a princess. You shouldn't be sleeping in the dirt's cradle. I keep thinking what would happen if I kissed you. Would it be like Snow White? With a single kiss, will you come back to me? But as I separate fact from fiction, I realize through the mental friction that yes, you are gone, and that yes, I am alone, living this fairytale I can't reverse with a thought so perverse - the wish of having you by my side so I can kiss you again, so I can tell you I love you. I don't care if you're decayed or not. I want another chance to share our love, for this fairytale to have colour and to know if your extinction was my failure.

Pack Of Wolves

The only thing worse than the ending of this poem is the gross misuse of semicolons.

She's running, trying to get away. Her footprints in the snow following behind; her beating heart trying to keep up with the pace. Exhaustion is sweated on her face; fear is colouring her eyes. She feels so heavy; her sense of balance is fading fast. How long will she last? Not long with her frozen bare feet and her naked body of ice. She's so cold and tired. In desperation for air, she tumbles into the glistening white. Her running has turned into a dead crawl. In slow, she pushes her way through the snow. Determination won't let her go. It won't let her give up. Even though there is no way out, determination won't let her fall easily to the situation, but she can't escape forever. She will be torn and severed. The forest will capture her wailing screams as her flesh is cleaned from her bones. Death is creeping up on her doorstep. She hears the slight movement of snow; it's racing towards her. She can't move anymore. She's frostbitten to the ground. She couldn't hide or get away. She's been found. Many breaths now roll around her ears, and without hesitation, she lets out screams like a machine gun as searing pain revolves inside her body. She's being ripped and mangled apart; blood is gushing in the snow. The red mirror is reflecting the feast: her body being annihilated by beasts. From this, her heart explodes, combusting from the waves of fatal punctures. In dying seconds, she lets out one last scream. And as the pack of wolves inhale her body, I wake up with eyes wide open and realize it was just a dream.

Put Me Out Of My Misery

God, it's been seventeen years and I'm still alive. Hello? HELLO?!

Nothing is okay. Everything is fucked up, twisted and mangled, coiled and tangled. Thoughts eating at my mind are driving me insane. Grasping from the pain, I shout. Ripping the hair out of my head; wishing I was dead. Life's not fair. I hate it! I hate it! This worthless pile of shit! I fucking hate it! I fucking care! Six feet above or six feet under, it makes a difference to me. Blow me away. God, kill me. Set off a holocaust of decay; put me out of my misery. I can no longer bear the person I am.

I'm an asshole, a jerk, a heartbreaker; I have no soul. I always feel hopeless and low. I'm an accident that went terribly wrong: built from the strong but I came out weak. Through my eyes, things are shown bleak; everything is shaded black and grey. Where's the white? Where are the colours? Where the fuck is the light? Inside I'm damp as stone. I'm an experiment that went far from right. Put me out of my misery; release me from this torment. Please don't leave me be. Kill me.

I'm beautiful on the outside but repulsive on the inside. It's my camouflage so I can get near people. Though I try and get close to make friends, to get a girlfriend, it always ends. I'm conniving. I can only hold back the creature for so long, then everything goes wrong. From Dr. Jekyll, I transform into Mr. Hyde. I have a black heart. It needs to be removed. I have nothing to prove, so just put me out of my misery. It's the right thing to do. I want people to forget I existed, that I was ever born. So, when you take my life... please, douse their minds with amnesia. God, with eagle-spread arms, I wait for you to strike me down.

Stunning Beyond Misty Falls

Tonight, on The Bachelor...

Stunning beyond misty falls; the sight of her makes my heart crawl. She's the ghostess of the waterfall wood. And here I stand in awe. Here I stare with emotions so raw, that I'm fighting to keep my soul stitched to my flesh. She's so breathtaking. It's hard enough to stop myself from melting. The sight of her is absolutely consuming.

Once existed but now extinct – she was the suicidal countess that jumped over the ledge. Her life pushed her past the edge. Now, she's a poltergeist that haunts this forest by the vertical water. Stunning beyond misty falls; forever enslaved within the rock walls. She has captured my heart and everything else within. Too bad it came a little bit too late. And that was the lie I lived by.

Now here's the truth I am dead from:

Beautiful to me she was. She was a desire that burned brightly. I had a love for her that was deeper than the sea, but a problem between us was always amidst. She was a virgin. And no matter how long I waited, no matter how often I asked, she wore my patience thin, bare right to the bone, and still, she wouldn't give in.

One evening I snapped and I stalked her. As she walked, I stalked; into the forest, I followed. As she peered over the river drop, cruelty struck with such malice, that my arms shot out like spiteful spears. And like Alice down the rabbit hole, she fell. A porcelain face of terror formed, and hollow thunder rang as her body crashed. Cracked and deformed, she wasn't beautiful anymore, just a bruised corpse bleeding profusely.

But as I see her now, stunning beyond misty falls, I regret what I did. The love I had for her is rekindling. Sadness is growing. I want to be at her side. I have to reverse time and undo the crime but that's not logical. But I know what is. I know what will work. I will retrace the steps I told you she took and commit suicide, then maybe we can be together. There's a chance I could end up in the darkest part of Hell, but she's worth the risk. So, as I close my traumatized eyes, I take my leap of faith, say my goodbyes to her just in case, and hope I'll wake to the glimmer of her eyes.

S.L.I.T.

I spelled "S.H.I.T" wrong.

G rey heart. Flesh bouquet. Tidal waves of red. No tourniquet. Is she dead? Not quite yet.

Damaged veins puking up blood, spurting like miniature volcanoes, her heart pumping empty, fluids circulating in twisted flows are running scarce. This is all she could be: a viral-induced entity. She has so many cancers and so many diseases: growths of deadly dancers. That's why she opened suicide's envelope and pulled out a blade of answers. Lacerating was her suicidal temptation.

In blood, she's drenched. By Death, she's clenched. The blood spills, enticing Death to drink. His tongue inside her wrist, drills, absorbing her taste. Not a drop goes to waste; she gives herself to him. With her naked body smothered in blood, she takes him in. Dying and wrecked – a knot of hunger pulls tight. She grows weak as he indulges with delight. Dessert of his thirst – Death's touch to her is amorous. This dark erotica has made her lascivious.

She can hear her black knight whisper, his coated lips whisking words into her ears. He tells her gently, "I will take you away." Softly he tells her, "I will take you to a world of rapture." Like a pendulum of trance, she agrees to his persuasion. She believes the things he says, so together they dance like beauty to the beast. She gives in. He gives in. Embrace. Circling into a puff of smoke, the two unlikely lovers vanish. Sadness, love, illnesses and trust.

Listening To The Voice

Totally disregarded everything it told me.

You're alone. You're crying. Inside you're dying. You need help, but no one is willing. Suicidal thoughts are drilling, pounding and breaking away your shield. When the shield shatters to dust, what will protect you? You need someone to ignite your flames, to melt the frost from your heart before time becomes too late. I know you well. In days, you will kill yourself. You need someone that can relate, that will contemplate. You need a person that will give you that hand, someone that will understand. You're strong but you're no Great Wall. You will fall, and with chaotic screams, their silence will extend. No one will hear your call. They'll be too quiet for people to even pretend, to pretend they care. You're a child separated by hopelessness and depression. You need love to fill that void. Love is what you're missing. Fill the gap and life will come into place. Its light you'll embrace. Its presence will make you smile. Your gallows-like life will combust, mutating into your well-fought paradise but you need a guide, a messiah to fix you from the inside. Because if you don't find a meaning to live, I can picture it as I speak: You're in the darkness of your room, in the foetal position with your head lying in tears, as your hands choke wrists that bleed. And as your eyes go black with fear, your body dies limp. No longer will your fingers coil your wrists, because you're dead in the cold corner of your room. And when you're buried, surrounded by only the falling leaves of autumn, all that will be left of you are the screams, the cries for help that were never heard. I know this because I'm you.

Hades' Hourglass

Sometimes hearts are hearts; sometimes they're glory holes.

Chest split open wide. Take a look; there's nothing inside. Feel free to stick your head in, past the skin and flesh, through the blood. Monitor the chest cavity, wander about aimlessly. Roam around; it's pointless. What you seek you won't find; there's nothing inside. What you're looking for is over there: the pile of ashes on the ground, my grained heart in the form of time, sand for Hades' hourglass.

Stop raping the fist-sized hole. Your answer isn't here. It's over there. If you don't believe me, here, grasp these scissors, cut right up the centre, vomit from the choir of flesh whispers, and pull the halves apart. See truth unfold – I don't have a heart. There's nothing inside. Please don't cry. Settle down. Let your tears dry. It wasn't all for nothing. I still feel. The reaping from the scissors was excruciating; the searing cuts kept my eyes shut. When you were clawing for hope, the scratches from the sharp shells at the end of your fingertips massacred my entrails. It felt like a waterfall of stabbing nails, but the worst feeling of all is knowing I can't love you back.

I'm a human-demon hybrid. I'm humon. I'm pain on display, sicker than yesterday. Hades has called my name. The grey crystals of my heart have lastly fallen. Heaven of the hourglass has drained empty, flooding Hell with my remnants. I'll be there for an eternity. There's not much time to say goodbye. Vision is sullen. Lungs are swollen. Breathing is impossible. Death by suicide inevitable. Before that final drop of blood loss drips, I want you to know one thing, to give you two things: this everlasting kiss and these words... *I wish I could have loved you.*

Anastasius Lykaios Watches The Sacrificial Fly

It's official. I'm the worst thing to happen to vampires since Stephenie Meyer.

Rising twilight erupting from the shadow of the sun; fear is unleashed beneath the stars. From a drowning flame and an exploding soft light, from the change of scenery, a frightening creature is released – the vampire, Anastasius Lykaios arises. Awakening with bloodthirsty cries, he is the predator of predators, a vicious raptor, wherefrom the heights of trees and buildings he watches the sacrificial fly: his victim that catches his eye. He hunts and stalks the most beautiful of women. When they feel a cold rush down their spine that's their omen, their sign that something evil is present, fate's signal of their demise coming forth. And before they know, he shows them their worth: absolutely nothing. He rapes them and absorbs their blood, quenching his thirst and uncontrollable lust. When they're corpses he abandons them to the night sky, the older brother of dusk. Anastasius Lykaios is an evil so pure, an evil so ominously vile, he craves the female fragile – a being so innocent, so breathtaking, he can't help but make them suffer. Their tender skin is a texture so soft that it reminds him of a freshly dug grave. And that's why he can never get enough because he loves the dead so much. This world is his slaughterhouse, his feeding ground, the star ceiling is the cage that holds his prey. Anastasius Lykaios watches the sacrificial fly, and before the sun can emerge above, he commits his sins, then crawls back to his catacomb until the next moon shines.

Zombie

Family reunions are so much fun.

I am not a hypochondriac, just a suicidal maniac. Come any closer and I will remove your eyes from your face, make space to fit my fists so I can engrave my sickness into your brain, then maybe you'll see what the fuck is wrong with me.

You're just like everybody else: a zombie without a conscience. It makes sense but so does me cutting your throat. Why won't you listen? You never understood me. You never tried. How can you be so cold? How many slits do you think my wrists can hold? Forget it. Never-mind. It's too late for answers. I don't care anymore, because I'll be smiling when you're dying... when I die, when I die.

Destruction: that is the path you paved for me, the only thing you have ever done for me. Why did you give life if you were just going to take it? I can't survive in this gas chamber. I can't breathe past the fumes of your words. I'm suffocating and all you're doing is staring. Does my pain get you off? Are you that sick and twisted? Would it be better for you if I never existed? Well, don't worry... You won't have to wait long because I know this is not where I belong. All the love I had for you is gone; there isn't a reason for me anymore to stay. I'll fade and resemble your heart's decay, and I pray when I kill myself today, that tomorrow you will do the same.

Mesmerizing Whore
That Wore Bondage Straps

This is exactly why I don't write erotica. Anymore.

Lascivious woman, beauty wrapped in leather, mesmerizing whore that wears bondage straps – she's a creative slut, a kinky misfit, a prodigy of peculiar sexual positions. When you fuck this dark maiden, look into her eyes; you can see paradise. Touch her skin and everything is pleasured within.

When she strips and her hands are adorned by chains and whips, see the phantom of the lust eclipse exist. Fall into a trance as you watch her dance. She's so seductive, soothingly hypnotic. Raging hormones will cause your heart to bounce and panic, becoming over productive, pumping blood rapidly, causing sweat to drip, filling you with nasty thoughts, making your mind filthy, and that's what she likes, what she wants you to be: a ruthless, horny fuck.

Her chamber of sex is of black décor: her palace where she fucks until she's sore. Mesmerizing whore that wears bondage straps: a dog that will straddle your lap, the nymphomaniac that will ride what's in your pants. She doesn't take *no* for an answer; you do as she says. Just obey, and on her satin sheets, she will lay, where she will command you to fuck her faster, order you to fuck her harder until ecstasy takes control and swallows the two of you whole.

But all good things come to an end. It happened during one fateful night; true love came in the form of sex. No protection was used during the amorous display and from that moment on she's been a mother. With her new life bestowed to her, she gave up the dominatrix inside, to enjoy the life every girl dreams of. And even though she's retired, she still has that burning fire, the same flame that has made her so desired. Mesmerizing whore that wore bondage straps – by many men she is remembered, still salivating from the sex she gave them. They were the slaves that were raped, fucked when she was in her prime, but all they have now are the memories, very erotic stories. For she has left them all for two males – her husband and son.

The Escape Artist

Life: "I see you have had your fair share of women problems. Congratulations, you're married. Here, have a daughter. Yes. I am aware your three cats and dog are female as well. Anything else I can do for you?"

My wings have broken through. I'm flying far away from here and never returning. And don't you worry, don't stress over what will become of me. It's none of your concern. All you need to know is that I fucking hate you.

Your life wasn't my life. My thoughts and words are mine. I'm not your puppet anymore. I cut the strings. I don't owe you a thing; you owe me everything. You're worthless, far from priceless, that is what you mean to me.

If you think I'll be coming back to you, you're sadly mistaken. If escaping you means permanent solitude, then I'm forsaken, but at least I'll have everything back that was taken. Your ball and chain couldn't keep me forever; they rusted away. You no longer control me. I escaped. Now I'm leaving as fast as I can, at the speed of my wingspan. You tried to contain me. How does it feel to fail? How does it feel?

Your beauty astounded me. I just wish your touch wasn't cruelty. Your perfect ensemble was a disguise, a cloak to shroud the lies. The beauty was the beast. It was too late to turn back. You had me trapped, my wings wrapped. For years you kept me motionless, enslaved to your commands. I felt damned but somewhere you got careless. I took the chance for freedom. I escaped and found myself outside, past the ramparts of your kingdom of slavery.

New pages for a newborn story – I can now live without you telling me how. I escaped. No longer by you can my emotions be raped, my heart scraped, my eyes be draped with tears. In your hand, I suffered and from it, I fled; in my heart, you're gone and dead. You thought you could be my world when I just wanted you to be my girl and for us to share a life, but you got greedy, you released the creature from within and tried to control me like a child. You're ugly on the inside like something died, that's why I disappeared, that's why I tore your heart out during my escape. I pray the wound never heals – revenge for every time you disemboweled me. Your suicide from a broken heart will be my victory.

Closet Creature

Not a bad vocabulary for a five-year-old.

It's bedtime. No lights. No sounds. Shadow-pasted walls and no mother – there's a creature in my closet. I know he's there. I can smell him by the thick scent of vomit in the air and his breaths that roll from underneath my closet door. Like morning fog, it inhales my floor. I always fear he'll pop up from it and get me. The only protection I have from him is my flashlight. The only place I can hide is under my sheets. Mom says it's just my imagination, that the night is just playing tricks on me, but she doesn't see what I see. Every time I scream for her, he disappears. He's very smart, vanishing quickly unseen. And when she leaves, he comes back again. My teddy used to protect me, but he ate him yesterday. Now I am an army of one, formed to be defeated. I'm only five, so far I've survived, but I don't know how much longer I can stay alive. One day he's going to get me, then my mommy will see I was right, that she was wrong, and I'm long gone, gone forever. Why can't my mommy save me?

Oh no! My thoughts interrupted, disrupted, the silence shattering from the creaking of my closet door. He's coming! I try to yell for my mommy, but the words won't come out. I can't shout. My voice just echoes in my head. I grab my flashlight and find haven under my sheets. I hear him slithering on my floor, knocking things over as he crawls towards my bed. There's a tug on my sheets, followed by a raspy roar. He wants me. He wants gore. It's either him or me. I pull off the sheets and point my flashlight to his eyes, the tiny circles that glow green. With closed eyes, I turn it on. I got him! I got him! I pry open my eyelids and there to my fright, I see drool dripping from his mouth, his vile smile of anger. The batteries were dead, irony, bitter irony. In last efforts, I throw it at his face. It doesn't phase him. He grabs me quickly and licks my face. His tongue is warm and prickly. I could feel his taste buds vibrating when they touched my skin. And with victory, he drags me to the closet. I flail my body parts, trying to break free. Pointless. Useless. I'm swallowed in the dark room, my closet. Inside I'm left in pieces.

Elizabeth's Demise

As I'm going through my old poetry, I'm starting to believe I have a vagina complex. I'm legit for a clit.

You wanted to be something spectacular, so from the kindness of my heart, I split open your jugular. And as the blood shot out from your creviced artery, it reached for the sky but only touched your face. As soon as that first drop hit, I saw you fall into space. There you stood with a suffocating stare; a dead glare accompanied by a blood fountain. Motionless you stood, patiently waiting for the signal to collapse. Seconds pass, then minutes. You need stitches but all I have is anger, so instead, I'll slice you again.

I call to you, "Elizabeth, are you there? Elizabeth... are you there?" No words escape your lips, just the sounds of someone gasping for air: failed breaths that highlight terrorized eyes. You bleeding to silent hills — I can think of nothing fairer. You deserve this more than I. I could have just made you cry but I'd rather you die than have to hear you say *goodbye*. You wanted to leave me for better things. I was always second in your life. My love was never good enough for you. You wanted to be a model, to fashion your beauty. Your dream was to expose yourself to the world. Well, guess what? Kind of hard to do that when you're dying. Why couldn't you just stay with me? Why did you have to be complicated? If you were rational about this, if you actually thought things over, my rage wouldn't have been stimulated, your neck wouldn't be mutilated. Why were you so blind? Elizabeth, why?

Your clock has wound down, no ticks, no tocks. Your time is up. Silence has taken its place. So, as our eyes lock for one last time I kiss through the red, leaving behind the outline of my lips. And as the blood drips from my pink flesh, I whisper to you, "I love you, Elizabeth." After those very words your system crashes, you die before you hit the ground. Your body smashes into the green grass; grazed skin appears from the impact. So, there you lay lifeless, adorned by rashes and gashes, looking more fragile than you ever have before. Peace awaits you now. In an urn and in the form of grey ashes, Heaven waits for your arrival.

Elizabeth, I gave you everything you wanted. Soon you will be famous, people all over the country will know who you are and you will be worth thousands. It seems you were right – you did have to leave me to get what you wanted. And don't worry, Elizabeth, don't worry, I'll make sure you're still beautiful after the autopsy.

Slaughtered The Bride To Be

Definitely. I definitely have a vagina complex.

You died before we became one, before you got to follow the falling of red rose petals. Your special day became your disaster. Your trust and love in me became your demise. I gutted your throat, slashed you, colouring your dress red, gave you a knife full of death. I slaughtered the bride to be, my wife to be. I turned our wedding into a funeral and made you the host.

When the blade pierced through, you fell to your knees, gasping for air but all you got was a mouthful of hair. A broken heart inhaled your face. Strengthened by devastation, I could see the reflection of my grin in your wide, blue eyes. I could see your shadow floating on your puddle of blood. Even when dying you were beautiful. When you died you became perfect.

Behind the tears, I knew you wondered why, why I turned my back on you. And you somehow gathered up time and asked past bloody lips, "Why?" With slight hesitation, I told you. Told you that after seeing you for so long, being with you for so long, I realized that you were nothing to me. No more important to me than an insect, so I had to squash you like one.

I slaughtered the bride to be. My ring and promise for her was a casket. My love for her was really a dormant hate that revived with a thick potency. I smiled for the first time in two years when my bride died. I knew we were never meant to be. I knew to escape her she had to die. She had to be a corpse. She just had to die. My freedom laid in her absence, so I slaughtered the bride to be.

She now lies above the stars and beneath the ground. And even though she's gone, I still have one memory of her. I remember how she was choking, dying so slowly, so painfully. I recall how sluggishly she began to crawl towards me, trying to reach for me like she wanted to hold me one last time. I remember when I bent down to her level and said, "I never loved you."

Overdose On
The Poison Rainbow

Not only can I not write erotica, but I'm also a terrible pharmacist. Those two things have nothing in common.

Want to die? Don't be shy. Won't you die? Here you go – take this glass of cyanide and swallow suicide. Overdose on the poison rainbow. Choke; fall back and feel the show, and maybe this time you'll suffocate from your woes. Just hold that glass and never let go. Guzzle as fast as you can, until you're restless and weak. Release some consciousness. Fuel the speed of your heart, then let it run empty. Drink until your heart no longer beats; show yourself no mercy. Don't think of an apology. Don't waste valuable time. Conquer yourself and forget a cure; die and rot from respiratory failure.

Breath in another flavour; have some arsenic. Ingest it until you're ill, too sick. Inhale until vomit erupts past your lips. Soon enough your body will be absorbed by slight tremors, then in an instant, expanding into deadly seizures. Just keep making these unhealthy errors and you will surely find all your desired pleasures, so overdose on the poison rainbow. Follow these instructions: Suck back and reload. Repeat. And you'll do just fine.

Heroin – grab the needle and stick it in. Get high. Feel your body soar and fly. Inject too much, to die. Flood your body; drown your veins. Don't fight the strain; accept the toxin. Over and over begin. Overdose on the poison rainbow. Feed your blood highway until you feel grey. Make the depression stay and rest as a delightful piece of decay. Just infect yourself until you're free because I know this is what you want to be: a self-sadistic disaster.

Perhaps add a little red to your self-destructing meal; try mercury in the thermometer. Break the temperature and drink the liquid milliliter by milliliter; prescribe this fluid to yourself daily, nightly. Consume it carelessly and you'll notice a difference – like complications in breathing, in walking, steps closer to dying. Don't stop drinking. Receive nausea and unbearable headaches, because that's the whole idea of dying: too diseased to be living. Continue to taste and organs might start to fizzle. Overdose on the poison rainbow; up the intake. Be in pain from lung damage, struggle from kidney failure, die from brain damage; towards yourself be savage. Embrace the carnage. And with the downward blink of two eyes, you'll be carried away by Death's carriage.

A Banshee Haunts Those Hills

My wife is never allowed to read this book.

A banshee haunts those hills...

Her throat was cut and her eyes were stitched shut. Her beauty was raped. She got fucked like a slut. She cried, "No more!" She said this over and over, but they kept fucking her like a whore. When she moaned in displeasure, knives across her flesh were scraped. The pain she felt couldn't be measured, but the distance drained her almost dry. Guilt came to their hearts when her tears flowed, so they sewed her eyes shut so she could no longer cry and wiped away the last of the tears that showed, then continued to fuck her cunt, ripping the virgin wide inside.

A banshee haunts those hills...

She almost got away, but instead of freedom she tripped and fell, crashing right into a knife's violent sway. A red rainbow was bestowed to her neck: a present from the slit that coloured horizontally and vertically, bleeding the rainbow red. As she struggled to gasp for air, they fucked her one more time. Her torn-open cherry was so sublime, that it added a true perversity to the crime. After the touch of sins, her life became a corpse that accompanied fallen leaves and decayed amongst the autumn trees. That night, tears, sweat, cum and blood poured.

A banshee haunts those hills...

Up in the hills darkened by clouds, to this day her screams pound, signaling sorrow and revenge. Her death was born at night up in those hills, so every time the black curtains drape and you hear those knives scrape, stay away and just let her cry. But if you want to see her stripped body and all the gashes that attend, if you want to see her stitched eyes, if you want to die then be my guest, but when she leaves you dead like the rest, remember before she does to you what was done to her... Just remember I warned you. So now you know why... a banshee haunts those hills.

Red As Wine

Not by Neil Diamond.

Red as wine – my neck wrapped in razor twine. Slicing through my skin texture, I jolt from coiling punctures. Stabbing at the outside, they slowly start to break in, sawing right into my throat and into my oesophagus. It is the mark of dying: a malignant, bleeding wreathe, the circular opening of blood and pus falling. Like choking I'm gasping, trying to capture every last breath, to stall, to hesitate, to pause, giving myself time to contemplate my forthcoming death. Never have I felt a pain so severe. Never have I been so frightened. And here I am dangling like I'm floating, as I take my last moments to grasp all the memories I held so dear. This is fear: my reality seen from dyeing eyes darkening red as wine, rarely whitening when somehow I'm able to inhale and exhale. But if I got another breath now it would be quite the surprise, for I have lost my airway and misplaced my sense of calm composure. I am useless just as I am helpless, near to being nothing. I'm hanging by this silver lining, this thin steel thread that's tightening, shredding apart the last inches of my neck, chewing away ravenously, transforming me into a pathetic wreck, a continuous source of blood dripping, iron-flavoured water that's red as wine, that's gushing profusely, furiously. Countdown for black curtains has started: Three inches... Ripping, tearing through. Two inches... Holding on as weak as possible. One inch... Failing to be strong. Horrible. My head detaches from my brainstem. I collapse as two. I'm deader than dead; grotesquely I've lost my head. I'm a corpse. I'm red as wine. Just another statistic for the records. Another worthless suicide gem.

I Killed An Angel Today

It's about an angel who kisses the Grim Reaper and then she fucking dies. There. Now you don't even have to read it.

I saw an angel today, bathing herself in the forest's lake, cleaning between her delicate fingers, between her long legs, between her perfect white feathers, ridding herself from any existence of dirt. In awe, I stared at her body in the raw, skin naked as blind eyes. I overindulged myself as she cleansed herself in the nude. Fighting against myself not to intrude, I hid behind an evergreen tree and watched, fantasizing about the act of intercourse with the woman created from a corpse – a lust overwhelming. Lust was my form of bravery that gave me courage. I took a couple of deep breaths and came out of hiding. And there I stood frozen as ice, nervously awaiting her notice of my presence while wind-pushed grass grazed across my dangling hands, soothing away the goosebumps that conquered them.

Her back was turned to me. I stretched my hand out and pretended I was there with her. My heart got carried away and I took a few steps forward. By the time I realized what I was doing, the sound of a stick breaking cracked the silence. She turned around and slowly put her hand to her mouth in shock but not in fear, and rising from the water with such weightlessness that I forgot she could see my face. She was smiling as she came near, walking through the meadow right towards me, still naked, naked as can be. And as my life flashed before my eyes, there she was in all her purity, standing a lean of the face away, stopping breaths apart from a sanction of our lips. My lips screamed for a kiss with all their might, as hundreds of eyes orbited around us. Creatures big and small were watching like they've seen this happen before.

It was now or never. I broke through her angelic spell she had over me, held onto my heart for dear life, and went to invade the space that kept me from bliss. But before I could move, her lips attacked first – the taste, the texture killed me. I died and went to Heaven. I kept my eyes closed to contain myself. Almost impossible by the speed my heart was exploding at. I opened my eyes with orgasmic relief, but something was wrong, not quite right. Her face was different. Tears were rolling down her cheeks, her lips were trembling. Then when I looked into her dying eyes, I found out why – my reflection woke me from her hypnosis, and I remembered who I was.

Her blonde, golden hair thinned apart from the scalp, the skin from her face peeled away to rot, her enchanting eyes melted into skull sockets. From skin to flesh, to bone, through the transformation of decay, I died listening to the dying tones: her fading voice from never-ending oxygen delay. I wanted to help but there was nothing I could do. I kneeled as she fell and felt my heart slowly crumble as it chased bits and pieces of the angel that tumbled from decomposition.

When she capsized, any pieces of her that were left withered to ashes and was whisked into the air by coaxing winds, retreating away from all my senses... forever, for eternity. Her demise was my curse, the purpose of who I am. Nothing I can do or say, for I am damned to be this way. I killed an angel today – a love I destroyed with a kiss of grey.

LIIAN VARUS LOSES
HIS PATHETIC SHELL

2004 was a very productive time for me. I was really coming into my own, developing quickly. Not physically. My penis stopped growing when I was eight. But when it came to my personality, I was claiming my identity. Let me tell you something: Self-confidence goes a long way when it comes to refraining from explaining the mating rituals of starfish. It's true. I had a bad habit of going into full-blown panic mode anytime a girl made a conscious effort to talk to me. My social ineptitude didn't stop there. I was a wreck. If anyone I didn't know tried to start a conversation with me, I would stutter like a mime discovering syllables for the first time. I couldn't walk out in public without worrying someone was going to stab me, because I happened to comb my hair in a way that was less than agreeable to them that day. I'd arrive at clubs, dressing like I've recently found last year's fashion trends hanging off a back-alley coat rack on the first day of school - I could go on. There was nothing special about me. Eventually, I began to hate myself so much I gave up and let myself go. After a while, not giving a fuck paid off in dividends. Not only could I carry myself as a respectable human being, but some of that confidence began to trickle down to my writing. It was still shitty, but you could see I was trying to expand and break away from the typical bullshit I was currently writing. My existence still had hope. Isn't this book so much fun?

Every Guy

Her name was Lesley. She ended up dumping me. That level of heartbreak fucked me up for years. We cool now, though.

Every guy that looks at you is another guy that wants to fuck you, but you don't seem to mind. I don't think you understand. Not every guy that's nice to you only wants to be friends. Some do but most have hidden agendas. When the time and day align, thoughts evolve in their head: different ways to seduce you, to take you away from me. Every guy so far has tried. All have failed but more keep trying. The thing that really bothers me is that you don't seem to learn, every guy is just another predator. Can't you analyze them before you befriend them? Can you for me just take the time to know they're honest? Because you never do and it's looking bad. I'm starting to think you want all this temptation around you. I fear that you've already been infected with lust and I can no longer rely on your trust. I'm scared I've lost the only thing I ever loved.

Prescription

My inner voice is kind of a dick.

It's alright. I will take your life tonight. Give me your wrists and I will show you how to play the violin. You'll feel the hypnotic music of tearing flesh: the chorus of blood dripping. You'll dance to the summoning verses that will enchant the virus, decay to come forth and suck the life from your body. Then with eager hands, we'll mould your heart of clay, constructing tiny caskets with great detail so we can collect the souls that die when your family stumbles upon your wretched corpse.

Darkness is beauty. You just have to lift a layer of skin. Become what you fear, and you will be beautiful. Two deep, vertical slits are your prescription. Repeat if needed. Precision is key. Make it quick and I promise you'll make it. Don't listen to anyone else. Suicide is an option so open your door to freedom. Enter and take everything you deserve. Don't worry, there's no lesson to learn. Don't think twice; take my advice. Just trust me. I'm your conscience. I know what's best so kill the hesitation. Take this blade and put your soul to rest.

Well Angels

I totally found someone else.

If I fall I can find you. Suicide angels go to Hell, and that's why I'm going to push myself into the well. I'll slit my wrists to lose my wings, tumble and crash into the place where angels never sing. I made my life miserable to conquer fear, the fear of suicide so I can grant my wish I hold so dearly: the fervent desire to be with you. I bottled up frustration, anger and sorrow inside to fertilize the suicidal yearning within me. When this emotional garden grows, the desperation for damnation will show and I will cut my wrists to go where you exist. I will bleed like a melting candle. When there's no more wax, the flame dies. When the ocean of blood runs to a river, a choking shiver will frighten my spine. My dying will stop and I will be dead. My planned fate will devour me down the well, sending me into the great fire where many before you fell. That is where I'll see you, where I'll hold your hand and say *hello*. I'll say *hello* and erase the goodbye you left me before you sent yourself to Hell.

Blood Pigs

This is the original screenplay for Babe: Pig In The City. It was rejected due to the lack of storyline, character limit and violence. In other words, it was too real for Hollywood.

Hang me upside-down, tie my feet together with vinyl, then watch my arms dangle as you slit my wrists top to bottom. Bleed me dry, drain the blood into buckets, pour me until red trickles from my eye sockets; let pleasure flood. When the capacity of sadism is swollen, dump the liquid raw into the trough. Feed the blood pigs. Sneak me inside the bellies of the beasts; let me feel what it's like to be the feast.

Hear the sounds of snorting snouts, stare into the eyes of greed, masturbate to the blood that drips from their gluttonous lips. Breathe, breathe, inhale. Breathe, breathe, exhale. Nourish the blood pigs. Save nothing for the angels to scavenge so they can't resurrect my soul, staple me with wings and take me inside their hands of their salvation.

Hellspawn, teething demons, cannibalistic couriers: the blood pigs. They will swallow the nectar from my veins. Engorging themselves with intense desire, until Father Time pulls the trigger and blasts a hole in my head, ending the road of a virus that failed to plague anyone but himself. When dirt is my bed I will ride the coffin flight right into eternal night without looking back, escaping the white zombies that tried to possess me.

I want damnation; sacrifice me to the dark. Slaughter all lights, anything that will make the tiniest spark. My pale flesh is made to grow in the night. I am the heir to nocturnal supremacy and I will bleed foolishly. I will be the red fountain. A sinner quenching the thirst of the sinned is my act of betrayal to the voice no one hears, to the ears that never listen. Acceptance from the eyes of evil is greater than toleration from the heart of God.

Lethal STD

Frightening that I wrote this when I had an erection, isn't it?

Give me your sleaze and implant me with your disease. Make me sick and infectious, impure and contagious. Fuck me, so I can taint others with my toxic seed. Trust me, hear me; I will succeed. If I held the venom I would poison all of them, as many as I could. I am a boy and you are a girl. I am persuasive; you are beautiful. We are the perfect plague to silence the world. With the lustful act of intercourse, I can be polluted as you. I hate the existence of mankind as much as you so if you don't mind, seduce me, allure me and entice me. Transform me into your replica and with the power of a fatal sickness, we can obliterate the planet. We'll rape the world. Like nuclear rabbits the lethal STD will spread, filling the mouth of humanity with its dead, until it chokes and dies. And if we by chance fade out of the apocalyptic spotlight before everyone reaches their inevitable plight, we can rest in peace knowing the heartbeat of humanity will cease.

Voodoo Doll Kisses

No. I've never done heroin. Needles are fucking scary.

Skeleton thin - his arms covered with needle holes. Blood and bruises stained, solitude in empty eyes; inside nothing remained. Existence left in shame. What a waste of creation ruined by heroin mutilation. Unable to be repaired, he will never be the same. It was too late. He pushed everyone away that cared.

Tenderized by voodoo doll kisses, he overdosed too many times. He died from nervous system failure. Brain no longer functional. It's a cemetery of dead nerves and tissue, a ghost town deserted. All the space in the world, but there's a sign that reads, "No Occupancy" hanging from the neo-cortex. Only a screaming voice allowed; nothing but echoes. The chamber is hollow.

Lifeless from the drug inserted, he couldn't stop the poison flow. Death was the late inhibitor. His expensive habit made him worthless, except to the maggots that are breaking and entering. To them, he's priceless. Heroin brought the maggots. His hallucinations transformed him into a meal. Hundreds of baby flies dine; so sickening, it can only be real. Insects devouring the flesh rot, drinking his blood like wine. It's a perfect horror scene: maggots eating through skin that's turning green.

The formation he died in is ghastly. Serpentine arms from voodoo doll kisses look like sticks of rot. His hands decrepit, resembling a vulture's clutch.

Vomit - his suit of choice. Disgusting by touch. Revolting by smell. Puke seemed to be his outfit of choice.

His green eyes are awful. A deathly, miserable stare shines. You can see the damaged soul trapped behind.

Stiff corpse in the shape of misery, eerie like an old collapsed tree. His body raped by voodoo doll kisses; evidence made by the masochistic needle. You can tell it's been overused by the rust and the macabre designs of blemishes and abrasions. He was weak; his self-indulgent urge was strong. Long story short - he died from an uncontrollable drug lust.

Morguetopia

So glad I won't have to read this poem again. It's the worst.

There's a place where the dead go before they're put to rest. They're stored in shelves, in their own individual cooler, awaiting the coroner's touch, so their cause of death can be found.

An autopsy reveals secrets, giving the cutter information on how they died. His days are long and gruesome; bodies are constantly filling the walls of shelves. Just when he's about done, more come rolling in on their death chariot. Silent and bagged, stiff and tagged, ready to be examined for the magician to work his magic before his apprentice, the lonely mortician prepares the funeral service where family members of the dead will pay respects, gather and spill tears, say last goodbyes, accept their loss and try to move on.

Bodies fat and skinny, short and tall, corpses of all sizes inhabit the coroner's kingdom, to be mutilated for answers before they're set to rest in their final destination. His job may not be glamorous or pretty, but what do you expect when you stab and smell corpses for a living? What do you expect when you're the only percentage of the population alive? What do you expect when you work in Morguetopia?

Lucifer's Thanksgiving Dinner

For more recipes like this, follow me on Facebook - @LiianVarusPoetry.

Flightless angel, captured angel, sky fish in my razor net so pale and silky. Your flesh is a godsend, so white and soft. Your wings will be a delicious trend. Lucifer will be pleased with me. Are you ready for torment and misery? Your innocent beauty, your face and body, you were created to be destroyed. Say hello to your bitter end.

That's right, panic. Struggle yourself into mutilation, slit apart the skin, and expose the flesh, fight the trap and bleed, drain empty into the cauldron below. Use fear to proceed. Use anger to persuade the blood flow. Don't give in; indulge the pain. Cut apart every vein, artery and tendon. Don't relieve the muscle stress; drown all the razors with your blood dress. Give yourself to Lucifer. There is no hope to escape; your accomplishment is failure.

Now while your blood boils, the soup that will accompany your carcass, I'll strap your half-lifeless body to this stone table and begin the gruesome act of plucking.

Feather by feather I rip them out one by one, laughing every time your body recoils. Every feather pulled releases the scent of turmoil. I can tell you don't want to be here. I see the desperation to escape in your tears, but this is not a dream because I can hear your screams and you know it by how the cauldron steams, and the feelings of discomfort as your wounds swell. This is real; this is fucking Hell. This is where faith leads you: Into Lucifer's palm.

Don't worry, it's almost over. Stop shaking; you're fine. Now hold still while I pull out your spine. It was nice torturing you, goodbye. Featherless wings and spine torn right out of your back; vague amounts of blood and flesh fly. She pulsates and twitches, a quick dance before she dies. Just look at her; she's perfect, a sacrifice suitable for warlocks and witches. But today is special. Today is Thanksgiving. Today, she is a meal for Satan. And how delighted he will be at what he sees. He hasn't fed on an angel in centuries.

She's just about done. Only thing left is the stuffing: two quarts of virgin's blood, feathers from angel wings, six cups of coral snake scales, four tablespoons of nun ashes, two minced crocodile tails, two litres of rapist cum, a dash of gunpowder, nine long strips of skin covered with rashes, and the secret ingredient, a flavour that is quite abundant and convenient: a handful of diced flesh from a pedophile. I mix it all into a bowl until it's thick, then by hand I shove it in past her rectum, ramming it in as far as possible. Then after, I glaze her with goat drool, cram a rotten apple in her pretty mouth and as fast as she was caught, she is ready to cook.

Sluts Of The Occult

Don't blame me. Blame - Eyes Wide Shut.

Whores all in a circle. Devil worshippers choosing their choice of meat: their partner for this special event. The masquerade ball of fucking: wear a mask and choose a cunt. All of them beautiful. Even though their faces are concealed, they are soft on the eyes, sluts of the occult.

Their skin is smooth and tender, flesh easy to sever. They're innocent girls doused with curiosity, which makes them demons. Lust is their sin. Unfortunately for them, they're blind as well and can't see behind their masters' masks. After the orgy, they'll be stabbed six times to Hell; damned to the fire well, a place they shouldn't be.

Tragedy starts here: an eerie mansion with many ecstasy rooms, completely filled with artificial lovers dancing in the mating position, creating moans and screams that echo throughout, doubling the sounds of sin that's bursting the eardrums and eyes of angels. Such atrocity shouldn't be heard, be seen, but that's what's happening. Existence is pouring from their ears and eyes and from it, they will fall. Their fate is in virgin hands. Dead angels will be everywhere when young harlots are scattered - an end of a climactic tragedy.

Beasts fucking beauties - sluts of the occult. Shades start to come down; the time has come. Mating season vanishes. Silent knives arrive. Misery blooms. Lives drowning in the red ocean rooms. Corpses floating angelically. Bloodletting set on automatic. Laughter conquered the cries while lured virgins died and the angels that fell to save them. And failure shows by angel rot that surrounds and the thousands of white feathers that cover the ground. An old saying once again reborn - "Two birds with one stone." Another victory for Lucifer.

Ghost Of The Ballet

Would you believe me if I told you I had an erection when I wrote this? I'm gross. I'm so sorry. I don't have one now though, so that's an improvement, is it not?

Disfigured ballerina dancing down the hall of 14th-century knights. Twirling and spinning, going in circles round and round, finishing and starting at the beginning. Never-ending circular rotations: continuous spurts of speed that could hypnotize the blind.

With her arms spread like wings, she glides across the red carpet, teasing the floor with dangling feet that are dressed in velvet white ballroom slippers that tickle the ground beneath them. Her black tights and white tutu shade her in as if she were alive, solidifying the transparent dancer almost perfectly, enhancing the clarity of her effortless movements. She looks so real you could touch her; too bad your hand would go right through. Untouchable is the ghost of the ballet. Just watch and be enchanted, it's all you can do.

Hollow beauty with swan white skin, white like bleached bones under the desert sun. Say hello to the ghost of the ballet. Falling in love with her is easy. Trying to stop staring is another story. Yes, she is voluptuous and hormones race because of it. But at the same time, you want to retch, you want to vomit when you see the eerie bobbing of her head, her bloody skull that dangles from her broken neck. The way it hangs and swings as she dances, you can't help but stare, risking the horrible chance her lifeless eyes will peer into you if her long brunette hair uncovers her haunting glare.

She's been wandering this ancient school of ballet since the day she jumped from the roof's ledge. The mystery is still unsolved; no one knows why she killed herself. No matter now, she's damned to haunt. You'll always see her dancing, mesmerizing and scaring people. It's no way for something so pure to spend eternity. It is sad her fate turned out this way, but maybe she's here because she wants to be.

The Burning

When it comes to chlamydia poetry - this is the best.

Trying to heal from the cuts and scratches, but infection has already taken form. Pus is building; signs of gangrene growing. My wounds and skin around them are itchy, irritated all over. Medication and herbs useless; the burning continues. A cure for a shattered ending of a downward spiral relationship does not exist. I can scream, cut my wrists, dream, swallow my pride and pray, but the burning won't stop. It seems the only way to put out a scorching heartache is by smothering the heat with body decay. Pathetic excuse to kill oneself, but when all hope fails, sometimes the cradling arms of suicide has the power to lure in a lost soul. Like me, like I. I love life. I just can't help myself from this urge of finding ways to die. It seems all I can do is shut my eyes, cross my fingers, hope to die and let the blade linger into my life valves, but in the end, I still know the burning will continue because, in one form or another, love is eternal.

Rodents And Insects

Well, that's the last time they put up Christmas lights.

Where's Katie? She's been missing since her school dance. Where's Katie? She's been gone four days now. Where's Katie? No one has a clue.

Days turn to weeks, weeks age into a month; still no word from Katie. Hope seems lost. And what's the cost of her disappearance? A shattered family coping with mourning hearts.

Thirty days has developed quickly. It's been a month since Katie's vanishing act. And all her loved ones are downstairs mourning, crying, praying that she'll reappear as nothing happened, but the heartache they feel is torture. They can't help knowing what life will be like without her. Sitting in a misshapen circle, they reminisce Katie back together, telling what seems to be just fairy tales about her. But for those sacred moments, joy and happiness breathes a little inside their hearts, easing the pain slightly so the hurt doesn't eat them whole.

A mouse scurries around the saddening conversations, runs through a hole in the living room wall and climbs up into the attic. Some dusty boxes, ancient picture frames and wooden chests lay about; you can tell no one has been up there in years. It's dark. It's cold and inhabited by rodents and insects: a great place for the suicidal to sleep.

A cockroach wanders past a few stray, dead maggots and starts to eat the rotting wood from an old stool. In front of the stool, there stands a cracked mirror. The cockroach sees his reflection, the stool's many small piles of starving larvae that hunger on top of it, and the reflection of badly decomposed legs that dangle just above.

A bat hanging upside-down from the ceiling sees it all: Katie's half-bald head, Katie's eyes popped from their sockets, her delicate tongue that's barely there, Katie's naked cadaver painted with gorgeous colours of green, blue and purple. Katie is a portrait of the decay rainbow.

Rodents and insects see and smell Katie's demise. They smell the scent of changing one's mind that came too late. They see the fear buried in her dead eyes. They feel absolutely nothing towards this tragedy. A heavy sound ruins their attention; someone is coming up the attic stairs.

Nightmare

Worst. Amusement. Park. Ever.

With the pages of a fairy tale torn, a nightmare is born. Everything is transformed, deformed; anything that made sense is nonsense. Light is now dark. Love stories are bloody tragedies. Nothing is right; every choice is a mistake. Fragility is a reason to break. There's no great castle just a superior prison. And the beautiful princess is an ugly whore; the prince is a repulsive boar. The secret meaning of "I love you" really means "I fucking hate you". Good luck is undiscovered misfortunes: guarantees without the warranty. No sun exists just a weary moon: the only real, true thing in this nightmare and it wants to be destroyed. Love notes are angry suicide letters. Death is the only cure to feel better. Anything that has meaning is dying. In this place, everything is pointless so consequences don't matter. Holding onto something is just a reason to let go. The point of kissing is so it leads to sex. No love... just lust. No truth... only lies and mistrust. To live is an excuse to find ways to die. Hellos are foreshadowers for goodbyes. If it's not tragic, there's no magic. In this nightmare, everything is as pure as plastic. This is the world in my eyes since the day you said, "I don't love you anymore."

Accident

Now I know how Bruce Willis felt when he survived that train wreck in Unbreakable.

Lost my girlfriend in a car accident. Since that day I've been feeling different like depression and sorrow fucked, and gave birth to an unbearable psychological illness, a haunting dark emotion, a pain more hurtful than suicidal yearning, more excruciating than a devastated heart burning. I feel like I'm the wrist of the world and everyone is cutting me. Like the guillotine is my god and I am bowing before it, taunting it, trying to get it to knight me. I'm being punished for being inebriated and seducing the wheel, for crashing and breaking her neck against the windshield. I want to run away, far away, somewhere safe, the place where Lindsay lays, so I can apologize to her until my words whisper apart, until the last beat of my dying heart.

Stuck on repeat, that days overplays in my head: her spine-shivering scream, the impact against the tree that caught me by surprise, her body shooting out of the seat, her head smashing against the glass, blood splattering from a wound of astronomical mass, her falling back into the seat, her busted skull leaning against the dashboard and her staring into me with dead eyes, as blood pours over her face. Tragedy struck violently and all I got was a bruised knee and a fractured arm. The accident was my fault, my mistake, but Lindsay is the one who died. I'll never understand the choices fate makes. I just know it should have been me! It should have been me! IT SHOULD HAVE BEEN ME!

Murder Scene

If this was a real-life game of Operation, the killer definitely touched the sides. More like got angry because they touched the sides and Hulk-smashed the game into pieces. You should try playing Monopoly against my uncle sometime... What an asshole.

Demolished like a massacred pinata. From her feet to her vulva, long brutal gouges bleed like geysers: macabre ravines ushering out blood before it coagulates, before it thickens and dries. Her pale skin valley is illuminated by red waterways. Haunting beauty slain, white velvet sheets stained, no signs of life, only the cause of death remains.

Eyes still bulging with fear. Mouth open; the jaw is locked. Murder relatively fresh; a duct continues to hold a tear. The further I look down the harder it is to stare. Bruises adorning the slit on her throat; hands of the culprit discovered. Angry fingerprints will reveal the identity. This lifeline clue to solve the mystery, it's priceless and fragile. It's the only witness to the murder.

Naked, red and dead; lying there without a thought in her head. Masquerading as the damned princess, she bleeds from violent lashes and amputations. No emergency; she's been stabbed into darkness. It's too late to crown her back to life; the killer inhaled her last breath. I have seen horror and it is here: slaughtered body with wounds too big to stitch; limbs butchered apart too luridly to reattach. Over-killed and over-destroyed; not a single heartbeat can be restored. The woman fell into the void. It is impossible for her to be resurrected.

Never have I seen something so sick. It looks like someone threw her to the wolves, into the hungry slaughter. Blood is everywhere; the dead smell is alive. Someone lost a daughter. When the identity of the deceased is released and the corpse is claimed, someone will receive a nightmare. Until then, pictures must be taken; evidence must be collected. Then I get to be a pallbearer to the streets, where an ambulance will be waiting to take her away. And I'll do all of that as soon as I finish vomiting.

Brenna

I am a straight male.

I fell in love with a girl. It all began with a dare. "Kiss Brenna," they said. "French kiss Brenna," they told me. And I did. It was all in fun, but something jolted. A reaction flared, surging hormones came rising in pairs, dirty thoughts swarmed my mind. Nothing made sense. I felt like someone else and I enjoyed it. I wanted more.

That kiss sealed my fate; I was a lesbian born. The taste of her lips ushered me out of my old skin that was damaged and worn, and brought me to a lifestyle of promiscuous sex with female whores that seduce new virgins, taking advantage of their weakness and curiosity, pleasuring them until all they breathe are breasts and cunts. When they were finished with me, the only things I desired were smooth, soft breasts and beautiful wet cunts.

A year went by. I was a toy and a dominatrix. I slept with and fucked many girls, but Brenna was the only one I wanted. We were so close; both ravishing lovers we were. I honestly thought we'd be together forever, but Brenna had other plans: like ripping my heart out and setting it in my cold, dead hands. I never saw it coming, especially when I was in the midst of orgasming. She fucked me one last time, stared right into me and said, "It's over." She put her clothes on and left. That was the last day I saw her. I never saw her again.

She brought the lesbian out of me, but now that she's gone, I don't know if I can continue. I am so confused about my sexuality. I don't know what to do. Am I straight, gay, or bi? I looked into the mirror, peered into my eyes; no answer appeared. I just want to disappear. It hurts so much. I don't understand what happened. She said I was pretty. She said I made her happy. She said she'd never leave me. She said... She said... She said she loved me.

Gone

Fuck you. Good riddance. Unless you're coming back to me. Are you coming back? Just want to know if I need to buy new sheets for the amazing sex we're going to have. Oh... You're not coming back. I see. Well, I suppose I still need new sheets anyway.

Kissing you makes everything go away. But now that you are gone, how do I make the feeling stay? Don't you love me? Won't you die without me? The loss of you is torture; without you, I've been an ugly creature. How can I be beautiful if bloody wrists are my best feature? Nothing breathes; I'm petrified inside. My dreams are suicide. My prayers are you, but they always turn into angry fists: punishers that beat me black and blue. It kills me that I don't know why you are gone and not knowing what I did wrong. All I know is that you brought me down with a brutal slaying of words, a surprise attack I couldn't fight back. And all you said was, "I'm leaving you." No kiss, no hug, just a single tear I watched fall: the climax of a tragedy being born. Your absence has been my destruction, my fucking nightmare. All my senses have failed except heartache. I've been eaten alive by the fact I made a mistake and it eats me even harder because I can't prove it. I want you back so much that I would die just to see your face again. Yes, I am alive but I'm not living, only waiting, waiting for the day you come back and say how much you love me, then maybe I would find out why you are gone.

Violent End
To A Peaceful October

And to think she spent all day putting her diaphragm in.

Enchanting necromancer without a head, spellbinding the sky a vermilion red. The voluptuous nymph coaxes her serpentine flesh and begins dancing for corpses sleeping in their soil lockets. Her dark magic is persuasive; the dead are awakening from their caskets. Zombies start to break through their dirty beds; they are following her lustful verses for necrophilia. She enhances the hypnosis. Like puppets on strings, they obey as she sings, walking hard as she tells the future about an orgy in a graveyard. Even with emotionless faces, surging delight colours the night. As empty as they are, the twisted maiden will be fulfilled before October comes giving birth to a splendid white.

Filthy sorceress, witch of darkness, grave-robbing succubus raising rot for the sense of touch. Decapitated but her minions are still captivated. Stimulated by the headless sounds, they continue to push up through the cemetery grounds. Enthralled to the curse, they drag themselves towards her. They can't repent; they urge forward to the sex serpent. Body parts are littered across the grass; some of the love-struck cadavers are falling apart. They have been hugged by decomposition for too long. Some of them won't make it to the powerful whore's song. Their journey won't lead them to her catalytic heart.

Hundreds, close to thousands surround her. She flirtatiously lures them in with the wave of her hands, giggling, laughing, teasing with her coquettish voice as she takes off her gown and bares her flesh, waiting to be dominated by choice. But something is different. She senses it in their glasslike eyes, past their ragged burial garments. There is a strong hunger but not for sex; they want flesh. Before she can remove the spell, reverse the necromantic curse, her slaves abducted from Heaven and Hell, bite and claw into her like starving gargoyles. Skin, blood, flesh and bone explode against the gravestones; the death slut is destroyed. With a violent end to a peaceful October and the disturbance slaughtered, the corpses slumber.

Pain

No. You have issues with women.

Red like garden roses: all my flesh melted from chemical burns. Pain: the ether that puts me to sleep. Hurt deep; I can't climb out of this hole you dug for me. Self-harm, mutilation up and down my arms - company for the corrosive chemical burns. I'm a bloody mess but I feel better. I'm pathetic, but what does it matter? I'm stuck in this hole you pushed me into. No point to try and escape; the quicksand at the bottom keeps me here. Sink - it's the only thing I can do.

You are the colour of destruction and I'm painted by you. Shrivel up and die, is there another option? My hands are so sore; thumbs shoved into my eyes; eight other nails impaled into my head. I can't keep it up. It's not enough. I need more. Pain - it charms the frustration away. Without it, I wouldn't be here today. Without it, it means I don't feel so I'm not real. You might as well fill in the hole; bury me because I'm dead.

Whore, you are the pain I can't sustain. My heart is slain; your lust slayed it. Betrayed; I trusted the succubus bitch. I loved a demon that lived for sex. I wasn't the incubus fuck she wanted. I was just the sacrificial quickie, the scratch for her hormonal itch, just a worthless rag doll fuck. When she left, that's when I found insanity. I completely lost it. I took out all the pain on my flesh, and still, two years later I feel sick. It seems the gash she gave me can't be stitched; it's a wound I will always have to lick. I'll never heal while I breathe. The day I die is the day the bloody lesion on my heart will seal.

Too Late

Found my reason to live. It was having sex with other women. Wow. Fictional me is a fucking asshole.

Somehow blinded, I couldn't see the poison you were carrying. The countdown for the sacrifice, I couldn't hear it. Completely unaware of the change of colour in your eyes, I couldn't translate the expression on your face. I didn't know with the power of suicide, you were going to leave with a trace, leaving me alone with nothing to embrace but a corpse, an image that will always haunt me. Maybe if I was more attentive to you, I could have realized there was something wrong, but I always played the game of distance and distance is what killed you. In your last days, your words and actions were strong; I didn't know they were cries for help because you were weak. When your lips trembled when we last kissed, I should have felt your pain signaling to me, warning me. But I didn't open my eyes to see that you were going to kill yourself in spite of me, because I was never there. When you desperately insisted for me to act like you existed, I never listened because I thought you were just being dramatic, overreacting that I didn't pay enough attention to you. I didn't see the big deal, until the day I walked in and saw what was too late: you leaning against your headboard, bloody and bare, portraying suicidal perfection: a lifeless stare accompanied by wrist mutilation. I could have saved you if I told you I loved you. If I wasn't so ignorant things would be different, but it's too late. You found a reason to die and left me wounded with the emotional poison I gave you. Now before infection takes over, I must find a reason to live.

Mannequin-Made

21-year-old Liian had a lot of issues, he needed to work out with the opposite sex. Proud to say it's less bad now.

So still in the night light, stained with dirt, dead bridal princess blanketed with darkness, with burial gown torn to rags, giving permission to the one who yearns for her: the groom that once knew her, a necrophiliac that loves and not lusts, her lover she left behind.

It was supposed to be a special day. Who knew her heart would give way? She wore the gown, went to show the mirror to see the reflection she gives. A face of joy fell blank when she saw. In an instant, she became distant, lifeless, and crumbled to the ground.

Silent, rotting pale, mannequin-made: corpse whore dug from the ocean shore, positioned to the delight, to the one who will fuck her this night, her lover she left behind. The scenery is right, in the cemetery by the water. It's warm, the waves are alluring, the owls are out singing their morbid song, and the grass and trees are dancing, tickling the gravestones that surround them. It's a perfect dark to rekindle the lovers' spark: a nightmarish fairy tale designed for the perverted.

The sickening ritual begins. He moans and thrusts, imagining she's alive and well, making love to her like newlyweds on their honeymoon, except his counterpart is breathless and without a beating heart. She's mannequin-made. Gangrene limbs and rot highlight her. To him, she's enthralling just the same. To him, she looks just like she did before she died. And that's why he cries when he sees baby flies devouring his fiancé. Because something so sweet shouldn't be so sour.

Enjoying denial, disturbing the maggot pile his bride is covered in, he finally stops and backs away. Seeing her emotionless, motionless has made him realize nothing will bring her back. It's unfortunate and sad that their wedding day had to end this way, but sometimes what doesn't happen in one life can happen in the next. Knowing this he dries his eyes and sets her back into the grave, re-enacting the funeral that should have been a wedding. Praying that one day, they'll be together. Her dressed in white, him dressed in black, with a ring on each other's finger, living happily ever after as husband and wife.

Safety Pin Butterfly

Failing that entomology course really did a number on my psyche.

I found a pretty, little butterfly gently fluttering its wings through the meadow, flying flower to flower, socializing with fellow butterflies and nearby insects as it goes, enjoying life to its full extent, floating needlessly, taking advantage of the summer warmth, using all its energy to take advantage of the day.

What a happy butterfly. What a sight this is. What a sight it is. Lucky butterfly smiling in front of me, taunting me, flaunting all it can. Fucking butterfly laughing at me, mocking the life I have, teasing me. Fucking butterfly! Fucking butterfly! I'm going to kill you!

You see me running. You sense the danger of the chase from the tears and anger on my face. You flap your wings in a panic, but I'm gaining. I'm right behind you. No escape for the winged one. The death of you will be my sunshine.

My hand comes down on top of you; my fist has taken away your day. I can tell how frightened you are with every wing flap that tickles against your cage of skin, that's padded by flesh and reinforced with bone. Your time of fun in the sun is over.

I slightly open the hold, use my other hand to pinch your body still, then with the hand that was once your cage, I pull a safety pin from my lip, grin right into your tiny eyes, and without warning, I impale you through. You jitter and convulse as your guts drip; your wings drop as your life slips.

Watching you die was bliss, but the best part besides playing God is having your corpse safety-pinned to my heart.

Trust Or Lust?

She chose to be faithful. Which was very disheartening to hear since this is a fictitious poem. Yup. I'm that pathetic. I can't even make imaginary sex happen.

'll fuck you if you ask me to. I won't pressure you into adultery, but if you give me permission, I'll fuck you into submission. I'm not cruel-hearted, just a man parted from morals. I won't force you into this. I'll give you an option: You can honour your vow of trust or betray it and bare yourself to lust. It's your decision. Just realize before you make up your mind, how bad I want to touch you, and how bad you want to let me before your conscience sits you down for another therapy session.

I'm not asking you for your heart or hand in marriage. Just to strip you down, lay you down, go down and suck you dry. I know you want to give in by the way you lick your lips. The impatient look on your nervous face foreshadowed the anticipating, subtle movements of your body. I can tell you're feeling like a dog in heat: all you want to do is fuck.

So, what's it going to be?
Trust or lust?

And you don't need to worry, this can be our secret. We can fuck from early dusk until late dawn. Orgasm for hours until our bodies are incapacitated. We can fill the bed with sweat, blood and cum, and no one needs to know. Your sinful expedition can be kept secret. This way you can still have your fairy tale life with your prince and have the family you've always wanted. Nothing will be jeopardized.

So, what's it going to be?
Trust or lust?

To be honest I want you to sin, to give in. I want you so bad I could rape you, throw you to the bed, tear off your clothes, hold you down and fuck you until you submit, until your disgusted screams cry into pleasuring moans, and you start biting me, scratching me, yearning for me to thrust faster, harder with every ounce of strength I have. But I won't violate you without your weakness for temptation. I won't rape you because I respect the friendship we have. But I am getting anxious.

So, what's it going to be?
Trust or lust?

Trust or lust?

Jake Loves Ashley

I don't know a Jake. I don't know an Ashley. But I'm sure there is a couple named Jake and Ashley, and I hope they're both just fucking miserable.

Staring at razor-engraved wrists to see if I still exist. The suicide hand twitching. It's urge to kill continues to persist. I take some deep breaths, a moment to relax, time to reminisce, I pause and think of all the things I'll miss. Nothing comes to mind but you, the hurtful thought of you.

Lovers separated by one; I took the scissors and cut us apart. A fatal mistake that was easy to make, but I can't believe I did it. I shattered your undeserved heart. Now without you, I'm so cold. Now that I don't have you to hold, I am so fucking cold. I don't know why I destroyed what we had, but it doesn't matter; it's too late. I wish I never let you go.

Actions are deadlier than words, but together they kill. I was vicious, malice and callous. My heart was boiling with so much of that puss, that I could not keep myself away. I wanted to watch something decay, so I made you the experiment. Your uniqueness made you the doll. I was amazed when I watched you fall. I laughed when your heart rotted, knowing you can never love again. I was the one that filled you with fear and drowned your eyes with tears. I was the idiot that did not realize true love never dies.

I love you, Ashley. Please, forgive me. I meant to hurt you, but I didn't want to. Sadism caught me by surprise. Surely, you saw it in my eyes. I was possessed, not myself. Ashley, please, I love you. Trust me and take my hand, just look at me. I am the Jake you once knew, the one you loved. I cry. I feel. Touch me. I'm real. The demon is no longer inside; your destruction massacred it. Ashley, please, believe me. Let us escape; leave it all behind. Just say you love me, and we'll run to the day where I fell in love with you. We'll run to the willow tree where it is carved "Jake loves Ashley".

Possessed

It all worked out. She had a rebound guy.

I've screamed all I can say but you still stay. Why won't my threats and curses make you go away? I don't love you. You see this heart? Notice how the colour isn't really a colour? It's black and cracked. And from the flesh tears, hatred poured in. Drowning. I am drowning as I speak. Crying. I am crying because I am weak. Love just disappeared, faded when I slept. I was caught off guard. When I woke, I vomited from what I felt, what I am feeling now.

I must be possessed. I must confess. Because I've never had an urge to hit you, to beat you until your white skin glows blue. I promise I tried to fight it, but the intruding entity was too violent. What's left of me is dead silent. I'm not myself. My hateful words are a warning for you to run, run away. I don't want to hurt you, but if you don't listen and decide to stay, if you try to save me, your beauty will rot into a mound of decay. If that's what you want then kiss me.

Twelve

Quite possibly the worst Advent calendar ever.

This art of suffocation was drawn by love starvation. I have mutilated pieces of my heart dangling and from it, I'm strangling, struggling desperately to hold together, but many failed attempts have made me suicidal. Now the only thing worth trying is finding the secret to dying.

Every time I see her with him, another nail is spiked into my heart. Impaled twelves times and bloody, I'm drowning from internal bleeding. My sadness is swelling from my anger's teething. My emotional flesh is bruised and damaged; most of it is rotten and there's not much left to salvage. *How much longer can I fight the heartache?* – a hopeful question with a negative answer. A heart invaded with twelve nails, to let them stay and infect is a mistake. I pull but they won't come out. I feel like I can't be saved. I will die because I can't take the pain; for some reason, I hurt but don't exist.

Being with her was bliss. From conversations to a kiss, from a kiss to romantic copulation; everything we did was some form of attention that followed with certain kinds of affection. We were unbreakable but I couldn't keep Eden. Our relationship became highly unstable; verbal violence made the downfall uncontrollable. Our whole paradise turned flammable and burned, not even strays of ashes were spared. It was a wasteland with a population of one: a stabbed heart pathetically holding on, waiting for the seed to return, to create the rebirth of Eden. But she will never return. And from this unwanted wisdom, the only thing I learned is that twelve is the worst number I've ever felt.

Deformed perfect for horror – my heart is a grotesque pincushion, twelve nails lodged deep within with lots of room left: sadistic, spacious vacancy for more brutality. A few more punctures and I will be a love-torn casualty. Being a dartboard, I thought there was more to me. I suppose falling in love was my penalty. Love brought suicide. I will be the fatality. Serves me right for carrying the thought, that together we would live on past forever, with hand-in-hand out live immortals and gods, but we could end it all with the slice of a razor and create our own eternity. If she could just come back to me, erase twelve days, remove twelve nails, bandage twelve wounds, heal my heart like new, just tell me that she loves me, remind me that I exist, then I would stop the calendar on my wrist.

Ogre

Beauty & The Beast in an alternate reality.

Hatred – that's all I am. How can I love someone if I can't even love myself? I am a fountain of lies, murky water to despise. If you can't see through the dirt, don't drink the water. Filthy, unclean; drag your fingers across me. Nothing clear; you can't make me disappear.

I'm not beautiful on the outside; rip away my skin and reveal the flesh. There's no beauty on the inside. I'm pretty like an ogre. You can dig further but there's nothing there. I'm hideous through and through. Positive qualities? I destroyed them all with obscenities. You could push your way past the red. If you're that desperate, try. But it's only black on the other end. It's pointless. I was born from darkness.

Remove the mask; unveil my dark heart. Hideously broken, isn't it? You can try to piece it together but none of the pieces fit. I don't really exist. I know I seemed perfect; the truth is I'm fucked. I'm not even real. Shoot me. I'm hollow. I bleed nothing but air. Now you see why I don't care, why I'm wicked. I am the climatic nightmare: a fucking story that has no ending.

Stop crying. Stop reaching for me. You have to understand – if you don't stop, I'll break your hand. It's over. There's nothing left to discover. I've already kissed both your lips, fucked you in every entrance. I fucking used you and you loved it, so quit the bullshit. I didn't tell you my perversity came with misery, that's your own fault. You should have opened your eyes instead of your legs. Do you now see the creature? It's over! Now shut it and fuck off! I'm warning you, bitch! If you don't stop telling me you love me, I am going to bludgeon you to death!

Drug Factory

Attempting to kill yourself by overdosing on pills is not as peaceful as Hollywood portrays it to be. It's Hell. Don't do it. Or maybe I've never used the right kind. Might try something else besides multivitamins next time.

Medicated to alter the design of my mind; many years later and something continues to infest. I'm still not fine; there's something wrong. Prescription drugs are having an effect. Their so-called operation is a failure; their medicine couldn't purge me. I'm still not pure. I told them but they refused to listen – my sickness doesn't have a cure. I'm not supposed to be here, but they don't understand – I'm trapped in the fucked-up Wonderland inside my head. The only way to escape is down the rabbit hole, a suicidal reaction to kill the abomination: the illness that's been eating away at my sanity.

Needle-poked and pill-choked; my body is a worn-out drug factory. All the recipes in me that were supposed to heal me have expired. Out-of-date recommendations are less than satisfactory; they're poisonous and corrosive. I feel the change boiling inside me. I'm venomous. My own toxins are turning against me. An eruption of mass proportion is brewing. My chemical romance has died; all the prescribed formulas are now fucking. I drink a glass of water to ease the future, but the water won't go down. Sticky, white chunks have blocked up my oesophagus: leftover pill residue glued together by my saliva. It tastes like pus. It tastes like a fucking catastrophe. My worthless end is not important. I'm not special. I'm not different. I'm just another fallen boy that forgot what it's like to smile.

I can feel it coming: the acidity of my meltdown. I feel it stabbing upwards like a bullet. It burns like my throat is running the gauntlet. Traces of vomit are starting to seep out past my lips. I'm fighting to hold it in, but the pressure is killing the eclipse. The force is too strong. My mouth will open, and I'll sing the terminally ill's song.

And as predicted, like an enraged volcano I explode. Pieces of food, stomach, lung and mystery bits burst out. I want to stop but the pain and smell entice me to continue. Now blood has decided to ride the regurgitation waterslide. Involuntary spasms push me to puke harder and harder; my insides have been drip-dried. There's nothing left to escort outside but still, I retch. I try and catch a breath, but the oxygen delays are starting to stretch. I'm suffocating from air loss and slowly dying. By the time the strangulation breaks, before the constant exhaling disengages, I will realize that taking that first pill was a mistake, and from a single tablet, I have created my own destruction.

A Hungry Maggot

Dinner reservations for one... please.

Blood-glazed corpse so lifeless, silently still on a bed of moss, decaying as the sun beams down on it. An unlikely barbeque for insects to enjoy, but they will feast just the same.

His body is mutilated. I can clearly see the colour of his departure. Dozens of wounds tell a story of horror, but the words on the pages are fading as starving phobias feed. With every bite, the gashes slowly disappear and soon there will be nothing left to read.

Countless bugs dine, eating flesh and sipping blood like a rare wine, savouring the taste and leaving none to waste. Water droplets sprinkled across the body multiply this terror by reflections of the horde shown in the morning dew. And the fucked-up circle of life continues.

Facedown, red, naked, exposed, not fully decomposed; I don't know where the body came from. I don't care when it got here. It's dead. It's soft and covered in shit. I can tell by the appetizing stain on the back of his pants. I feel no remorse for what I am about to do to this corpse because I'm just a hungry maggot.

Wounds Of Cupid

The wounds aren't a metaphor for herpes, but I wish they were. It implies I got laid.

Let go of my hand or I'll punch you with the other one. I've said it all. Now release me so it can be done. Don't you understand? I'm not the one your hopes sent. Yes, Cupid struck me down with his mighty arrow, but I pulled it out from my heart and shoved it through his head. He missed his mark. I wasn't the target. I know it's hard to accept when the wound on my heart strongly shows. Trust me. It'll be better for you to turn away and forget. Try searching somewhere else. You will find nothing here. Lady, my patience is wearing thin. Remove your skin from mine. Speak no more words. Stop telling me I'm the one; that is absurd. I don't love you. I don't want anything to do with you. Look at my so-called love wound – it's gangrene and rotting. Love does not look like that. I am sorry for what has befallen you, but I'll never say I love you. So, turn around and walk the other way.

I remember after saying those horrible things to you, you bared your chest and there it was: a similar wound of Cupid. It was gangrene and rotting like mine, just as putrid. I was at a loss for words. I didn't know what to say except that I was sorry for not believing you. You cried and said, "No, I'm sorry." You pulled out a gun and threatened your temple. I begged and pleaded for you to drop it but instead, you shot it. Sequenced to the blood and the crack of thunder, painted red, you fell dead. I couldn't save the girl I didn't know I loved. I just watched her tumble as my heart crumbled. And as I knelt down at her side, holding her lifeless hand, I leaned over, kissed her and whispered into her bloody ear, "I love you, too."

Orchestra Seven

The whole ghetto blaster outside her window thing didn't work.

If I died today would you bleed for me? Would you cut yourself and imagine I'm right there beside you? After the funeral, after the six-foot burial, when you're at home drowning in sadness, would you follow misery and meet me at the cemetery? Would you hug my grave, scream my name and sacrifice an artery, or would my selfish kill be my unseen exploitation?

My suicide will be instrumental: music without sound. Only a sharp cry will disrupt the silence. My wrist is a seven-string violin; this rusted machete is the bow. Seven severed veins; no more pain. I've lost everything. I can only gain. But if you want me to stay, if you mean it, then seduce the conductor to cancel the orchestra. Kiss my frustrated-bitten lips, wet my heart and stop the clay from hardening. If you want to tell me you love me, if you mean it, whisper into my ears and repeat it until disbelief clears. Just don't quit until I say I love you, too. But if you want me to go, if you mean it, I will show you a bloody song of seven slits.

I've tried exhuming the past to build a future, to learn from mistakes and tame the creature, but my virtuous efforts have gone unacknowledged. Your dark heart still beats without any cracks. Will I ever have you back? Of course… you're not here to answer. You are trauma. You are cancer. You are the tumour in my brain that ticks, the nightmare in my dreams that sticks. Will you ever come back and extinguish the flames that melt me? Of course… you're not here to answer. I forgot. Already I'm dying in denial. While I'm exiled, I'll never smile. As long as we're separated, I weaken.

While I wait, I will always know heartache. Will you ever love me again? Once again, I fell back into fiction. Once again, you aren't here to answer.

A Dying Rose
That Can't Be Saved

Not about my mother. I'm fantastic at lying. Er, I mean at storytelling. Should I put a trigger warning on this? The subject matter is sensitive and dark. Fuck it. You're on your own. I hate it when people ruin surprises.

A single ebony-glazed rose tilted against my mother's grave: a present of mourning to keep her company. Its sorrow reflects my own. I can describe it by the sagging, wilted petals beaten by many nights of rain – a dying rose that can't be saved.

She played her game of roulette and as suspected, lost. She wouldn't take heed. Even when her ulcers would bleed, no signs of quitting approached. She told me and I quote, "Just never-mind." She took her cigarettes and smoked, and would choke when her gag-reflex provoked, enticing her to hack up pieces of tar and lung, past her throat and out her mouth until the charred bits rolled off her tobacco tongue. Not even tasting her own burnt insides subsided the ravenous craving. She never stopped until the day she dropped.

Cigarette after cigarette her condition worsened. She couldn't break from the addiction until it was too late. She passed the point of no return like a dying rose that can't be saved. My mother was once a beautiful woman, but cancer made her hideous. Sadness and hurt trampled me. I couldn't bear seeing what she became. Her state reminded me of something revolting, something contagious, someone I could not recognize. Even her eyes were different. Something was sneaking around in them, something I despised. Death was lurking about and was taking over fast, preparing to rip my mother's soul out of her body. And all I could do was watch, watch him take her away from me.

Not dead yet but looked like a corpse. She was ahead of schedule, already set for burial. Her resemblance and smell were so realistic, so identical to the dead that she could've been buried alive and no one would've noticed the difference. She was already a corpse before she died. No wonder the whole family cried. They were devastated, knowing they would have to say their final goodbyes because God didn't answer their prayers. That was the day everyone questioned their faith.

On a windy, cloudy, summer day, my mother finally passed away. It killed so much because just before she died, I felt a pain so great that I knew she was too far gone to ever come back - like a dying rose that can't be saved. I wish I could say she went peacefully, but that would be lying. I wish I told my mother when she was dying that I loved her and forgave her. I wish I had said something instead of nothing at all.

Ms. Macabre

Here's a lesson: Drugs are an expensive habit, especially when that habit isn't yours. Keep that in mind the next time you fall in love.

I fell in love with a drug queen, a harpy with needle-stabbed skin, a body that's sickly thin. She's almost reptilian with her overdosing stare and the hundreds of bruises that colour her, scales that represent the sweet spots, places where she loves to indulge. She's addicted to needlepoint bliss: destruction in a syringe. It will eventually kill her, but she doesn't seem to care. She's amazed by all the tiny punctures that her body is covered in.

I was looking for love. I found Ms. Macabre: a whore of holes. I can't deal with her, can't handle all the things she does. I think I bit off more than I can chew but I love her. And that's why I ask myself – Am I in over my head? Am I in over my head?

This relationship is unhealthy. It's pushing me away and dragging me in. We never talk. She never has the time. If I'm not intoxicating, she doesn't have time for me. Even the sex is horrible. It's like I'm fucking a corpse. She's too stoned to react, too high to know what's going on. If I wanted to fuck a corpse, I'd be a necrophiliac and go gravedigging. And that's why we're falling apart because she doesn't know I exist.

No matter how this ends, how our path bends, I know I'm stuck to her. I'll always be there for her because I love her. Maybe in cleaner, better days, we could try again. When her eyes clear, holes and bruises disappear, we could try again when she realizes what she is. Until then I should go my separate way. When she leaves the reptile, I promise myself I'll come back for her.

I was looking for love.
I found Ms. Macabre.
I was looking for love.
I found a whore of holes.
Ms. Macabre.
I love her,
couldn't deal with her,
couldn't handle all the things she did.
Ms. Macabre,
I know I bit off more than I could chew.
So, tell me,
am I in over my head?
Am I in over my head?

Diamond In The Dirt

Talk about 24 carats of regret.

Romantic kisses and serpent-like hisses: definition of our love/hate relationship. You are the diamond in the dirt I've spent my life looking for, but some of the dirt doesn't come off. Without a doubt, you are beautiful, almost perfect, but the filth that stays, poisons you and by it, I'm affected, quite infected. Your presence sometimes frightens me. The depth of how contagious you are must be dissected. Unfortunately for me, you're the one in control. You're holding all the knives, allowing your sickness to strive, but if I can find something sharp, I can make you feel alive.

Your temper is only defeated by your lust for it. It could be a mentality malfunction, some kind of brain dysfunction, but I don't think so by the way you enjoy it. You are your own personal holocaust, a replica of Faust, except you sold your soul for anger. Too bad it wasn't for knowledge as well, because then maybe there could be a chance you would repair yourself, and finally be able to sparkle to your full potential. I try to cleanse you but that only makes you red. You sweat, cry, cuss and throw fists. In the end, causing yourself to bleed from wounds that once bled: a dreadful reminder to show yourself that you are real. I want to save you, but I don't know how; your marble heart seems impenetrable. And it kills because it could mean something, that you and I might not be a reality, only a forgotten fable, a story lost to the ages. The loss of you will be a pain strong enough to take me under, down into a place where I won't be able to remember. And sometimes I wish I were already there. Sometimes I wish.

There are days where you surprise me with your sweet words, actions and subtle shine in your eyes. Kissing you, your laughter, and hearing three words I barely hear makes me happy that I found you, but then as quickly as it comes, it goes. Kissing alters into biting, laughing melts into screaming, *I love you*s rot into *I hate you*s: a rare feeling of paradise violently torched. And there have been many times where I've been scorched by your blaze. You're two-faced and I don't think you're even aware. You're so fragile, it's frustrating. I tell you there's something wrong, but you say you're fine. I don't know how to handle you. Sometimes it seems you are so far gone, a distance travelled where I've lost you for good. You're delicate like a worn portrait: the smallest thing can cause a lot of damage. I try to help but no matter what I do, nothing works. You always turn back into what I despise. I don't know what to do with you anymore. You keep getting worse and worse, and the end result is me always getting hurt. I don't know what to say or what to do now, except I know I'll have to live with the fact, you were a diamond in the dirt: a stone I never should have touched.

Black Silk Scarf

Seems like a whole lot of work just to get sodomized.

Dressed in an elegant gown of ebony and her identity hidden by a mask shaped like a pitiful creature, she runs from other decorative monsters, from the masquerade ball, and finds solitude in an open field of autumn. The trauma of a broken heart is driving her insane. There's a war going on inside her head. Her subconscious is battling, rattling. The fight is vicious but it doesn't last long; the angel catches the Devil's pitchfork by the throat. Fate is given a path for the girl: the damned will choke. A sick decision quickly desired: hanging for fire. No sympathy, no empathy, no remorse. Her fatal ending will be dire, ugly by vision for those who see. From a dead angel, the bravery for suicide appears. She has the motivation to disappear. With her black silk scarf, from a leafless tree, she decides to be an ornament. She climbs and ties a knot to the highest branch, wraps the noose around her neck, tests the distance with her tears, inhales, exhales, closes her eyes and falls back. The rope is tight. The weight is great. All that exists black.

Tortured damsel in disguise floating under a moonlit sky, she hangs where the complete breakdown occurred, where sounds of desperation to breathe failed, where struggling stirred from a suicidal act that couldn't be cured. She couldn't swallow the heartache, the tears, regret and the realization reality isn't fake. She was pure but insecure, which made her vulnerable. She was easily manipulated by dark forces, provoked to die by manmade sources: a black silk scarf. She obeyed, caved, made it too late to be saved. She chose to fill her grave, to be the victim enslaved in a darkness she can call her own. No Heaven, not even purgatory, no option but damnation. The Devil wooed her down under with a sour promise of salvation. Yes, her heart was repaired – a promise kept, but for eternity she'll be his, playing his favourite game, a game called sodomy. His slave, his treasure, his slut. The gates are shut. She can't get out; suicide trapped her forever. Her fault or not – she welcomed death's decay and the Devil received his pay.

Strangers At First Sight

Ugh...

Face-to-face - an opportunity given by fate. What would be the stakes if I waged this to be a mistake? If I'm right, is the risk great if I follow through anyway? What would happen if I said my name, asked for hers? What would happen if I tried to hold her hand? What are the consequences if I do more than stare? She's so beautiful; I feel ugly. But face-to-face, it's a mirror image; she thinks the same way. I can see the same thought in her eyes that swims in mine. This could very well mean something: a vague sign of a classic case of it's meant to be.

We are strangers at first sight. A glitch in the solitude machine is the cause for this unsuspecting night. And I hope the error is never repaired, or at least reconstruction is put on delay until I figure out what to say. I need to think of something fast to get her to stay before she decides to get up and walk away. I am worried though because I'm enchanted. Stuck in a trance; I'm speechless. Words won't make a sound unless my eyes refuse to dance. But the glow that beams off her is blinding, her spell shining so hard that I'm hypnotized. And if I can't fight it for one second, then I'll never know her name. I'll never know if we're meant to be.

My heart is racing and hers is chasing. The speed and force are so strong, I can feel the vibrations through the pavement. Her beats are almost synchronized to mine. Two hearts pulling at each other to be one - that's the cause of the awkward silence. And all I need are words to complete the sequence, only a few words to guide the arrow to its mark, then we'll be able to create a flame from a spark.

Her face is turning restless from the void between us. She's too shy to try and say *hi*, and so am I. My smiles and subtle gestures aren't comforting enough, not open enough for an introduction to occur. Building a relationship from strangers at first sight, could anything be any more complicated, more complex? Maybe none of this is happening, perhaps I'm heavily sedated and hallucinating, I'm dreaming and none of this has any meaning, or I'm dead and this Heaven I see is Hell. And no matter how long I wait for her, I'll never know her name because she's never going to tell.

Killing Flowers

Note to self: Next time you have a pity party, maybe not do it on her property. It won't have the effect you think it will and it's borderline psychotic. Also, you wrecked a bunch of her flowers, so that's not going to help your chances any.

Hundreds of petals of she-loves-me-nots quickly floating from profusely gripping thorns; blood from mutilated hands chases them downriver and a part of me washes away. I shake as my heart mourns; with every drop, I feel less complete. I clench my fists tighter to feel whole, but the punctures are great and blood still pours. My hands spotted with these bloody sores are at risk of infection, that's the synopsis of my inspection. And I won't do a damn thing until I have her affection, not a thing until there's a change and I don't feel so strange. When the pattern alters, I will quit decorating the water.

I picked apart rose by rose, cleaned many arm-reaches worth of landscape bare, and still, every petal was a not. I guess that's the way it goes when you're ugly like me, disfigured, badly configured. When a mask is your only friend, I guess that's the way it goes. But if I could manipulate one rose and have it say she loves me so, I would stop killing flowers. I would leave the river and run to her; as fast as I could, I would run to her.

But hope seems dismal; the amount of time I'll be withering in solitude seems abysmal. With every negative tear, I remember failure. With every desperate rip, I hurt for her. I'm worn from being scorned, left forlorn. My purpose is critical; every rose born is a rose to be torn. I'm going to keep killing flowers until one says *yes*. I'll speckle rapid waters with dark petals, massacre my hands, watch blood trickle, cry pathetically and scream. I'll do it over and over again until a rose says she loves me so.

Gunshot Ready

I survived. She had the safety on. Couldn't figure out how to turn it off. Got bored of waiting, so after twenty minutes I just walked away. Couldn't hang around. Had meatloaf in the oven. You understand.

Dwell and choke; drown in every word we spoke. All your words are red. All your words are red, screaming inside my head. Haunted, exhausted, I'm plenty tortured. I'm lost, confused, but I know one thing: dying can make me dead. So, let me control your strings. The stage is set; be my marionette. Perform for me, shoot a bullet past the scent of your perfume, ignore that whispering feeling of regret. Remember, one shot to the chest and I'll forget... I was yours to ruin.

Prepare your hand to kill. Easy now; nice and steady. Are you gunshot ready? Open your eyes, aim, twitch your finger, pull the trigger, murder me, be my savior.

I never forgave,
never forgave you for making me your slave.
I will never forgive you unless you do me this favour:

Put me under, bury me in my freshly dug grave. I surrender; put me under. If you won't kill me instantly, leave me in a terrible state so I can't be saved. Take me out; make sure I can never come back. Because if I revive, survive, I'm coming back for you and I'm going to attack.

I sense you want this. I know you want this, but I want it more. I want this more.

Prepare your hand to kill. Easy now; nice and steady. Are you gunshot ready? Open your eyes, aim, twitch your finger, pull the trigger, murder me, be my savior.

You are an empress wearing an executioner's mask. You say you love me, but you treat me like a prisoner. You say I can trust you, but why do you stutter? You're nothing but a deceiver, a self-absorbed liar. Chained, restrained, obtained – explain. You cheat. You put me down. You're violent. You pushed my friends away, so why should I stay? I want to break free, but I can't shake your spell; love is holding me still. Please... gun me down. I've gone berserk. I don't want to live. Free me. Shoot me. It will work. JUST FUCKING LET ME GO! LET ME KNOW! LET ME GO! LET ME KNOW!

ARE YOU GUNSHOT READY?!

LIIAN VARUS WANTS TO DIE BUT DOESN'T

Ah, 2005, you son of a bitch. Thought you could take me out, didn't you? Oh, sure... very smart using love to get me to lower my guard and then barbarically have HER rip my heart out. Well played. Well played. But you've forgotten one super important detail: inebriated Liian has the grip of an arthritic old woman. Pretty fucking difficult to slit your own wrists when you have the dexterity of a bowl of JELLO. But you were close. Got me in that hospital for a psychiatric evaluation. Impressive. Don't feel too bad. I still have the wrist and forearm scars. Consider them your consolation prize. Got to say though, they're pretty cute. They look like little tracks from an adorable cast iron train set. Choo, choo, asshole. Oh now, now, you mentally ruined me, absolutely. I can't take that away from you. Did you know I was only able to muster up a measly four poems because of you? Four. And they were before your assassination attempt. You struck a heavy blow. Be proud. You should know, despite years between us, I still think of you. You were my greatest foe. After all, how could I forget? I hope you think of me from time to time, too. It was an epic war. You can't forget battles from wars like that. You are always with me, my friend. May we never meet again.

A Girl And Her Stranger

Her first clue should have been the ten Block Parent signs in the window.

Tied and gagged; a heavy hand brings her to her knees. She panics with fear as she's pushed into the snow, in between the winter trees. He yells and curses at her. From violent verbal rage, she cries. From silent surroundings, all hope dies. She's bound to the ground; there's no way to get away. Muted and immobilized, hysteria infects her senses, unveiling the frightening truth that this is not a dream or a dark fairy tale. No knight in shining armour is coming; the lamb is left to the wolf. Terror now consumes the girl. And like a chameleon, her skin turns pale as she waits for the beast to bite.

Cold... cold situation darkens. It worsens from a black sack pulled over her head. Her cries turn into optical waterfalls and shivers become desperate shaking. But it's useless, she can't escape. She can't even crawl. No movement, no words, no sight, only the capability to hear, but with sudden silence her breathing quickens. Her sixth sense awakens and wails like rapid sirens, warning her that something terrible is about to happen. That's when she hears it: dull nails tapping against a rock. She tries to pray but it's too late. The handheld meteor repeatedly crashes against her head and shatters her skull into dozens of fragments. Now lifeless, this girl is this: bone shards in a bloody sack made by a vicious attack. This is the risk, the possibility, the danger when you trust strangers.

My Favourite Gender

What you must think of me by now.

Beautiful females always in my line of sight. Obsessed. Hard-focused. Lost in tunnel vision. Optical perversion. My brainwaves are neurotic. My lust is sick and erotic. My actions automatic. I am a killing machine with a dick, and I get what I want.

I get what I want.
I get what I want.
I get what I want.
I get what I want.

I follow them, stalk them, chase them because they are my favourite gender. I catch them, steal them, kidnap them because they are my favourite gender. I fuck them, stab them, kill them, because they are my favourite gender.

Sex - it's etched into all my senses; murder is just the mishap that seems to follow. I want to fornicate, copulate, but I always take it too far. And that's the reason why, why there is a corpse for every star. Maybe if I could love, maybe if, then the Hyde in me would die, the incubus in me would subside. If that were to happen, I would finally know what it's like to cry, to be human. But the Jekyll in me is weak. The throat of what is right is cut, severed to a depth where not even stitches can fix it. I only know what is wrong so those are the things I do. I will probably never be saved, but one thing is for certain – I'll be a monster even after I'm slain.

Him

Probably would have saved myself a lot of trouble if I continued living as a recluse. Stupid heart wanting shit. FML.

Red hands and heavy heartbeats; the situation got out of control. Silence tells it all from the reality splattered against the walls. She didn't have to do it: him. I loved her but that wasn't enough. She made me do it: murder. I knifed him too for stealing my life. I killed him for fucking my wife. And when I fall into Hell, when I see them both there together, I'm going to do it again.

I could have spared her but what I saw, what I felt, I couldn't hold myself together. The splitting of my heart, the excruciating tearing had the power of manipulation persuading mutilation. I fought it for as long as I could, but there's no strength in heartache, only weakness and hate. From their first touch to my shattered heart, it was fate. Their deaths might have been uncalled for, but how would you treat a thief and a whore? Will you tell me? Because I would like to know.

In a room of red, holding the limp hand of a dead lover, I curse. I could never forgive her for fucking him. She knows this well from the loud whispers I spit into her ear, the hurt I tell her over and over. Taking his life, taking her life, it didn't make the pain go away. It's worse. Already I'm haunted by their fall. It's unbearable. Suicidal behaviour is seeping in. Living no longer seems suitable. It's clear. My future status is inevitable. I am going to die. So as a too late last goodbye, I kiss my wife's lips, apologize to the stranger, and with a dream of flight known to fall, I walk onto the balcony's edge.

From this sky-high apartment,

from the bullet-speed drop,
I will touch pavement.

A Boy Of Bullet Wounds

But the amount they must have saved on daycare, though.

Holding onto the respirator, struggling to breathe, fighting for survival, gasping for permanent revival, but the bullet wounds are superior and are quickly taking over. The boy has no chance of winning. His fate is irreversible, no longer invisible. And it's terrible, so tragic, the boy will never be six.

Modern technology did all it can, but the intelligence of man only spans so far. And the boy is left to chance. He does feel some comfort with his mom and dad at his bedside, holding his hand, stroking his hair, kissing his forehead. They try to keep themselves together as they try to help ease his pain, but every fragile minute that breaks, their son fades further and further away. And all they can do is watch, watch him fall, die this day.

His wounds are repaired on the outside, but he's far from healed. Internal bleeding floods his insides, that's where damage is fatal. Many attempts to stop the flooding have failed; there's no hope but prayer now. So, as they wait for a miracle, the little boy drowns. There is no God this day, only death.

Proof is suddenly revealed from a breathless mouth, a limp body, lifeless eyes, and the haunting sound of a flatline that tears through his parents' eardrums, as the continuous high-pitched beep crashes against their hearts, exploding them upon impact. Doctors try to revive him but it's too late, his ending is shown on the heart monitor. It's fate; they lost him. The boy is a flatliner.

LIIAN VARUS MIGHT BE A WRITER AFTER ALL

After the complete shit show of 2005, I thought about throwing in the proverbial towel. Mostly because there was jizz on it. No. That's not right. Writing. I contemplated giving up writing. Besides, who the fuck reads poetry anyway? No one according to my infinite wisdom which holds less insight than an empty fortune cookie found at a Chinese restaurant named after some Caucasian dude. But time did heal my wounds. Sure, it could have done a better job keeping the scar tissue to a minimum, but despite my heart resembling Freddy Krueger's nut sack, I was healed. 2006 was the year of Liian. I spent a lot of my time working on my craft, trying new things - mostly cocaine and promiscuous sex. There was A LOT of debauchery in my life that year. However, I was able to fine-tune, filter, polish my ability to coerce thought to paper more clearly. Like years before, garbage would still make its unannounced visits like a social worker holding a grudge because you pronounced their name wrong. I trudged on. I knew there was a hill I was climbing and the horizon was almost in view; vague hues of what I would be capable of started to seep into the skyline. If I kept my head down and maybe even keep my dick in my pants long enough, I could be so much more. Could it be possible, that this train wreck of a human being could be the next Poe? Hahaha! No. Yet.

You Live In A Box

I chickened out. It's not my fault. Death is hella scary.

You live in a box, done up pretty in a nightgown, not wearing any socks. Six feet under, you live in a box. Your body is distant but the scent of your perfume, the reminder of a death too soon, well... it still lingers inside my room.

You live in a box. Your corpse... well... like a knife, it cuts. I know I'm alive by the way my blood runs red, but it doesn't matter because you're still dead. You live in a box, but I can hear your voice in my head. You live in a box, but I know you heard every word I've said.

You live in a box, but you won't be alone much longer, not with these suicidal train tracks I built: the railway I made from forearm to my wrist. You live in a box but don't worry, I'm already at the station, sitting, waiting for my train. Just one more rail, one more spike and we'll be alike.

You live in a box so I'm taking a trip, purposely going to slip, sever a vein too deep so I can rot beside you, and together we can sleep. Together we can forget we cut too deep. You live in a box, but suicide will take me to you. As long as you love me and I love you, together we will always be.

A Girl I've Come To Hate

So yeah, that infamous girl from 2005... Here she is.

Inside I'm badly decayed from hurtful thoughts that overplayed. She was a girl I loved, a girl I've come to hate. She was a mistake, gave me the knowledge of heartache. What the fuck happened? I don't know but the damage shows. All the pain is in my head, but you can see it by the expression on my face. And I don't think I'll ever recover because I'm always thinking of her. I can't stop this memory slideshow; every day it plays over and over. Because Lesley, my first love, a girl I've come to hate, continues to haunt me so.

Without her I became sick. I fell into addictions: alcohol, drugs, cigarettes. I've overdosed, almost fell into a coma. From all the trauma, all I wanted to do was decompose. And yes, somehow I'm still alive, but suicide still tries to rock me to sleep, making sanity hard to keep. But if I could find meaning, get out of this state of fatal dreaming, then maybe I could sew myself back together and understand that I don't need her, a whore named Lesley, a girl I've come to hate.

I loved her so much, but now I can't seem to hate her enough. She's the reason my heart is gutted. She never fought for us. It was always me and that's why our relationship rotted. I tried to keep us tied, and in the process, almost died. I love her. I fucking love her, that cold-hearted bitch, a girl I've come to hate. And I might be slightly psychotic, neurotic now but I'm not worthless. And she won't be either when she's breathless, so fucking lifeless. Sometimes the pain is so unbearable that I just want to end it all, finish myself with a gunshot to the head, but I don't even bother because I know it will all come back again. Because something tells me, constantly reassures me, Lesley will always haunt me so – the nightmare I can't seem to let go, a girl I've come to hate.

Confessional Rot

I've never confessed sins before because I'm too FUCKING fabulous.

In this room of secrets, the priest and I talk. I confess and confess, revealing my mental mess, and he does listen, but does he really give a fuck? Because I'm repenting but I still feel dirty. I'm afraid there's no salvation for me and everything I say is just confessional rot, verbal mold to stain these walls because I can't be saved. And I think I know why – my path to Hell has been paved.

This large wooden box is a gas chamber. I'm choking on the fumes of my sins because the Lord won't take them in. I'm drowning in confessional rot, suffocating from every sin I've got because the Lord won't take me in. The screen isn't filtering out my sins. I feel damned. In this pine stall of Heaven-starvation, I'm tightly crammed, wedged inside this fucking church closet, stuck in my own confessional rot. I know I'm damned. I can tell it's too late for me.

My soul has been bought, sold to the highest bidder. The priest doesn't make me feel better, so I know I belong to Lucifer. I guess not everyone can be saved. I failed at being human but when I die, I hope I pass at being a demon because I don't want to know a worse place than Hell. So, if there's a confessional, another purification box in the Devil's well, I'll go inside and give it a shot. I'll try to give myself one more time and pray my words don't rot.

Meth Beth

Beth really, really loves meth.

Beth so pretty. Beth so lovely. Five months go by; Beth all of a sudden is going to die. She looks like death because she's addicted to meth. Beth has no friends, no family, no life because she fell in love with meth. Hit with all the signs but she didn't stop. That stupid girl didn't mind and look at her now; look at her now. To fix her quickly, doctors don't know how.

Beth quit track because of meth because it gave her shortness of breath. Beth quit dancing because she's always convulsing. She does too much meth. Now Beth can't do anything. She was in good health, then she met meth. Now Beth's really skinny. From rapid weight loss, she's anorexic. From sleep deprivation, she's overly alert, very disturbed. Every expression on her face is death. Twitching, jerking, shaking, teeth grinding and jaw clenching; Beth can't be controlled because meth tells her so. Beth is alone and she doesn't even know.

Beth is a wreck, very sick. Meth is running up the score. I know this sadly because Beth the virgin is a promiscuous whore. Beth the virgin always wants more, but it doesn't stop at sex. Beth is paranoid and extremely depressed. Beth is no longer gentle. Her behaviour is violent but soon she will be silent, either from a meth lab explosion or complete brain corrosion. One way or another, after she suffers, Beth's toxic indulging will be over.

Her continuous state of hallucinating, her long vacation away from reality is tearing apart her mental stability. Beth doesn't seem to understand that living permanently in Wonderland will put her in the graveyard society.

Meth will make her deathbed and she'll be sleeping in it soon because just look at her – she's raped with sores. For months she's been digging at her skin, trying to get at the meth mites: imaginary bugs under her pores. But nothing's there, nothing bites; Beth's not alright.

She's burnt here and there, disfigured from chemical spills. She's scary like a creature from an Effexor nightmare, except this isn't a dream. Beth is proof: in different ways, meth kills. But in Beth's case, it's obvious, she's going to die from a natural meth death. And when she does, Beth will become something. It happens to all meth heads. Not only do they see them but when they die from meth, all meth heads become them. She'll be a part of something terrible. Beth will be added to the population of shadow people. I know this to be true because I died from meth.

Self-Destruct Android

Definitely not doing science fiction any favours with this.

Disassembled. Can't be reassembled because all my parts are busted. All my pieces are broken. I can't be put back together; nothing fits anymore. Game over. I've given up and rolled over. Allowing myself to rust in the mud, I've accepted my fate. I'm garbage, absolutely no good. No revival. In this state I'm in there is no such thing as survival. I'm lost and scattered about. With the amount of damage and how often I malfunction, the possibility that I can be fixed, to be repaired and be operational again, well... I have my doubts. This android will always be rubble.

I'm completely annihilated. Blankly staring with my one good eye, I see my mechanical limbs. They're destroyed all around me. I'm scrap, unusable crap, rubbish machinery. I was a product of vast technology, now I'm just junk. Even my intelligence has faltered. I'm so severely altered that my thought process is juvenile. Useless... shock, shock, shock... Worthless... zap, zap, zap... I'm a robotic mess. Help. Help. Help; I can't rebuild myself. Affirmative. Affirmative. Affirmative; that bomb explosion was destructive. All motor skills are inactive; this android is no longer effective.

In this forced horizontal position with circuits showing, barely glowing, with battered insides exposed, I am having troubles staying composed because severed wires keep electrocuting me. And from this unwanted electroshock therapy, too many irregular power surges, I sometimes shutdown. I can't help myself. I'm permanently disabled from colossal obliteration to my body and dozens of ruptured hydraulic cables, not to mention handfuls of cracked computer chips. I know I will never again be functional. I'm incapacitated, vulnerable, clearly disposable. There is no hope for this

android. My warranty ends here. "Self-destruct sequence... activated."
Certain death is inevitable; the countdown has started. It's finalized. I will
be terminated.

Happy Anniversary
(Whore! How Could You?!)

I was so unstable when I was young. Now I just shrug my shoulders when people treat me like a piece of shit. It's easier on the brain. And to be honest, my body as well.

How could you do this to me?! You whore! You fucking whore! I loved you! How could you do this to me?! How could you?! He's my best friend! Ah! My head! I'm falling apart! My heart! My fucking heart! How could you do this to me?! I'm so confused. Too… Too much mental abuse. The hurt is unbearable. Suicide? Yes. I'm capable. No! Don't fucking touch me! Leave me alone! It's too late! You're the salt on my wound, and my death can't come too soon!

Red roses and champagne –
happy anniversary!
Dead flowers and alcohol poisoning –
fuck you for the misery!
Happy anniversary!
Happy anniversary!

Do you even fucking love me?! My heartache is spilled across the floor. Will you clean it up? I didn't think so. How could you do this to me?! I can't believe what you've done! You whore! You fucking whore! Where else have you been?! How long have you been doing me wrong?! I should fucking kill you! I should throw you off this balcony! Crazy? Maybe slightly. You bring the worst out in me! I loved you! But you sucked the life out of me! I'll never forgive you! Not this time!

Chocolates and a decorated card –
happy anniversary!
Stale sweets and torn cardboard –
fuck you for the adultery!
Happy anniversary!
Happy anniversary!

My spine is mohawked with knives from you stabbing me in the back. I've bled to death for you. Over and over, I've bled to death because of you. You fucking whore! You swore! You promised me no more! You lied! You're the one who sinned but I'm the one who's going to die. Heartbreaker! Heartbreaker! I FUCKING HATE YOU! I HATE YOU! I HATE YOU! How could you?! HOW COULD YOU?! I can hear the lullaby in my head; my will to live is falling asleep. Here… take my heart to keep. I won't be needing it, not when I'm dead.

Love and compassion –
happy anniversary!
Hatred and mutilation –
fuck you for the history!
Happy anniversary!
Happy anniversary!

Happy anniversary, whore.

Pulse

I am going to assume I told the wrong person to go fuck themselves.

Two fingers against my wrist... What is this? My pulse isn't pulsating. Don't I exist? Did I die? Two fingers against my throat... I don't float so I'm not a ghost. Something is wrong though; I don't feel alive. Two fingers against my thumb... There's no pulse. Perhaps I'm dumb and I just can't find it. If this is true, then why do I feel so numb? Long gone is my pulse. Did I die? I don't remember. Was I in the back of a hearse? What is this curse? I move and talk, but how come I have no pulse?

Like a zombie, the resemblance in the mirror is uncanny. My facial expressions are cannibalistic, but I have no hunger for flesh. Matter of fact, I have no hunger for anything. This all seems too unrealistic, maybe too realistic. Frantically I search for life like an addict looking for heroin. There's no sign of it. Lost pulse can't be found, no pulse to make a sound. Am I dead? Am I already underground? Is there a line I must cross before the blinds are pulled from my eyes? This must be purgatory because I don't feel anything.

I'm breathing. Well, I think I am. My chest moves up and down, and I'm not struggling for air. Oxygen must be flowing through me. But still... If I'm alive, where's my pulse? Do I bleed? I wonder. A knife and my body touch; it doesn't hurt all that much. Come to think of it, it didn't hurt at all. The knife falls and blood very slowly glances out, then suddenly stops. Coagulated - it's almost a solid mass. This human is dead. I'm a corpse. I see it now: zombie-like reflection, pulse missing-in-action, blood that doesn't run, no oxygen either, it was just my imagination. How the fuck did I die? I don't recall saying goodbye. And if I am dead, where the hell am I?

Crying hysterically, I panic. I have to double-check. I need to make sure I'm not rotten, so I furiously rip off my skin. Still no sense of pain. Pull off chunks of flesh. Still no pain. Break apart my ribs. Again, no sense of pain. With my chest easily massacred, I grab my remains and lift them up enough to see. I take a peek, look underneath; it's true, there's no heartbeat. Mystery of the missing pulse solved. I found the reason why it dissolved. Then it hits me. Somehow I always knew having no pulse was the truth, I died, damned to forever walk the earth. I see this clearly now. So with an extinct pulse, my heart stiff as a post, all confusion is gone, except this one thing: I know I'm a ghost. I know I died. I just don't know how.

Crack Whore Reward

There are so many poems in this book that show so much disdain for my mother, yet, none are actually about her. I've got a whole different bag of issues I guess.

Addicted crack whore, faceless being, my mother facedown on the floor with her crack pipe tightly held in her right hand. There's blood on the counter, blood on the door, blood still gushing out her fractured skull. I don't think she will be getting up, not this time. Her puddle of red is bottomless, deep enough to be dead in it. This fall looks final. This dramatic scene is too real. It just oozes *curtain call*. It appears true enough; she looks dead from here. And it's sad to say I don't care. I'm not kidding; good riddance. I told her. I fucking told her, but she didn't listen. I told her, "Mother, this shit will kill you. One way or another, it will kill you." She didn't listen and now she's dead. She's fucking nothing. She got what she deserved. And with no memory of her preserved, once she's buried, I will forget who my mother was. But before I lose my memory, mother, I just want to say there will be no tears from me to you, not this time, not ever again. Mother, you earned this. Enjoy your reward.

Actress (Murderer Of Love)

And the Oscar for "Best Actress" goes to... a lying bitch.

I never had the chance to see your play until today, and I must say what I saw, blew me away. That climactic kiss you gave was grey. It must have been because my heart is no longer red.

Seeing your lips against his says it all: you've forgotten everything I've said, or you just didn't care. Actress, murderer of love, my love must be poison, it must be a disease. For you to leave me for him, there must be something wrong with me.

Your trigger-finger was restless. Do you agree? I know the gunshot to my heart does. Thank you for the backstabbing honesty! Sorry, I shouldn't be angry at you; it's not your fault. Serves me right for playing with a loaded gun. Beauty is a fucking killer – a lesson learned but I don't feel any better.

I must tell you though, that kiss, that act of passion was incredible. I can see why you've secretly said goodbye. And honestly, I would love an encore, to watch your mouths dance together again. Unfortunately, my heart is completely torn. My existence is relying on me to walk away because if I decide to stay for the second act, suicide will find me. I'll make this day night, absolutely pitch black. There will be no resurrection. This zombie won't be coming back, not for you, my cherished actress, my murderer of love.

I don't know how long you've been lying to me, but I never suspected a thing. To hide your hush-hush agenda that well, you are a terrific actress. And if I may say, even though you are the murderer of love, you look

251

beautiful in that dress. I still love you. Yes, I know I am a mess, but I know what I still miss. Actress, murderer of love, I want to applaud you for your fantastic performance. Excellently done. But the show dies here. At the end of this barrel of this loaded gun, it all stops now. From here we're Shakespearean – Romeo a Juliet in the 21st century.

"Good night, Good night! Parting is such sweet sorrow,
that I shall say good night till it be morrow."

Bang.
Bang.

House Of Dead Siblings

I have one sister. To clarify, I don't mean one sister left. Just in general, I have one sister.

My parents are away, gone for the day, so I'm running with scissors. Cutting, cutting, cutting, stabbing, stabbing, stabbing, killing sisters, running with scissors. Piercing, piercing, piercing, slicing, slicing, slicing, killing sisters, running with scissors. Slashing! Slashing! Slashing! Killing sisters! I'm an eleven-year-old boy, a warped kid mutilating sisters.

This will be the house of dead siblings and in this place, they scream. With sharp scissors in and out, the girls scream. One by one, it will all be done. With bloody wounds open, all my pretty sisters will be gone.

Gutting, gutting, gutting; like fish, they squirm. One, two, three... their entrails fall out. Two sisters left; their turn. Blood loss drags their escape, so they just stay. They bleed and cry. Their time has shattered. Fate has spoken. They are going to be murdered, to take their place, their spot in the house of dead siblings.

There is no sense for this psychotic nonsense, no motive, no particular method, no personal vendetta. I just for no reason want all my sisters dead. Perhaps I'm insane, not completely normal. Nonetheless, all five of my sisters will fall. Even the one that for some strange reason has the strength and the right amount of blood to crawl. Too many horror movies, too many scary stories, dreams of autopsies – if I am crazy that could be why... why not one sister will be left alive.

Two sisters remain bloody, ready for disaster. Brand new shears stare down at the one lying on the floor, reflecting her tears, showing her what's in store. And before she can even muster a word, like an angry barbarian's mighty sword, I thrust the murder weapon into her throat. Back and forth, side to side, I take her worth. She struggles and cries, blood flies, she dies, and I just stare.

One to go. The female that's crawling for the front door. No chance for her, for I am armed and filled with blood. Slowly I walk up to her, kneel beside her and tell her, "Shush now." I grab a handful of her vibrant red hair, snip off a generous lock, then gently sniff her scent as I wave it in front of my eager nose. She looks up at me with drowning eyes, eyes deadening, begging for mercy but there's no such thing as guilt. So, anxious scissors attack, impaling through the top of her head. All five, all my sisters, all destroyed: Jessica (6), Tess (3), Emily (5), Ariel (10) and Hailey (17). All my sisters, all five, all destroyed.

In the house of dead siblings,
I have no sisters.
I wonder what my parents will say.

My Pulse For Your Hearse

I remember writing this and thinking, people are going to cry when they read it. Fuck. Was I delusional? Yeah. They cried alright; cried tears of laughter because it fucking sucks.

Dark cars moving in single file, carefully chasing a varnished coffin, and I can't contain myself, my girlfriend is in that box. She's dead because she can't swim. She fell into the water. No one was around, so she drowned. The river's current took her down, kidnapping her for almost a mile. We found her the next morning, facedown, pale blue on the rocky shore, being picked at by crows. We scared them away. Sadly, the damage was done; early birds got the corpse. Samantha will have to be laid to rest, buried without some of her flesh.

Driving down this winding road, cautiously following the death car, cars slither their way to the graveyard like a mourning black snake. With no bright sun, this day is grey, but the scenery is beautiful. On both sides of the road, there are tall, tall trees side by side like giant pillars holding up the vapid sky. The grass is long and green. Birds are chirping as they fly. It's loud and heartwarming, but even from the other cars, I can still hear people cry. Beauty doesn't matter today; this day is grey.

I wish I was a powerful force so I can resurrect your corpse, but I'm just a man. I can't trade you my pulse for your hearse or turn back time and give you my hand to pull you from the icy water. I can't revive you, can't save you. You're stiff and there's nothing I can do, except say... *what if?*

My heart is torn in half, which is nothing compared to her family's. Theirs are shattered and will probably never be repaired. As we get to the gates of the dead, I can feel devastation grow stronger. It feels like being in a dark room with fifty-three people, all of them holding a sharp knife and committing suicide: I can't see them, but I know fifty-three people just died. I know they would easily take their lives if it meant giving back hers. There is no happy ending to this tragedy. You can't rewrite this story. This is not Disney.

We've arrived. And as we slowly get out, we do the best to hold ourselves together. So, like zombies, we reluctantly walk to her gravesite, choking on happy memories of her as we drag behind her deathbed. Holding hands, we watch her coffin lower into the dirt; a perfect fit. Some people fall to their knees and some have to walk away. The priest begins his prayer; it starts to rain. This day will never be forgotten.

Samantha, if you can hear me, know this: I'm not any kind of force so I can't resuscitate your corpse. I'm only human. I can't exchange my pulse for your hearse, or reverse time and allow you my hand to rescue you from the freezing river. I can't revive you. I can't save you. Samantha, you're stiff. There's not a thing I can do, except say... *what if?* And hope I'll see you one day soon.

Pistols Seem More Attractive

There is no hope. We all die alone. Kill yourself.

Breathing with a concrete heart, a solid mass that won't come apart is how it feels when love fails. It's like walking down a hallway, a never-ending aisle of doors and finding they're all locked. Claustrophobia kicks in, anxiety and depression become overwhelming, you go into shock, and pistols seem more attractive. Feeling like you only have one direction can pull their sensitive trigger, submitting your body to decomposition. A bullet convincingly persuades it's an answer, but you still question it – *Will a gunshot to the head make things better?*

Losing love is shattering like glass falling from a building, or even from your bedroom ceiling: pieces fly everywhere. You can pick them up, but some always go missing. You never know where they all are. You don't feel complete. So, you fill the void with drugs, alcohol and promiscuous sex, anything that's negative, making pistols seem more attractive. You might never again be whole, but you'll never know if you pull that trigger. If you don't let go, if your sweaty finger slips, you will never know.

Yes, you feel like Edward Scissorhands: unique but incomplete. Don't let dangerous emotions infect you. If you allow that poison to course through, you won't ever be new. Brainwashed and wrists slashed, you'll just be trash. Don't give in. Don't let pistols seem more attractive. Your empty for a reason. Love is what goes there. So, find a girl, know her, care for her, make her happy, and the concrete will crumble, exposing your red, red heart. Just don't give up; stay away from triggers. Do this and you'll smile, you'll be better than ever. The past won't matter because she loves you and you love her.

Reanimation

You would think someone like me would be amazing at writing horror. That's it. That's the punchline.

I was walking by the river, that is where I found her barely on shore, beached lifelessly. I wanted to run. I've never seen a corpse before. Instead, I carefully approached her. There really wasn't a rank smell but I could tell, if she were dry, I'd be able to feel my nose swell. I didn't know how she died, or how she got in the river. I didn't really care. I was too mesmerized. Completely in a trance, I could tell she used to be beautiful. So, I held my stance and continued to stare at what is now my new nightmare.

I started examining her body; it wasn't difficult. She was naked and badly wounded, in perfect shape to be studied. Both her legs were cut up and bruised, probably from the sharp rocks in the river, but there was something stranger: There were bite marks on her breasts, all the way up to her left shoulder. Dozens of them closely overlapping each other. It was vicious. The bites were so deep, it was like someone was eating her. Her arms were bad too. They were ravenously clawed. I could see broken nails in her still and flesh barely hanging on. Some of her fingers looked broken as well. They were too flawed for them not to be. I saw both hands busted on a corpse that was rusted.

Her face was perfectly deformed. It was raped by teeth and stabbed with nails more than anywhere else on her body. I had trouble looking at the horror and glancing at her eyes drowned in terror. Her face was fucked with mutilation, which was only complimenting when I matched it to her decomposition. There wasn't much but with a single touch, I knew she was beginning to rot away. For minutes, I watched her hair in the water, waving side to side, slowly letting the reality sink in, that this girl died. It's gone. She has no life left inside.

Hypothermia got her too. It's on her wounds, anywhere there's trauma. It was stained on her skin and deep inside her pores. Any part of her that was left outdoors was the part that turned blue.

Ravaged from an attack so savage, this girl is Mother Nature's garbage, food for whatever will devour her, to finish what's left of the girl from the river. One thing is for sure, it won't be me.

Dead body stiff and contorted, the crime, the cadaver had to be reported. So, I pulled her to shore, dragged her through the wet sand to keep the river from taking her again. It was pretty easy like pulling a mummy to safety. When I got her to a good distance, I put her down, and that's when shit got really fucked up. She started jolting and shaking. She stopped, looked up at me with her ice-like eyes, bared her teeth, growled, and quickly started crawling towards me. I couldn't believe it. So, I ran as fast as I could through the trees, across busy streets. I ran home and locked all the doors and windows.

That was two days ago. My house is now completely fortified. I'm armed with my .22 and a belt of kitchen knives and ammo. I looked outside today; she's still there with hundreds more by her side. They're banging and smashing; they're trying to get at me. I can't believe what I see. It's the undead, Frankensteins, zombies. It has to be. It's the only nonsense that makes sense.

I don't know how much longer I have before they figure out how to get in. I just know I'm heavily outnumbered; there is too much decay today. I'm one person in a zombie nation, in a world where the dead are given the gift of reanimation. Unprepared – I'm more ready to be dismembered. But no matter the odds, I will fight this losing battle. I will fight.

What was that?!
Oh no!
I hear boards breaking!
They're coming in!
THEY'RE COMING IN!

Haunted

I'm not an idiot. After fourteen years, it's safe to assume I'm not getting my heart back.

Broken, smashed way open. I couldn't hold myself together; my skin isn't leather. So, when I crashed, I shattered like glass. Frantically, I drained out my emotions. And sure, I continue to feel pain, but my conscience has been cleared. You can tell by the blood painted on my walls, by the handprints spotted here and there: clues on how my blood was smeared. I know I did no wrong, that's why I can still hang on. Even though I know dead love, a rotten dream. Even though I'm bare, when I fall asleep, I always relive the nightmare. Haunted by your reoccurring scare, you've given me despair. Its toxicity is killing me, but it's the only thing I can afford to keep. I'm terminally ill but if I can just hold still, collect myself, I know everything will be well. I'll be okay if you just do me one favour: return my heart so I can stop tearing myself apart.

Dark Flowers

Roses are black, violets are black, black, black, black, black.

I know I care about you but when I give you bright flowers, I don't feel the same. I'm just not sure. Lately, it seems automatic. I believe I love you but when I speak to you, my words are unclear. Muffled by static, I'm finding it hard to sound sincere.

Forever and ever and ever, hand-in-hand, I'm struggling to keep us together. We promised eternity but I'm having trouble keeping my part of the deal. You've done nothing wrong; depression is the reason. I'm sorry for the trouble. It's how I feel but we can be together; misery loves company. If you really want me, take my hand and join me. Together, close together, we can continue to live our fantasy forever and ever and ever.

Heart crawling. Petals falling. Bouquet turning black – dark flowers, dark flowers. Love fading fast. Counting the hours. How long will it take for you to say, "Yes, let's make this life ours."? I'm waiting patiently with both hands holding roses – dark flowers, dark flowers, dark flowers, dark flowers.

I wish I wasn't mentally sick. This is hard for you and it kills me I am this way, but I don't want to split because I believe the pieces still fit. I'm confused and you're being abused. I'm trying to snap out of it. I want to be okay, look into you, hold your hand and say, "I love you, too." I'm ill though. My heart feels like it's smothered with decay; it's falling to pieces. Do you know how to sew? Please stay.

Understand, I love you. If I could paint these dark flowers, if I could give them colour, I would. I should walk away from you before I really hurt you.

I don't want to be your doomsday device, your heartache suicide but I'm failing. I can't seem to take my own advice because I want to be with you. I want everything to be alright. Everything. What is wrong with me?

Outside your door, drenched from midnight showers, holding twelve dark flowers, I wait for you to answer my questions: *Will you stay? Will you love me even if I'll never be okay? Will you accept these dead flowers and make this life ours, or do I have to keep counting the hours?* Beautiful girl, if our hearts aren't meant to touch, then take this match and incinerate my world. If I can't be with you, I don't want to live.

I Love You And I Hate Myself

I don't love this girl anymore, but I still fucking hate myself. Nice to know my poetry holds some relevance after all these years.

I love you but the masochist in me can't be killed. I tried, tried so fucking hard; repeatedly I've failed. It's no use. The hate I have for myself can't be distilled. I thought I could win. Until sanity wore too thin. I couldn't keep it together, so I destroyed my heart, self-destructed. Taking you down with me, together in flames, we burned away our fantasy disastrously into a pile of ashes, because I love you and I hate myself. I didn't want you to crash with me. Not much I can do about it now, except hope your landing is gentle as I brace for my catastrophic impact.

For a little longer, if I only had it in me to fight a little longer, perhaps I would have gotten better. Maybe I'd be alright. But then came night. I called you and once I heard your voice, my brain unraveled and fell to nothing. I made the fatal choice and murdered the only thing that ever felt right. Know that you're not the reason I am this way. So, I ask you... Please, don't take our downfall personally. I know you despise me as of this moment. I don't blame you since it was me who ordered the curtain call. I wish it could have been different, but I love you and I hate myself. Just do me one small favour – take care of yourself.

I know there's going to be a day where I'll be begging you to come back to me, but I have to learn to live with my decision, my dictating depression. I rolled the dice, lost, had snake eyes slither me into this vise, in a lonely dimension, this dark place where there's no communication, just a shadowy corner in my room where I'll cry and regret, want to die and forget in a tiny corner where I'll rot, rot, rot. There's no doubt you make me smile, no doubt I need you, no doubt you are great. There are absolutely no traces of this to be false; you make me happy I have a pulse. But I love you and I hate myself. There's nothing really left for me to say besides, I think I've expressed myself enough. And maybe I'll tell you more. Maybe I'll breakdown and say I love you over and over and over and over... when you come by to get your stuff.

Once I Was King

#Meds

Beaten and drugged down, I slept and lost my crown. I owned you and everyone else, even the dead, every corpse. Iron fist constantly tight; I told you what was wrong and what was right. I was emperor, emperor of this universe. Ladies loved me, fucking me in the back of my hearse because I was God. Water, trees, air, dirt, people and animals – I gathered it all. I ruled the globe. Once I was king of the world. Once I was king. Once I was king. Now I'm a mental patient that's force-fed different types of medicine.

Learning to assimilate, to join the vast population of zombies, I'm having complications adjusting. The process is staggering. Why do I have to be a peasant? Don't they know, once I was king? Insanity is a possibility; slowly I'm realizing I might be crazy. My castle, my throne, my gold – the saner I get, more of my belongings are sold. Reacting perfectly to the pills in my system, I'm losing everything I used to hold. My brain might have been damaged, but it gave me something to call my own: a planet. These treatments I'm receiving are taking it away. I try to make it stay, but in a padded room, in a straitjacket, sedated, it's hard to make it stay.

Delirium, it's not an issue. I don't need or want your precious serum. Let me be. Don't make me tear open my scar tissue. Your medicine is stealing my powers, bulldozing down my silver-coated city. Once I was king, which means, if you're demolishing everything by tampering with my mind's fragility, you can at least treat me with dignity, like royalty, treat me right. Come closer. I don't bite. Do you have to be so cold and hard? You're lucky we're not in my place of origin, in Necrotopia, because I would have you killed by my guards. They would not stand for such treason. How much longer do I have to be here? How many more seasons? GET ME OUT OF HERE! No, no, no, no, no, no, no, no, no! Put away that needle! I'll be good! I'll be very good! I won't be a problem! I won't be a problem! I'll be good! I'll be good!

Please, can you put me back where you found me? Can you crown me and put me in my rightful place? I detest telling people, "Once I was king." I want to be king. I'm not hurting anyone. Give me back my palace, tall gem-filled throne, my chambers of gold, everything I had before. Your gift of sanity is my frailty. Leave me in my make-believe world. Who cares if it's not proper? Let me live my life how I want. I'm sick of being a pauper. I don't want your help. I want out, no more padded room, uncomfortable bondage jacket, pills and electroshock therapy. Let me free. Hey! Don't walk away from me! Don't you dare shut that door! Hey! I'm talking to you! Get back here! Hey! Fuck! Fuck!

Once I was king. Once I had it all, then I was kidnapped, imprisoned, tortured, stuck violently with a needle and was forced to watch myself fall. Once I was king! Once I was king! Hahahahahahahaha! Ahhhhhh! Ahhhhhh! AHHHHHHHHHHHHHHHHHHHHHHHHH!

Ghost Letter

This is a love poem I wrote for my cat.

Before I wrote you, I hung myself. I had to make sure there was no saving me, to prove to you that I can't get better. I collapsed inside, fell, got caught up in a noose, found suicide, came back hollow-alive and wrote you this ghost letter: spiritual literature, a cluster of emotional words, things I couldn't say breathing.

I know I'm dead. This doesn't mean I don't love you. You are still my everything. Brainwave patterns vertical; depressing impulses made me suicidal. I know I'm dead but you're still vital, very important to me. I apologize for any pain I left you. Reality was too real for me, too dark for me to see. I love you. I love you. I love you. I'm right beside you. Always.

Dead today.
I accept my body will decay many tomorrows later.

Don't cry. You're not alone. I'm not gone. You feel that cold around your paw? That's me. I'll never leave your side. I'll always be right there beside you. I wanted to live life with you and experience it all, but I was too fucked. I'm sorry I wanted to fall and made your heart crawl. I'm so sorry you saw me dangling from my basement ceiling so motionlessly. I never meant for you to see. I never meant for you to see me hanging from my basement ceiling so lifelessly. I love you so much, more than you could ever possibly know.

Do you forgive me for my neck suspension?
My daredevil asphyxiation?

My selfish execution?
Do you forgive me for being a ghost?
Do you forgive me?

Without My Prescription

Effexor was my best friend.

Grabbed by two unseen hands and bent; my mind is badly proportioned. I can't vent. I'm spent, off-balance, about to crash. I must level my mental stance. Where's my medication? Oh yeah... the doctor took it away because of my attempted overdose yesterday. This is wrong. Without my prescription, I'm vulnerable to any type of mutilation: Calm, frantic, hard or elaborate, there are so many different ways, ways I can take my flesh and slice it. It can be simple or complex. Either way, it's a bloody mess. Anytime now, I'm going to implode. Watch me. I'll do it. Without my prescription, I'm human beach wood: something I love carving to any shape I like. Without my prescription, sanity is no good. My mind is starving. I have to strike, pierce my skin and flesh, make myself alright. Without my prescription, without mutilation, if I stand and do nothing then I'm with suicide.

Far Too Frail

You've got red on you.

One glass of poison to make my blood run thin. This way when I cut myself open from my neck to my stomach, I'll bleed like a hemophiliac. One deep wound and I'll drain to death. Don't worry; there is time left. You can save me. I'm not bleeding yet. Dissect my wrist. Suck the pollution out like a vampire with an uncontrollable thirst. Save me and infect yourself; it's the only way. Or let me bleed myself out. Allow me to drop my guts on the floor: my dangerous entrails and everything they entail. You know you should let me die. It has to be this way. I'm far too frail. Life can't seduce me otherwise.

Don't you see I've given up? Motivation of an anemic – my purpose is stale. I'm far too frail. Life's weight is monstrously great. Uneven balance, at the top, the scale tells my future. It shows there's no hope: reason for me to admit failure, commit over-exaggerated acupuncture, bleed, bleed, bleed. Fight. I know I should continue to fight, but life's choking-hands has my throat squeezed tight. The venom is already injected. I'm toxic. Depressed. Stupid. I'll take the credit. I'm disposable just how I projected. Knowing how far I've gone off course, I've changed my mind. Don't rescue me; put away your heroism. It's done. Hand me that knife so I can free myself from this prison.

Fragile a lot longer than awhile. Built up to the climax; ready to be thrown in a dead man's chest. I saw it coming from countless dropping of tears; optical waters foreshadowed this for years. I've seen my fate before and now I'm here – far too frail. I'm prepared to break the score: die to kill the tie. This is the finale, the climax. Goodbye.

Knife shoved into my throat. Blood spews out. Cutting myself in two as I drag it slowly to my stomach. Blood running down like red candle wax. It's excruciating, but pain to me doesn't matter because I don't. There... I've arrived at the destination, been emptied, hollowed less red: an accomplished permanent disfiguration. Denouement: a perfect end to a perennial struggle, a resolution, some peace at last.

I appreciate you for letting me go.
You are my hero.

.44 Calibre Of Mine

Like Hollywood Squares only better.

I want to be surrounded by a morgue and have its inaudible talent of stiff tongues, exterminated population, no voices for my ears to hear a single whisper to remind me of the terrible thing I've done, not one person alive telling me I should die for hurting her: Devil woman I was possessed by, a lady I loved. Manipulated by a witch; everyone on her side. Blinded, they don't see the transformation: the bitch. Unjust — she holds my family's trust. And I hold this .44 calibre of mine. She's taking things too far because I broke her heart. She'd be damned to let the pain scar. She's gone psycho.

Left alone. No one around at an acceptable distance where I can't feel people's footsteps on the ground, that is what I desire before any more drama transpires. Solitude. Quiet. Sweet, sweet tranquility. Absence of tormenting memories, contagious flashbacks. I want to be fenced in by rotten mimes and own their ability of staged silence. If this is impossible, then to be deaf... being capable to fail to listen to her witchcraft, her heart-killing songs, background music for her dead love spells, then that will be just as well.

Amnesia, erase the contents of my brain. I don't want to know anymore. Delete me until I'm sane, perfectly sane. Desperation, construct me bigger hands to push scum away: people who follow her lies' sway. Could you do it today? Single. By myself. Must escape turmoil before I spoil. I want to be circled by cold drawers and gain the muteness of its corpses. Exiled. Forgotten. .44 calibre of mine, it's time. Send me home. I'll take the real estate property of a morgue drawer. Make me leave the Jezebel, her worshippers: my family who turned on me. .44 calibre of mine, blow a hole in my head and pronounce me dead.

Drowning

The only thing that's drowning is the quality of this book.

Deep in love, light as a feather, walking on water, footsteps barely touching the surface, small ripples pass over my face, smiling reflection staring back at me. Happy as I've ever been; soul melodic like a violin. Euphoria-coloured. Heart beating an exquisite red. Permanent smile floating for miles. I'm so in love. I hope this lasts forever and awhile. Treading lightly on water so gracefully, here she comes. She glides beside me; beautiful as always. She looks at me blankly. I wonder to myself why does she stall to say she loves me so? Then, a man comes to her side and says, "I love you." She replies, "I love you, too." She floats for another. She doesn't care I love her. She doesn't love me. No! It's happening again! Growing heavy and sinking as they kiss and hold hands. I reach for one, trying not to be submerged. I purge words for help. They don't turn their heads to break their kiss. Helpless, below love, lungs filling with water, blood flow going slow, vision blurry, stuck in an undertow, quiet dark, alone.

Drowning.
Drownin..
Drowni...
Drown….
Drow…..
Dro……
Dr…….
D……..
………

Blue Mercury

Yes. I am well aware of how stupid the title is. Thank you.

Yesterday, my wife shot herself. Now tormented with lights out, I've barricaded myself in my room, rocking slowly on an old rocking chair, being careful not to make a sound. I don't want to wake the baby. I shouldn't leave my child, but she'll only be alone for a while. Someone will hear the gunshot; someone will rescue Violet. I need my wife. I can't live without her. This is one action I won't regret. I'll sacrifice everything to be with the one I love, even you. I'm so sorry, Violet. Daddy loves you. Always.

Gun pressed against my temple. One bullet in the chamber. Losing grasp on reality has set me here ever since I lost the one I loved, the one I held dear. Prepared to violently return to her the same way she left. Very anxiously, I sit and wait for cowardice to die out, so I can die in. When I fall to Hades, I don't know if I'll have the money to pay Charon, the reclusive boatman, but I'm not worried. If I can't afford the toll, I'll swim to her if I have to, across the river Styx to give myself to her, my heart, my soul, every inch of my being.

As I speak, I know she's looking for me. She won't have to search long. Fear is withering, tension around my trigger finger is slithering, tightening, forcing it to bend. I'm almost ready to descend. Knowing quite well, love will take me to her. Love will take her to me. I'll find her. She'll find me. I solemnly vow I will not stop seeking her until our feet touch the same ground. I'll be Hell-bound until I hear her heart's beating sound, and our lips connect, embracing our damnation together. Forever.

Window open. Heavy snow falling. Temperature well below zero. Gun barrel half-cycling, twisting back and forth against my temple, contemplating when. Barrel twice as cold, colder than blue mercury. Finger pressing against the trigger, contemplating when. Snow falling faster. Finger getting stiffer, tighter. Thoughts of her coming in clearer. Contemplating when. I hear her voice; she says she loves me. I can't take it anymore. Gun forced hard against my head; I scream her name. Finger pulls full strength. Violet cries. Dead...

Pinstripes (Dressed To Fuck)

The amount of unprotected sex I had with multiple partners is gross. And although there is a lot of truth in this poem, I've actually never fucked a girl named Nikki before. I don't think so anyway. I've slept with a lot of people. Makes it hard to keep track of names and faces. Like I said - I'm gross.

Skinny-thin, covered, white shirt with black tie, pinstripes overtop, up and down like Jack Skellington. Dressed to fuck. Attracting the opposite sex. Black boots a military shine. Reflections I see, that is what's mine. Cancer lung black: hair darkest shade hanging barely above pretty irises. Hypothermia blue eyes over-lined grey, underlined black, highlighted. Mysterious aura I set with automatic cigarettes resting on perfect lips. Blowing smoke. Lessening the days, I'll exist. Free hand dancing, boney fingers tapping, black nail polish up and down rhythmically against my knee, secretly counting girls staring at me. Confidence on high, self-esteem flourishing, choosing a girl who deserves my attention... Hard decision. Beautiful women everywhere to pick for a dance and a kiss, an overnight fuck. Night almost over. I must find her. And sure enough, I do. Her. Yes, her. The one with the purple dreads, in the black and red Medieval dress, smoking against the wall. She is the one who quickens my heart. She will be the one to take my hand. Putting out my cigarette, I get up and approach her. She smiles. I introduce myself. She blushes, takes a second while, inhales her smoke once then discards it. She says her name is Nikki. Curiously, I look at her, take her hand and coax her to the dance floor. No struggle. She eagerly follows. I have found myself another whore.

100mm Cigarette

I miss smoking. It's the only thing I'm good at.

Midnight balcony sitting, smoking my 100mm cigarette, counting burning stars, numbering forearm scars, dwelling on regrets, trying to forget painful memories of the past. Over two hundred nights, many moonlit hours I sat out here. Every night my thoughts get darker, my lungs blacker. I'm fading like rising smoke. At least I don't choke, cough anymore, not with the callus burned into my throat. I love it outside. It's so peaceful listening to crickets, watching bats, as I inhale and exhale smoke from my 100mm cigarette. Every night I flirt with cancer. It will find me soon if I keep coming out to greet the moon. On this balcony, this is where my addiction takes place, where I shorten my lifespan. What's therapeutic for me is what will kill me. It seems complex, but to me, it makes perfect sense. It's okay if I die. I won't be leaving anyone behind. It's just me and my 100mm cigarette. Time. I have no idea how much I have left. I only know this: Depression, a 100mm cigarette, this balcony, they will be the death of me.

Love On All Fours

This is going to start off sounding like a poem about rape. I promise you it's not. It's consensual. I just dated some freaky girls in my time. That's all.

She's on all fours, moaning and whimpering as I ruthlessly fuck her from behind, pulling back hard on her red shoulder-length hair, digging my nails deep into her flesh while I yell at her, telling her she's ugly, she's a whore, I hate her. Reminding her nobody loves her. She's mine forever.

She begs me to stop. I tell her, "Shut up! You'll do what I want." I fuck her faster, screaming more obscenities at her, traumatizing her, making sure by the time this is over, she'll be a disaster.

I have both hands pressed into her now, pushing nails in, luring blood out. Blood is everywhere. How she got in this position, I'm sure she's forgotten how. She's too exhausted, too dehydrated to think.

No longer on all fours, flat down in her torn-up gown, I can tell she doesn't care anymore by the way she doesn't react to my insults. She's stopped crying. In a catatonic state, she's probably thinking about dying.

She might be still as a corpse, but I'm not done. Lying right on top of her, my teeth inject themselves into her neck. I can feel blood hitting my taste buds. I go wild like a vampire, a starving zombie. Every time I thrust, I bite her more viciously. A mouthful of blood, flesh under nails – this is paradise.

I can see it. I'm about to orgasm. And her? Well... she's motionless, only slight breathing moves her. About to cum, I pound her savagely, smearing her blood around with my chest. I moan "fuck" repeatedly. I kneel up and my body jolts back and forth as I cum inside her. Emptied, panting like a dog, I collapse back on top of her.

Both completely out of breath, I stroke her hair behind her ear and whisper softly, "I love you." She turns her head, looks at me with satisfied eyes, tells me she loves me too. We passionately kiss. I lie down beside her. We hold hands, kiss again, and stare into each other as we watch one another fall asleep.

I Fell In Love
With A Scarecrow

Even scarecrows can't stand clingers.

Ugly as sin, far from thin, sores dotted on my face from me picking at myself, looking to see if there's beauty beneath this layer of skin. There isn't. My body is covered with moles: unattractive brown spots. I'm gross. I'm all the way down. I have no friends. I don't fit in. My parents won't talk to me; they resent me. I didn't turn out how they wanted. I feel soulless but I do have emotions because I fell in love with a scarecrow: the body of hay, a rotting pumpkin impaled by a large stick. I visit him every day. Deep in the middle of the cornfield, I talk; he listens. Crows sometimes interrupt, disrupt, but I know his attention is fully on me. I love him because he's always there for me. As gorgeous as he is, as monstrous as I am, he loves me. I wish he was alive so we can get married, make love and have children, be together for eternity. But life is cruel. In it, I'm buried. I'm worried. The wind is constantly blowing him slowly away. His pumpkin head is decomposing. The one I love is dying. Soon I'm going to be alone. Staring at him, I see we don't have much time left. And this tells me life is not a gift.

Boogeyman

If I don't make it as an author, I might fuck around and direct some B-horror movies. I don't know.

Vivid nightmares,
night terrors,
three covered mirrors keeping struggling creatures at bay.

Hiding under sheets, sweat dripping, frantic heartbeats, sun dying, moon rising. I left my closet door open. Now there's something lurking in the dark, sneaking inside my room.

Good or evil, from Heaven or Hell, I can't tell. But the smell, the way it dwells, its scent has my hair standing on end.

On alert,
waiting for the worst to happen.
No vision of it,
only the unsettling feeling of another presence.

Open eyes. Staying awake. Can't be vulnerable. Lying in the middle of my bed, defending, pretending I'm dead. Not from inside my head, the monster is here, all around me, everywhere. Do I dare take a peek? I might be bigger than it. There's a chance I could kill it.

Petrified. Unstable. No fable. It's going to get me! It's going to kill me! It's going to eat me! What do I do? It's over-top of me now. Claws in chest. Painful. Blood leaking. Still not peeking. This is the end. Dead end.

It's breathing heavy, grinding teeth. Stuck underneath, I'm squirming, screaming. Through my blanket, it bites into me. I go into shock. Roommate comes in. Light flickers on. Like a flash, the Boogeyman is gone, back inside my closet.

Pouring red. Traumatized. My roommate and I look at each other. With hearts temporarily stopped, our jaws are dropped, as our skin changes to an ultra white. I think I'm going to be sick. Bleeding to death; I need stitches. But I'm not concerned about it. My eyes are fixated on my closet. I know I will never sleep again. I won't be able to. Fear won't allow it. What am I going to do? What the fuck am I going to do? Oh, God! Oh, God! OH GOD! No! NO! NOOOOOOOOOOOOOO!

Kiss Me On The Mouth

When you're that desperate, oral herpes is no longer a deterrent.

Do you love me? Tell me the truth. Either walk away or kiss me on the mouth. Succumbed with frustration, I'm turning grey. Add distance to this equation or press your lips firmly against mine. In any direction, cross the line.

Please take my hand. Do you feel it? My heartbeats through my fingertips? This is how much I love you. All this blood to sacrifice – I would die for you. I would coagulate myself if you asked me to. There's not a thing I wouldn't do for you. I would steal. I would kill. Anything you ask I will do. I am your obedient slave. If you pull my leash I will heal. I will behave. I am yours.

Are you listening to what I am saying? By a single command, I would turn Heaven into Hell, and Hell into Heaven. All you have to do is ask. Please, I beg you. Let's touch lips and exchange tongues, connect hips and share oxygen between lungs. Have me. Step once. Step lightly. Take a chance. Come forward; kiss me on the mouth. If you don't want me, then get off my shadow. Prove it's not meant to be.

Your eyes are looking distant. Will you hug me now? Hold me tight before I lose you? Press your palm against my heart; tell me you want me. Tell me you love me. Kiss me on the mouth. Tell me everything is going to be alright.

Fear-injected eyes crying. Your flesh off my chest. You take a step back. I start dying. I knew it. How can something so assembled love something so destructed? You blow a kiss in my direction, but the wind carries it away:

permanent dissection. I reach for you; the fog swallows you whole. Gone. I have failed to make you stay.

Grey clouds.
Cold wind and heavy rain.
The weather is perfect.
I think I might die today.

New Body Alteration

Would you believe me if I told you I treat women with the utmost respect? It's true. I'm not a fucking psychopath.

Gone distant; you have simply vanished. But if I knew where you are, I would drag you back to me. If I found you and by chance you are still too far, I would dislocate my shoulder so I could reach and pull you towards me in great agony. You left me, but I still want to find you. Where did you go? I need to know. I have to show you something. Reveal your unknown destination so I can show you mutilation: this mighty gash slashed across my neck. There was no vaccine, not for this. It was inevitable. You never knew but this whole time you were a murderer.

There's no antidote for this slit throat, no medicine to stitch this wide-cut thin. It's too far past my skin. Come to me, see the devastation, my new body alteration. I want to feel your fingernails deep inside my wound. I need you to feel the full effect of this drama. Touch me; absorb my trauma. Let's both fall into an everlasting coma.

You have wrecked me for the last time. My suicide is your crime, not mine. It will be your fault, your guilt, not mine. With you gone, I didn't know how to survive. I had to eat my own heart just to stay alive. Now fully devoured, I'm sour. Now hollow, I can no longer swallow. Now choking on the taste of my insides, I struggle to scream your name. Way beyond helpless, I fear I will not see your face. My ending is here.

I see time is no longer on my side because I'm seconds away from bleeding to death. And I still can't see you or hear a single breath. Without you present, my mission, my kamikaze decision has no worth. Unsuccessful to lure, I'm alone. Too late to change my mind; there is no cure. Seeing myself dying in the mirror, I realize... I... I am the epitome of failure.

Sara, where are you? WHERE ARE YOU?!

Mother

Dial down the hatred a little bit and there may be a grain of truth in it. Mom,
if you're reading this... I was an angry kid. Sorry. We cool? Cool.

Junkie mother of mine, I wish I was your abortion. I have had it with you, your skin speckled with needle punctures, your rotten mouth and its falling of brittle teeth, your forgetting of my name and existence. There is no love in you; it's been drained out from all your nose bleeds. Now only drugs circulate underneath. Mother, I fucking hate you so much. Not once for me, not once were you ever there. I have come to believe you never cared. I have come to believe I would kill you on a dare. You are the worst mother in the world. Your abandonment sickens me; your addictions worsen me. Knowing you still breathe, I can't. Your carousel is shameful. Your men and location keep changing, but your bad habits and rent stay the same. I hate you for making me play this game. You are not beautiful; you are not human. How can you be when everything about you is automatic? Mother, you're the only creature I want to smother. Mother, to murder you, you are worth the trouble and the bother. This is the power of hate. I remember I once traced your circle. I remember almost being your duplicate. I don't know how, but I found my way off course. And I'm glad because when I die, I wouldn't want to be your corpse. Mother, if I knew where you are, I would make you read this then stab you in the back, in the dark. I hate you that much. Mother, you are not my mother. You're just a stupid whore that keeps walking through the same fucking door. Mother, when you die, know this: I won't be at your funeral. I'll never visit to say goodbye. I will leave you alone. By yourself, you will decompose. Alone... you will be bones, and for eternity, insects will remind you what you lost: a son that loved you.

LIIAN VARUS VERSUS VAGINAS

If you're a woman and have made it this far without wanting to track me down and stab me to death on my porch, while I'm drinking my morning coffee, I applaud you. By now, you and I both know if there is ever a #MeToo literary award, *Is Stranged.* isn't going to win one. Without a doubt, I may have some deep-seated issues with women. Not so much hate, but fear. To me, women are these little, fragile creatures. They seem so vulnerable. The power they wield is like nothing I've ever seen. Women are not to be trifled with, and I suppose in some way, my violence towards them in my poetry is my pathetic attempt to control their existence. I fear what I respect. A woman's spirit floats on untamed whims. They are capable of anything. Don't doubt that for a second. Influence is etched in their DNA. Men get to be men because women allow it. So, I believe. To this day, they scare the living shit out of me. What can I say - their mystique makes me cower. With that being said, 2007 wasn't an overly busy year of writing for me. That doesn't mean I threw women to the metaphorical wolves any less than usual. Wish I knew what I wanted to accomplish with that amount of bloodshed. Perhaps other issues were boiling over, and for whatever reason, women became my scapegoat on how to deal with my shortcomings. I know it's fiction, but I feel like I have a lot to apologize for. Can't apologize yet, though. The book isn't over. Women hate premature guys. You know exactly what I just did there.

Run (I'm Addicted To You)

To be fair, even if she did a light jog, that would have been fast enough. Yeah, exercise really isn't my thing.

Knuckles across your face; blood on the back of my hand. Fist paintbrush – pretty canvas. Art made, domestic violence, sad silence, your fractured jaw damaged and raw. Obsessed. Disturbed. Control, control. I can't seem to overdose on you. I love you and I'm sorry that I do. I want to make you smile. I want to stop hurting you, but I can't help myself. I have no control.

Half a dozen steps back, I brace myself by placing my shaking hand on my chest, desperately trying to catch my breath. I'm addicted to you; you're my drug of choice. Another attempt to overdose on you, once more I have failed. You're never enough, never enough. My heart won't let go. I'm sick, deeply infatuated. My grasp on your heart can't be separated. I've tried. I fear this will always be until one of us has died.

My love is sadism. At war with myself; you're the tested specimen. My problems are yours and you are mine. If you don't run, there's a chance you could die.

I'm feverish! Run! I'm delirious! Run! Fucking run! This will never be over unless you run! I'm troubled. Things will never get better, so I'm asking you to run! Leave me! Are you listening to me?! I'm not well; something is wrong. Love must end here before murder entices my sadism. I'm addicted to you. You're never enough because I can't overdose on you. This is the reason why my actions are no longer pleasant. Pure love can not satisfy me. This is why I've turned violent. This is why you must run!

Run!
Damn you! Run!
Run!
GET AWAY FROM ME!
RUN! RUN!!!

Holder Of The Zombie Heart

I'm as threatening as a fitted sheet.

It takes me months to crawl out of the dirt and when I finally do, you touch me once and I fall. My eyes close and tear, lips tremble, heartbeats skip and crawl, skip and crawl. Everything goes numb then I stumble and fall back into the hole, the abyss you enslave me in.

How many times do I have to resurrect myself before you stop burying me? Because I don't know how much more I can take. I am not your puppet. Stop cutting me down and setting me up. I am not your toy to destroy. Quit splitting my strings with your malevolent scissors. I am not yours. From your morale-sucking games, my mind is mangled into a knot of panic and my heart is soft as a fist-sized bruise. You are slowly killing me. I'm warning you now. If you don't spare what is left of me, you are going to get the full extent of this blow.

Altered and deranged, faltered and changed, continuous absorption of evil deeds, emotions die and a mannequin takes its place: the holder of the zombie heart. Spit more cold words, act out more devious plots. I have the patience to watch you rot. Thrash and flail; get the best of me. Get the best of me and fail. Higher and higher, looking down, I see you getting smaller and smaller. You have slaughtered me endlessly, attacked ruthlessly, so profusely that I'm echo-empty. What's inside of me – that's all you'll ever be.

Mannequin, holder of the zombie heart, torn down to the skeleton, I now carry the axe. You, the girl, you are mine, my puppet, my metaphorical corpse for me to bury. Karma has changed its sheets and now, I lie in the bed while you struggle for sleep on the floor. I get to fuck with your head and twist the blood from your heart. I finally get to ruin you. Unfortunately for me, luckily for you, I'm hollow. You have swallowed me whole. I have no urge to be vindictive, no need to have revenge, but I am going to leave you where you're buried – in that fucking hole you left me.

I Seduce What I Kill

And to think I'm married.

Sadists and their two faces: whores and their evil schemes always out to get me. Every day it seems fierce battles are fought on dreary war grounds. In my pathetic surroundings, constant aggression is faced. But I'm protected by my endless skill to counterattack. Making vicious harlots know black. I fake dead until the time is right to empty their red. This is the way the war will be won until all the succubae are gone.

Love is in the eye of the beholder and I am blind.
Love is in the eye of the beholder and I have lost my mind.
Cutthroats and rolling eyes.
Bloodshed and fatal goodbyes.
I murder because I can't be loved.
I seduce what I kill because I can't be loved.

Pushed and shoved by ones who tear out hearts for enjoyment. I know their trickery well, so I let them play and I lure. I wait, stay, be still, then at the perfect moment I run them through until blood loss is sufficient, and their ruby lips are blue. When there is no life left, my shovel conceals them with dirt.

Backyard cemetery where dirt mounds are spread like landmines and corpses push up fresh daisies like white flags of surrender. Beauty far under, filthy morgue filling fast, war showing no signs of being over. Where do I keep the dead? When enchanting thieves continue to march, where will I keep the dead? This epic struggle will not end well. I'm already halfway to

Hell and no soul to sell. But it's too late to return. I might as well continue to fight and prepare my flesh to burn.

Girls of sorts with identical missions,
coming at me like they're coming off an assembly line.
Overwhelmed,
my knife stays in the ready position as they approach one by one.
Opened jugulars and bloodshot eyes.
Red streams and unaccomplished lies.
I murder because I can't be loved.
I seduce what I kill because I can't be loved.
Failed decapitations and lifeless eyes.
Attractive stiffs and hungry flies.
I murder because I can't be loved.
I seduce what I kill because I can't be loved.

My fallen enemy, you will love me because without me, you have nothing.

Corpse Lake

The lake your summer cottage is on has dead bodies in it.

Human hair suspending a bloody scalp: hair held by a murderer's cold fist. Take a look down. There's a girl facedown on a blue tarp, spread like a dead star. A young woman bleeding from her undressed skull and the impalement through her heart: the original attack that killed her. No life lingers. Still fingers. Dead body. Her wounds will never scar; the killer knows this. So, he grins and reminisces on past sins while tiny chuckles sneak to his vocal cords, allowing laughter to coincide with his victim.

In the middle of nowhere, on an old farm, in a broken-down barn, far in the middle of nowhere, there she was given no chance to escape. She was stripped, raped, and exploded like a squished grape when stabbed and scalped. Screamed she did and died she did, in a nightmare no one saw.

An hour passes by; the rush of the kill has faded. The man has settled down. He kneels and firmly grabs two corners of the blue tarp. Very neatly he wraps it around her like a cocoon, like a street woman's gown. Like a blue tarp that's covering a stiff, he wraps it around her. With thick twine, he coils it around her. Like red wine, blood leaks through holes and tears. Through the bloody mess, he ties off her coffin tight and begins his journey to the water, dragging her slowly in the wolf-howling night, to Corpse Lake where he gives what he takes, where she'll drop down, be sunk and lost, where she'll meet others. And there she'll stay, greeting new company until she is found.

Autopilot Off

Don't let my constant suicidal threats fool you. I'm super fun at parties.

U p and down blood tracks: suicidal behaviour on autopilot. This is it – walking the tightrope between life and death, between asphyxiation and a breath. Mentally I'm shot. My soul is so close to the Devil's hand, I'm pretty much bought. I'm falling but haven't quite descended yet. I could turn my life around, but why should I when there's more room for me underground? Sure, this could be pity or just a mere extension of someone's misery, but it doesn't matter with all this weight I carry. Everything, everyone has failed me, including myself. I can't be saved. You might as well chisel my name on my grave, on my stone that will advertise what was, because as soon as I wipe this mud from my eyes, my vision will clear. And when it devours all fear, I will have left myself for maggots and flies. For me… there is no final destination, just this hole that calls out to me. Reality has bitten me hard and has sunk in. This is where it ends. Tonight… I'm crashing this flight.

Autopilot off.

Groom Kills Bride

I mentioned I was married, right?

Shotgun murdered the romance, ended a lovers' dance. One twitch of a finger squeezed back the trigger and shot off half her skull, splattering blood from left to right, straight across the bedroom wall. This was the argument that went too far: anger-possessed groom kills bride. How bizarre. Both in love, both close to being wed, but instead... instead of a diamond ring placed on her finger, she wound up dead, had her corpse pulled off her bed and dragged throughout the house, out the door to his car, leaving a thick trail of blood behind. During late hours of the night, she was shoved into the trunk of his car, driven an hour from where her blood stained, and when she arrived, there it was: trees for miles and miles. Deep in the forest, that is where she was discarded, somewhere among acres and acres of burial ground, concealed, never to be found.

It started with a fit of rage which let madness out of its cage, unlocked and let loose from a simple spark: a disagreement about the location of their honeymoon. From this progressive heat, it brought in the dark because he wanted Rome and she wanted Spain. It took twenty minutes for words to turn into a melee. Groom victorious. Bride left without a conscience, without half her brain. Swollen vexation stopped the yelling with a traumatic resolution. This was not premeditated; he didn't mean for her to die. He just got emotional and careless. He loves her. He loves her more than anything. It just happened so fast. He couldn't grab hold of the situation. Now struck with grief and panic, he can't come up with an alibi. He really doesn't have a choice but to turn himself in. Besides, it won't be long before someone finds the body because he hurried, didn't pay attention to detail. He didn't quite finish the job. Fingers like roots painted pale and the blown side of her head acting as a well, collecting rain as it starts to pour - they both stick out, out of the dirt, showing clearly for the next passer-by.

Back on the road, the man is bombarded. Memories like flash grenades come out of nowhere, hit him hard. One after another he's blinded; the only thing he sees is her. From 60km/h to 80km/h, faster and faster. Everything at once comes real. He loses it. The guilt was vicious enough to devour him whole like a cannibal with fresh meat. The mental breakdown is now the driver, so the groom lets go of the steering wheel and leans calmly back against the seat. Now at 120km/h, he's right off the road, aimed right at a giant tree. And before he can take a breath to embrace the hit, like a kamikaze missile, the car smashes into it, splitting almost in half. Bark, leaves, branches, large sections of tree are scattered everywhere. And, where is he? Well, he flew through the windshield, nosedived heavily into the mangled tree, where the impact mashed his entire head into birdfeed. And like a broken hood ornament, he was leaned over, bleeding a six-litre lake on the field. This... this is how it ended. After this ordeal, the rest is obvious – there was no wedding, only funerals.

Love Is Absinthe

I've cut myself more times than someone who's received a hand job from Edward Scissorhands.

No one loves you like I love you. No one can tolerate your bullshit like I can. I am the only person that is immune to you. So, why did you leave? I remember how we fought and how it weakened us, how it warped our thoughts, but I loved it because we always kissed and made-up. We fucked each other like we meant it. Our angry spurting of words brought us closer. But this time… this time you ran, and I don't know where you went or where you are. I only know until you come back, I won't let these multiple wounds on my body scar. For days, my brain has been swelling from the insanity that has sunk in. Its continuous growth has enlarged my head and has made me question my worth. Living seems so deceiving. I should surgically remove my brain with a chainsaw. The loss of a lot of red will only make me a little dead. Somehow, I must relieve the pressure, but I don't know how. I have come to believe that love is a myth, a dream soaked in absinthe, it doesn't exist. What am I without you? I tried to figure it out, but I can't do the math. Come back to me. Come back to me and I'll forget… I'll forget what I was becoming – a psychopath.

Whitechapel Grapes

Butchered this poem worse than one of Jack's girls.

Whitechapel 1888, where a shade used grapes as bait to lure in the dirty tramps and the hungry vamps. Into the darkest corners of the streets, this is where he introduced them to their untimely fate. In an instant, between one suspected last breath and a painful death, they would lose their bodies to sell, resulting in vacancy openings at The Ten Bells for any duplicates willing to take their place. Nonetheless, it is no concern to them. Money has no worth in Hell. In Hell, whores fuck for free.

More grapes from the vineyard; another unsolved murder. Was it ever going to end? Morning corpses, stiff lips not even the blind would kiss, middle-aged women mutilated, with organs stolen and uterus taken. Why were these gals forsaken? Especially, girl five of twenty-five? I guess the beautiful get it the worst.

With a combination of stealth and skill, the Ripper was born to kill. Incisions were professional, precise. Possibly he was psychotic, but he knew what he was doing. London was his playground. There his victims were already dead. They just didn't know it yet. Entangled in his cobblestone street labyrinth, it was just a matter of time before they felt their throats slit. Back then every day was chance, that tonight could be the night where Jack would ask them to dance. It was mass paranoia.

Through shadows and alleyways, he was like a ghost. With darkness on his side, grapes and surgical equipment provided the seductions and the merciless slaughters. Maimed ruthlessly to satisfy his blood addiction, these girls weren't spared; torn to pieces like it didn't matter, like no one cared. The attacks were ferocious like he knew he would never be caught. He knew, so bodies continued to rot. Police were helpless. No self-confidence. From crime scene to crime scene, not a single answer could be bought, not even with the letters Jack sent. Suspects with no concrete evidence, it was all they had. And this is why, and they knew, Jack would never be caught.

"One day men will look back and say I gave birth to the twentieth century."

-Jack the Ripper

Death

I've resurrected myself more times than Jesus stuck on a time loop.

Body shivers: quakes strong enough to disrupt the intricate blood rivers, that flow throughout your entire circulatory system. There's a war inside your head: you versus them. Outnumbered; you fall into a state of numbness and lead desperation in front of the charge. There it takes command, raises its sword and fiercely hacks at your circuits. Left, right, up, down and centre, veins cut like wires, like stems from a bouquet of roses. The blood patterns are so spectacular, even the sane would admire them. You're a fountain of blood and that is why shock hits. Every part of you freezes, seizes. Dripping like a leaky faucet, vomit creeps past your sealed lips and drips down your chin. Pressure engages. Gone by too many stages. The give in. You erratically convulse, shaking loose the digested garbage held in your mouth. Climatic eruption. Waste smothers your exposed pulse. Eyes roll lifelessly. Vertical crash. No heartbeat showing. Light in your eyes no longer glowing. Everything is still, ever so quiet. This is it: What you dreadfully feared but wanted more than anything.

Why Should I Have To Snap Your Neck To Get You To Look At Me?

Damn you and the sexy way you flip your hair. Ugh! Why do you always smell so good?! Agh! Notice me! PLEASE! Is that lavender? Sigh. I love lavender.

Passed over – my heart overlooked by you. You don't even glance at me. How do you know if I am ugly? The slight breeze as you walk by drains me. The side of your face is venomous; my heart stalls permanently from paralysis. So, here I stand, holding my own hand. Here I dwell in what feels like Hell. Forgotten. I'm rotten. Realizing I am invisible, I've found out I'm divisible. My heart is really two halves: a bloody pair badly misshapen. It's a mystery how they fitted together at all. I know this by the way they harden and the sickening feeling that I am about to fall. No first kiss. No first love, only a pitiful dance, this lonely waltz where I pathetically go through the motions while I burn in the spotlight, waiting for the cue, a somber moment where I wrap my arms around nothing, around something that should have been you. Step, swing, step, swing – I wish I could forget everything. Step, swing, step, swing – I wish I could stop the bleeding: the aerodynamics of my knife's acrobatics puncturing inside me like a murder weapon. But I am terribly stained by emotions that aren't quite human, which has resulted in the complete loss of my sanity. My early extinction is imminent because you won't answer this simple question: *Why should I have to snap your neck to get you to look at me?*

As Lovers

I did it! I wrote a poem that doesn't involve a woman getting murdered! Now, where the fuck is my gold star?!

Break the fusion of our hands. Cool the sweat from our palms by untangling our fingers. Unlock water-underlined eyes and turn our backs against one another, hiding any piece of evidence of how much this hurts. Take a deep breath in. Shout it out and engage into the unknown distance by forcing one foot in front of the other. We have our own destination, a place that doesn't involve us but will evolve us. The greater the space between us will be fact. When the swelling of our hearts crush our kneecaps and makes us crawl through past memories that will never be repeated, we will know nothing stays intact.

I know this doesn't feel right, but we've travelled as far as we could as strangers, as friends, as lovers. Sadly though, our road has ended. Things that were have unraveled and are dying as I speak. We can't ignore this and continue on. It doesn't matter how much we pretend. We will fail, for we are cancer-weak. One way or another, our Yellow Brick Road is gone. Yes, this separation is pale; there is no sense behind it. We only know it has to be this way. By the discolouration of the sun when our hearts are as one, every day is greyer than crematorium ashes. That is how we know. So, let's get this over with. Place one foot in front of the other and let's end this story as lovers.

Worms In An Apple

Feel like I lost out on a business opportunity with all those worms in my head. Could have opened up my very own bait and tackle shop. Damn.

Depression-chewed brain: eight pounds of bridges opening up freeways to intensify the pain. Faster, quicker, it resolves, making the disease harder to solve. Like worms in an apple, in time I will be hollow, one misshapen hole. I tried to medicate myself, but the pills were too sticky to swallow. I've even prayed but the sinned have no faith. My ability to accomplish a mental balance has failed. Years of being eaten by emotional piranhas, my sanity is almost inhaled.

I would kill myself to feel right, but I am unsure. I feel like my wake, my rest-in-peace would be no answer, only an open coffin banquet. There is no surrender, no mercy, no end. I can't think right now, scaring myself with this death threat. Maybe one day, one day it will be a reliable bet.

There's life against me, inside of me like worms in an apple. Irreversible damage has shown me this sickness has rabies. It can't be putdown, not in this human. I have no immunity to this disease. I can feel myself shriveling up, hardening like sundried clay. I see the formation of grey: decay lines and spots. They are a part of me, as much as I am a part of them. I am fully deformed, living dead. There is nothing I can do now but sit here and try to remember... remember what it was like to have a brain inside my head.

Mummified

Did I ever tell you about the time I lost my job as a pharmacist?

I am a pharmacy addict. I swallow mass productions of pills to fight conflict: the overgrown tumour of an out-of-control mental state. I do what I can to keep myself at bay.

Because I've widened my throat to accept the overflow of my dependent fix, I breathe without sense of panic, stress, or fear, only to suffer what it feels like when my emotions fail to generate. Nothing exists within; all I am is misused skin.

Emotionless. I can't operate, react to situations like I normally would. I feel broken, no good. I am stuck between a pill and a hard place. You can see it on my face - I am drained dry. Dead and wrapped; I am mummified. The continuous intake of this little pill, that is the reason I am alive, but recently I have found myself questioning its purpose. Everything is still. Anything that can harm me is frozen. If I stop this medicating consumption, I will be ill again.

Open palm spotted, speckled with anti-depressants. I take these to stay calm. These blue pills... These tiny machetes keep me gutted. I don't really see a reasonable choice. If I take off this zombie uniform, if I stop and attempt to conform, be normal without medical science, suicide might be able to reassure me it's safe.

I'm in checkmate. My army of pills is my protection, except they are renegades, grenades. For the price of life, I am stripped of friends, love and family, robbed of everything I need because they have taken away my ability to be human. But at least I am alive, so I try to tell myself.

Far off in the distance, I can hear a faint sound of a clock ticking. It would probably be louder if I weren't choking on a few pills that are sticking. I'm noticing my oxygen intake is getting smaller, but I can't deter my attention away from the tocking. I hear it getting louder and louder. The more the pendulum-like beat closes in, my eyesight becomes shorter. I think I'm dying and it's about time.

Secret

Strong enough for a man but made for a woman.

Everyone has skeletons in their closet, as do I, except mine are still bound with some flesh, because my secrets are somewhat fresh from consistently being repeated. Continuous reliving of actions and thoughts that taint, coats my entire soul in dark paint: denial that someday it will go away. I am my greatest threat, my fiercest yet. Sometimes I just want to faint, never to wake.

There's only one secret that never stops damaging and that's - who I am. I am a wolf in sheep's clothing. My charismatic bark is really an infectious bite. My words are right, but my thoughts are grey – replicated night. This careless being inside me chooses to stay, to make sure everyone eventually goes away. Suppressing the inevitable only creates more decay.

I realize I am potent. I can attract almost anyone. I suck them up and spit them out when I am done. My buried emotions never resurrect; they stay down covered in rot. This must be why I can hurt anyone without regret. Whether I do this on purpose or not, it doesn't matter. I am cruel. I am not user-friendly. I'm deadly – a hard punch to the heart.

I am your perpetual wasteland. My secret will probably never let go of my hand, not until the day I die. I care about no one, including my own mother. It's sadder that I hate myself above any other. Solitary confinement, my feet off the pavement, off any direction to someone - that is how it has to be. Some things are the worst kind of strange. Some things just don't burn brightly.

Victims

The only victim here is you because you're about to read this toxic waste dump of literary bullshit.

I remember a girl long ago. A girl with such beauty and grace, she could bring royalty to their knees. A girl who would put her hands on both sides of my face, look hard into me and say, "You're the only one for me." She was perfect in every sense, from the inside to the surface. I remember a girl, a future I looked forward to, to a paradise where nothing would matter because we would have each other, a son and a daughter. But in two years, everything crumbled brick by brick. Paradise was bulldozed down into a gutter. I've been trying to rebuild but I am starting to feel all is lost and I'm left with the sick.

Somewhere between the beginning and now, she became a multiple addict somehow. I can't pinpoint the cause or reason because she won't talk. Not since the last passing season was the last time we spoke, but I see her almost every day.

My love for her is dwindling because she's mummified. She doesn't care; she's petrified. She doesn't know I know she doesn't glow anymore. It's her fault for failing to hide the evidence. I've smelled the rum and cigarette smoke. I've seen the crash scenes powdered against her nostrils: multiple accidents from her white lane highways. I've noticed the inconvenient nose bleeds and handfuls of bloody tissues in her pockets. I've stared at her town-worth of needle punctures: heroin jabs populated across her entire body. She looks like she's been pecked apart by vultures. I'm surprised she isn't dead yet. I'm starting to believe she doesn't remember me.

I live with a zombie where sometimes we secretly roleplay what used to be: a memory jolt with touching lips. But it's weak, not the same. There is no spark because she lacks movement and passion. Her show of love feels like a jawless kiss. My devotion seems a lot like sin. The girl I once knew I can't recognize. My loyalty goes unseen under radar. I can't pull things back to the beginning. Failure to do so brings amnesia, and amnesia tells me to forget her. I knew I should have done something about this sooner, but I thought it was just a phase, a phase that now has her mind lost, stranded in a catatonic state between the drug walls of an addict's maze. The price of my ignorance was not worth the cost. I want to make everything new again, make the present like the past, but I can't remove the rust or the dust. I waited too long; the wound has sealed and scarred. I am at the bottom of a pit that guilt dug, and I am about to burst.

In different ways, her and I are weak which makes us the same. It makes us victims to each other. Vocals that won't speak – We are mimes towards one another. No communication will be our destruction. I am a fighter, but I wish the weight was a little lighter. I love her and want to help. And my love fails me because I can't make her stop. Time is on my side except I can't move, and on that side, I have no arm to grab it. Amazingly the gears in her life's clock still turn, and my sadness grows as my hopes burn. There is nothing really any of us can do now. We don't give a shit so the picture shows. It feels like too late. There is no breaking the stalemate; her and I are stuck. We can only do one thing out of this fucked up rhythm, our frail existence we call life, and that's playing this game where I'm the victim and you're the victim, a game we will both lose.

Choke Me, Frankenstein

When you can't even convince a dead person to fuck you, you might want to think about giving up your search for love. Shiiiiiiiit.

Choke me. Put your hands around my neck; tell me you love me. Choke me. Put your hands around my neck and tell me you hate me. Give me every one of your emotions; give me anything. Empty on me like an angry trigger-finger holding a machinegun with a full magazine. Be truthful. Be loud. Be obscene. Redeem. Scream. Come clean. Show me you are capable of feeling something; prove to me you're alive. See this hand? Count my fingers – one, two, three, four, five – five fingers on one palm. My hand is on your chest, listening for a heartbeat. Come alive. At least cut me once with this knife. Please, Frankenstein – react, feel, speak. Tell me you want to be mine. If the dead can walk, then the dead can talk. Choke me. Choke me; say that you hate me. Choke me. Choke me; say that you love me. Please, Frankenstein – don't leave me buried.

Pack Of Crayons

I miss smoking so much... So... so... much. It's better than sex. It's the greatest invention ever created. Fucking quote me.

Shaded cigarettes stitched to my lips. They live there so often they're like an extra appendage: mouth tenants. Probably the reason why I am always coughing. Within two days I inhale twenty sticks to take my life bit by bit, my pack of crayons I use to colour my organs black. This cycle is broken on repeat. Addiction has made me its host. My throat kills like it's been sliced by razors, and my stomach aches from a couple of bleeding ulcers. I am sure cancer will pay me a visit soon. I am sure it will find me and kindly usher me to the closest hospital room. I am certain.

I try not to be an addict, but I am reliant. Lobotomy, lobotomy, lobotomy – one missing chunk of brain could make me less dependent, could make me less me. Is there a fix to fix what makes me tick? Because I feel sick. I can't stop. My fingers continue to flick, tossing butt after butt. I have a mouth that won't shut because I have a nonexistent willpower. I am a corporate puppet, a slave, a Muppet, another smoker with one foot in the grave.

Djarum Black lungs, tar heart, other choking organs brace yourselves, for I am Chernobyl. I am what is going to smother you down. Completely lifeless and still, you will end up on shelves, in jars of alcohol. As for me, I am dinner. Maggots will devour me pound for pound. For beneath the dirty ground, I will be wearing my death frown with a lit cigarette burning in my rotting hand.

Old habits die hard.

Rubik's Cube

Rubik's Cubes are fucking stupid. But hey, so am I.

Trapdoors and hidden passageways: a vast network of tunnels and secrets. I am a maze, a labyrinth, incomplete. I don't know me. I follow different paths endlessly, but I always find myself standing at a dead end. I am perpetually lost. Sometimes I can see a ray of hope, bright spots, but I can never connect the dots so bright spots turn into knots, knots I get myself tangled in. But hand me a rope and I can make a noose.

Like a chameleon I wear my skin in some new way, to adapt to every new day but I'm not fooling anyone. People know I paint with knives, own a gun. They see the bullseye pressed into my forehead. I show signs of contemplating. Grey eyes tell me I'm losing lives. I am one emotional relapse from being dead. I'm one case not worth investigating. I'll be dead before I am solved.

Surfing on my brainwaves; can't stay above the depression line. I wipeout hard into insanity, hard into many graves: a burial hole for each one of my personalities, fatalities. Multiple character disorders have my brain in thousands of pieces like one giant puzzle. Waiting for people to tell me how to put it together, the only feedback I receive is silence. Billions of people and the whole population happens to be wearing a muzzle. It's up to me to correct myself. But how do you fix something if you are blind? How do you repair yourself with a fragmented mind?

I've decided to leave this Rubik's Cube on the shelf. I'm quitting while I'm already far enough behind. So, if you don't mind, I'm going to paint myself with my knives and play Russian Roulette against my shadow, until I run out of lives. I'm going to tease, flirt with death, give myself completely backward as far as I can go, begging for torture with a pretty please, to the point I can't even stand on my knees. I will be my worst enemy until I am as shattered as upstairs and daylight has burnt out forever.

LIIAN VARUS' FOREST

In 2008, I was shedding loops: the old skin of bad habits. My mind caved, dared to cross the tree line and into the forest of my psyche. Not too far but enough where a compass gave it comfort. I wrote about different things. For the first time, I didn't rely on the perpetual relationship between violence and women. In this forest, there was understanding, corruption and haunted houses. Of course, I could never shake my ghosts. What a weight off my shoulders, though. Seemingly I was capable of so much. Chipping the tip of the creative iceberg to accompany my rye and Coke, I was drinking myself to new life. After all these years, my brain opened up and branched out like infectious constellations. There were unearthed roads to venture more than ever now, woven and spread out like sheet lightning interlocking, unveiling untouched stories at every juncture. Where would I go? How would I do it? Liberation was exhilarating. Almost. Despite the expansion of maps, a forest is still a forest. No road was brash enough to pave through it which was unfortunate since I remained trapped in that forest. Leave it to me to discover a pristine world and instantaneously want to leave it. Peering through the promising, yet, debilitating trees, I couldn't get my feet on the pavement. Looks like I still had some hiking to do.

Lanterns

Why am I so pathetic?

Love is lost. Emotions took their surgical tools and opened my chest; took their filthy hands and removed my heart. This was not a surgery. This was an autopsy. Flowers and romance: an assault that could not win the day, the woman who stood close. My arms couldn't overcome the distance. Transparency ruined attempts. Ghost-like resemblance kept me from reaching. Why was there so much resistance? Am I bleaching? Has my existence been completely whited-out? Am I invisible? Or does my being have no significant importance? If it's just ignorance, then I'll just be dead.

Small hollow: a fist-sized hole. Missing heart killed my soul: strings that gave this flesh life. And now I'm without both. Now I'm a different cut of cloth. I'm pulled butterfly wings. Achromatic replacements spread out its wingspan; I am a moth. I fly myself into specks of light: lanterns revealing what's left for me to live for. Electrocuted; the light kills me every time. Executed; life is a jokester and its trickery is murder. Lanterns are no guiding light, only cues for suicide. Life is a clown playing with fire and I am the burn victim.

So, here I am crashing into lanterns, repeatedly torching myself because I cannot come up with alternate patterns: better flight plans to move forward without scorching myself. Cupid pumped me full of arrows; I'm a Valentine pincushion. I can't move on and go forward, not while my heart is in her head. It's just too hard. My mind is in no shape to help me escape. I'd pull out these arrows and regain my composure to move ahead, except I risk bleeding to death. All those signs I should have read. I knew she had no interest, but I couldn't help myself. Drawn to her with permanent marker, dragged me right into her mouth even when I knew she hated me best. And now I'm drowning, drowning in acid in the pit of her stomach. I'm just another boy for her to digest because I sat there and let her chew me up. I let her swallow me like a cough drop. It must be true what I say, "Love is a Trojan Horse."

Devoured and left with misleading lanterns; movement is something I don't desire. Every forward motion I'm fire. Any motion backward I'm a leftover meal. I call *stalemate*. I'm in a frame of mind that is foreign to me but is very real. I feel like I'm in Narnia except I'm the population, though voices from others do seem to carry. This is a new world, a new phobia, a fully developed mental disability, possibly insanity, but I'm not going anywhere. I'm setting up camp in this nightmare. Here, I will be related to Stonehenge: ready to corrode when elements tell me to. Welcome to the great unknown. Welcome to desolation. I am never leaving here. This is where I will stand. This will be my forever.

Do not disturb.
Statue in progress.

A Lobotomy Is A Furnace

Hope you like your meat extra crispy and pumped full of GMOs.

Everybody wants to know what makes me tick, the cause for the way I think. This is why I'm strapped to this gurney and my vision is a little blurry. Monotone morphine shots every hour help me stay calm, help keep the sweat off my palms, as I stare at these white walls in a padded room where I giggle, laugh as hallucinations run free. I'm kept in this safe place, so I'll be okay for the doctors to torture me later, torture me with their electroshock therapy: their brain blaster. I've been electrocuted so many times with the voltage increased after every attempt, that I have scorch marks permanently burnt into the sides of my head. That has to be a crime, especially the one time when the electrodes caught fire. Why can't they give me pills and send me home? Because by the time they're done with me, I fear I'll be stiff, stiff, dead.

So, the worst has happened. Doctors say I'm too crazy and that deep-frying my brain isn't working. They tell me I am going in for surgery. I don't care as long as they keep the morphine train coming. They tell me they can only do one thing to help me, that a lobotomy fits my case and it's the only option left. I don't care as long as they keep the morphine train coming. They pump me with my best friend a lot more than usual, tell me everything is going to be okay, wheel me out towards the operating room, as my eyes roll into the back of my head and drool pours out my mouth like an opium waterfall. For now, it's squeaky wheels rolling down a dark hallway.

By the time I get to the operating room I'm in a full catatonic state. I can't move for the life of me. That's when I notice something isn't right. Must be this small room I'm in with the giant furnace. Panicking, I rock back and forth trying to escape, but I'm not moving. My brain is just working at the speed of petrified. I have never been so terrified and not have an expression on my face. Doctors fold up the gurney's legs and left me up on their shoulders as if they were pallbearers and walk me slowly towards the crematorium. Closer and closer; I'm sweating so much it's like I'm melting. Closer and closer; my hair singes. Closer and closer; my skin is peeling. Closer and closer; the white sheets catch fire. There's nothing I can do, except scream inside my head and listen to the echo – "This can't be real! A lobotomy is a furnace! This can't be real! A lobotomy is a furnace! This can't be real! A lobotomy is a furnace! This can't be real! A lobotomy is a furnace!"

THIS CAN'T BE REAL!
THIS CAN'T BE REAL!

Jack-O'-Lantern

If you're wondering if I was listening to Smashing Pumpkins when I wrote this, then you would be sadly mistaken. Clearly, I was listening to The Nightmare Before Christmas soundtrack.

Kneeling on the floor in the dark, staring at the haunting glow of television static. You can't see me moving but believe me when I say I'm frantic. Insanity is running wild throughout my entire circulatory system, causing an impenetrable mold around my brain. Holding still is how I keep myself under control, but as I ratio white spots to black spots, I am contemplating letting go. Curing the crisis that has found a home inside my mind was supposed to be destroyed by a single pill. Not believable considering the number of containers I've already gone through. If anything, modern medicine has left me far behind.

Zombie characteristics are fluent, evolving faster and faster, much stronger because they have hitched a ride on insanity's current. My face is now faceless. Body movement is down to a crawl. Hunger, extra thirsty, thirsty to keep myself down, extra small to keep myself locked in the stranglehold of misery. I'm hard as rock. I've never weighed so much or had the urge to hear a loaded gun cock, but as tears collect on the palms of my hands and puddles form, the tightrope I've walked my entire life reduces to a few strands. I'm sagging to the bottom, into an abyss of unlimited depth. Life is a hook and I am a worm. You can tell by countless bite marks I've endured, scars and missing flesh, all the close calls. It has come to the point where I want to be swallowed whole. Dangling. Struggling. Someone, murder me.

Like a jack-o'-lantern I'm hollow. We're two of a kind, except a jack-o'-lantern has a facial expression and our method of becoming is slightly different. My scalp was removed by a perfectly long, circular incision around my head as if the scalpel was spinning on a merry-go-round. A bone-saw was the culprit that opened up a large section of my cranium like I was being prepared for a lobotomy at the local asylum, then with unseen latex hands, my brain was removed, thrown down hard and stamped heavily into the ground. Like a jack-o'-lantern, I'm hollow, except it lost its orange flesh and seeds, and I've lost my mind, except it is brightened by a lit candle carefully placed inside it, where I am left in the dark in a state of loneliness I just can't handle. Like a jack-o'-lantern… Like a jack-o'-lantern… Do you see the pattern? Burn, jack-o'-lantern, burn. All I want is for me to return, to be normal once again, so burn, burn, burn.

Symbiote (Oh, Love Of Mine)

I could have gotten a cool symbiote like Venom or Carnage, but no... I got this fucking psycho instead.

Coma-attached mind separated from a heart struggling on life support. Our emotional boxing match has put me in my place, pulverized any happiness that once inhabited my face. Your incredible talent to destroy a human being with a vast verbal arsenal kills any meaning, any meaning on wanting to continue with continuing. This knife in my back is fairly deep. How long have you been conspiring against me? By the force of the jab, I would have to guess awhile. Any harder and I'd be lost to the ages in a state of perma-sleep. Any softer my frown would still be a smile. Oh, love of mine, hate guides your way most treacherously. Do not take it seriously. Oh, love of mine, your brain is beating faster than your heart. Relax and gather your senses. Work your lungs. Utilize your mouth. If you want me to take you seriously, you are going to have to work your lungs.

Arguments and fights; sometimes you make me want to punch out your lights. Your over-exaggeration of every situation is ridiculous. Your drama is clearly venomous because I'm terribly poisoned and still struggling to find an antitoxin. One way or another this has to end. One way or another, things have to mend. Stop blowing everything out of proportion. Things can be crystal; stop the distortion. For fuck's sake! We've been at each other's throats for so long, I can't recall what turned us into enemies to begin with. I can't remember at all. But for fuck's sake, everybody makes mistakes!

Your decibel range of your screams can put a banshee to shame. Evidence poised from shattered eardrums has resulted in constant earaches. Now deaf, I see you moving, marching in your rage parade, arms flailing and legs kicking, looking like you're about to explode. Oh, love of mine, pantomime grenade, breathe before you blow a hole in the road.

We should be able to fix this with a perfect kiss, a kiss that would disarm your fists: missiles that gave birth to these busted lips. But now, you're saying you want space and I don't know if I can do that, because I know I'd have to break my fingers to stop myself from calling you. I know I would have to paralyze myself to keep myself still. Now, you're saying this could be it. And with the number of wounds smothered with salt, I'm beginning to believe this is my fault. This mass confusion between two is way too much for us to endure. Oh, love of mine, let's spin together and intertwine. Let's be one with a double-fused spine: an invincible vertebrate with a mammoth-sized heart. Oh, love of mine, be my symbiote. Come into me; take a chance to make things right. Let's transform ourselves into one formidable force, and that way we will never lose faith in one another, for life without the other would hold no future. One without the other is failing against all odds. Without each other, we are nothing but corpses.

Please, take my hand.
Let's spin.

City Of Desolation

There's no place like home. There's no place like home. There's no place like home. Man, I could really go for some fucking heroin right about now.

I live in a city of desolation where buildings are ruins and people are broken statues: sculptures that fail to keep themselves from crumbling. I live in a city of desolation where superheroes are lynched, long since been extinct. I live in a city of desolation where villains are kings and victims hold their tongues because the closest hero is six feet down. I live in a city of desolation where there's no law, no justice, only sacrifice. I live in a city of desolation, a spreading mutation. I suffer in the worst part of Hell.

Murderers scurry the streets like rats, picking people off one by one like an unstoppable plague. Bodies fall one after another so quickly that they are put into stacks like random piles of raked autumn leaves, revealing the knives and gunshot wounds stuck in their backs until their graves can be dug. Here it seems the new dead always outnumber the old. Prostitutes line sidewalks and brighten them like streetlamps; every district is a red-light district. Sex here is ruled by rapists and tramps, where countless abortions are performed under the gun. Life can not flourish if everyone you trust is corrupt. The harbor is a sea of drugs where dealers fish past their limits and set up new hatcheries to increase the size of their wallets, causing a massive tidal wave of addiction, bringing an entire city to its knees. Criminals and politicians are allies: two against one. Robbed, robbed, taxed, taxed – citizens kicked when they are down. Empty pockets gather a fine collection of lint. Empty pockets force them to join their ranks. Here it's like guns versus tanks. I live in a city of desolation – the cesspool of the entire planet.

Grass is greener, much greener on the other side of the fence, but it's hard to escape when I replaced my mother with heroin and have to rely on a new source of sustenance. Freedom seems as far away as a journey in a fairy tale when I've been looted and looted, purged of everything I've owned. Because of that, I have let myself be recruited. From a murderer to a john and everything in-between, I have lost my way far into the dark. I have allowed myself to become scum of the Earth. Left behind; my sense of morality is gone. In the cave of my psyche, there is no sun to bring a stunning dawn. It has been conquered by my nocturnal override. This lifestyle I live has killed me. Blood on my hands and needle in my arm is proof that I have died and I am no longer human. I am a cockroach. I live in a city of desolation where there is no such thing as redemption. Because this... this is damnation. This... this is home, sweet home.

A Single Kiss To Kill

What I'm saying is - I loved someone and ruined it, because I was a fucking whore who couldn't ignore the whimsical spontaneity of my GIANT penis.

Walking with my head hanging down with a heavy shame. As I protect one-step worth of sidewalk from falling rain, I flip through thoughts like an unorganized index. Frustrated. I try to gather on what the hell just happened. But as not so tiny droplets strike against me like gunfire, I find myself swimming in these thoughts, drowning in the whole complexity of what the hell just happened. I'm finding it hard to keep my composure afloat, especially when persistence has come so difficult to acquire, though my determination for it is something to admire even if it isn't keeping me dry.

I feel uneasy, hopeless, so drenched like descending down in an ocean's darkness. Entrenched: sinking but secure, stuck. Walking forward pushes me backward, but it doesn't stop me from adding distance between love and failure. It doesn't stop me from remembering her. How could I forget when these raindrops stick like regret and sting like flashbacks? How was I supposed to know the situation was a trap and I was going to fall through one of the cracks? By my own stupidity, I am dumbfounded on how I neglected to keep my heart grounded. I am beginning to believe maybe I deserve to capsize.

Rain like memories — I am flooded by them. To stay buoyant and raise my lungs from becoming soaking wet, I would need to throw my sense of reason a lifejacket. To be rescued, I would have to seduce amnesia so I can forget and be able to lift my head above water. But this liquid curtain has been following me since I stepped outside, almost as if I had these grey

328

clouds on a leash. How am I supposed to recover when I can't erase everything that is a potential reminder? How can I move on when I won't be able to hurdle any emotional obstacles? Lust once again has wrapped me in its tentacles, force-fed me what I secretly desired, and left what actually mattered partially devoured. It is obvious. I am the worst out of any possible good.

I am trying to take this all in stride even when oncoming headlights come through the billowing fog like vague ideas that seem promising but are hard to define like a centuries-old corpse pulled from a Scottish bog: You have it but you can't quite make anything of it. To me, a liar, a concrete's umbrella... these blurry, yet beaming yellow orbs are bright stars: possible chances to solve my problem. But just as they come in clear, they disappear. And I am constantly reminded redemption, a solution is nothing but passing cars.

Sometimes all it takes is a single kiss to kill.

Burn Victim

See? This is exactly why I don't write inspirational shit. I'm the worst at it. I'm not kidding. I fell asleep four times, trying to edit this piece of garbage. It's one of the most boring poems I have ever written. By far.

Burn victim, burn victim, glance away from cycling mirrors. Look up; grow your stem. Rise above your reflection; take the time to bloom. Burn victim, burn victim, you are not ugly or the furnace's daughter. You are violently pretty, not Freddy Krueger so pull your vengeful claws out of your face. Trim, smile and glow. I know the horrors of your flashback attacks, how you are set ablaze every day. You melt more and more with every inferno; your scorched eyes tell the story. But you are not candle wax or ash grey. Defying the odds is glory. You are a beautiful immortal so stand tall. It's not your fault. Don't apologize. There is no need to say you're sorry. Burn victim, burn victim, I don't see scars, only a cocoon: damage you will overcome soon. Physical matter is not always fantasy. If you really want to be okay, you could heal yourself today. Don't you know anything is possible? Burn victim, burn victim, I know every now and then your skin boils because trauma is still scabbed to your brain. I see you struggling to fight off such pain and it can't be easy with only half a face. You can't solve an equation if it's not entire, so erase it and write your own; you will find your answer. Burn victim, burn victim, it must be hard to live where Hell came to visit. Walking inside your home must be excruciating like being pushed into a raging bonfire, but life is not all fire and brimstone. You're looking at the bigger picture with the wrong side of your face. If you don't peel away the past, you will never escape the fireplace. Burn victim, burn victim, you have suffered enough so do yourself a favour — change elements. Drink this glass of water and remember... nothing lasts forever.

Identity

Ever play that game - Guess Who? This poem is similar to that, except it's always me and everyone loses.

The great affliction of an identity crisis – I have touched this virus, known this virus for years. For I am its twin and it is my dead foetus attached: my reflection still breathing. I've tried to separate from it but it's an itch that can't be scratched. Attempts to cure myself have died terribly, leaving behind a spreading rash. Mass confusion of oneself – where a theatrical mask has become nothing but an excuse, an unwanted muse.

For years I've been hovering like a mangled neck broken in a noose, locked in a knot that won't come loose, swaying a lifeless body side to side. My name is this... but the sickness is serious. Gouged flesh revealed no answer. Cuts and open wounds acted as portals, gateways for a transplant that stole my blood and topped me off with some strange sludge. I feel dead, a corpse once human.

In a tiny secluded room behind a secret door, hidden beneath the attic floor, I sit with ripped out hair wedged between my fingers while I stare blankly out a small circular window, watching the sun spit out days like vomit, as the moon scavenges behind, chewing and swallowing them up like rats in steel dumpsters. This regurgitation of time is painfully slow. I need to look away, but my identity is smoke and mirrors: lit cigarettes and shattered glass. It's not my name I've forgotten, it's my purpose.

A change of scenery would do me good, a few hours out of this room, but my feet are bare and the floor is scattered with smashed objects: jagged spikes that once held my duplicates. I am so frustrated. I can't think. My brain is running out of ink, causing me to draw nothing but blanks. I might as well be a statue, a decorative piece in a museum, something to take up space in an empty corner because I don't know what else to do. The only thing now is to adapt with no identity, accept that I'm an unknown entity, and do the best I can to keep my sanity.

Not being able to pinpoint a reason for existence is just as bad as not having one at all. The miracle of life is pointless without importance.

I'm falling because I'm failing.
I'm failing because I'm falling.

Haunted House

Not scary but at least it isn't terrible.

Dark hallways stretching so far that they seem to lead into an abyss. And with no glimmer of light, I can't push through the blackness to extend my sight. Straight, straight, a perfect line, not one bend. Insanity tends to repeat itself no matter how often it tells me it's a friend. These passageways are ominous but I'm curious. I'm curious because I have a spine. How can I not walk down into possible oblivion? Every time I fall asleep, I awake in them as if they are starting lines, where I face fear and see if I will be rotten or live to turn pale another day.

Long red curtains – capes of glory specifically made for great rectangular windows that stand tall like powerful generals. These windows are open mouths inhaling cold wind, pushing red curtains in a twisted manner like butterflies escaping cocoons ready to flutter, lifting them high until they are horizontal. And when the breeze stops, red curtains float down like sheets as if putting these dark hallways to sleep. But horror never rests. You can always hear something creep. No time not to panic; fear is an insomniac. This cycle is continuous, carelessly leaving clues, making it obvious my imagination resides in a haunted house.

Winding staircases spiral up like Jack's beanstalk. Hungry giants wait above high at the top, licking their lips, hoping I will accept their dinner invitation. Safe to say these massive trolls will starve to death. There are too many other things to worry about than dealing with digestion. Like ghosts in the attic: angry poltergeists who have declared war on me. Their spirit brigade dominates in numbers, so I cut down the number of hours I slumber. Less chance for possession means more days human.

Then there are carnivores, morbid creatures who wallow in an unfinished basement: mounds of dirt, no cement, a wonderful place for an indoor cemetery. Down there is an illusion: filthy demons throwing beautiful promises at me like fireworks, trying to lure me in, crossing their slimy fingers to help ensure I will listen and come down, where they will mutilate me with teeth, maim with claws, devour me until I'm skull and crossbones. Needless to say, I don't go near the basement anymore.

Cobwebs are spotted here and there randomly, but with a sense of purpose like constellations waiting to be named. Black, black spiders inhabit these dens of death. And when I pass by, I can feel them stare as they suck the life from captured flies. If I were any smaller it would be a danger too close. At least there is one thing here I can easily decompose. Watch. Tomorrow, they will be a thousand times bigger, then I'll be a fly, a body pierced with venomous fangs, paralyzed, blood drank from underneath my skin, drained mummy-thin. It's a cruel way to die but that's nightmares for you.

Every step on these old floorboards there is a creak politely followed by stalking pictures that peek, glaring at me with infectious eyes like they are secretly casting spells, or seeing if a ghost will pull me through the ceiling, or a demon rip me through the floor. With chilling air where I can see my breath - morgue temperature, I would suspect Hell is freezing over but lack of ice means monsters stay alive. Will this haunted house ever be condemned? Related to Death or just damned - why I run this gauntlet every night I might never know. I only know I fucking hate it here but I have to sleep.

Felo-De-Se
(A Lost Game Of Hangman)

If you didn't have to look up "felo-de-se" in a dictionary, congratulations, you just impressed the hell out of me, kid.

Hanging with no real importance like a vague idea. Bloodletting from storm clouds - whole wrists divided. Under the circumstance, above a bloody area, floating here stranded, I'm about to find out if suicide, if this torture will be worth the ride. What do you think my chances are that Heaven can be resurrected from horror? Cowardice is an effective way to stay alive when your heart stings like an angry beehive. But I'm not afraid anymore. The nest must have been abandoned, because there's no more buzzing, no honey weakening my heart. It's vanished insects and dried honeycomb. Hence, why I sway from this noose, exposing wrists chopped like butchered meat. I had to make sure I wouldn't be able to shake myself loose. I couldn't go through this again. Blood loss drags me out slowly, pulls my head toward my feet to show me what I wanted has been given to me - asphyxiation and decay, my felo-de-se, a bruise necklace, eyeless face, skin choked blue, wrists open wider than floodgates; what a mess I have gotten myself into. Strangulation puts me in checkmate, allowing my blood to coagulate one last time. After many, many botched attempts I've achieved my freedom of choice. I'm dead... dead... dead, a lost game of Hangman. Finally, a promise kept.

Pumpkins
& Jack-O'-Lanterns

Best believe this is about a girl, and you better fucking believe it's not about my wife, and you better, better believe she fucking hates her, and better, better, better believe, I'm not telling her this poem is in this book, and you all better, better, better, better just shut the hell up about it.

Two jack-o'-lanterns reflecting shadows, graveyard scenery: a deformed skull and a Halloween tree. These shapes hang above our heads like a mobile, except no music compliments and no movement shows. They stay still like scorch marks in the ceiling. Pumpkins we carved with imagination and steel, glows, glows brighter than anything we've dissected before. Tiny flickering candles, miniature fire placed inside their hollow interior separates black curtains, revealing you and I, big eyes and bigger smiles, bodies half-submerged under water looking like prey in a rabid animal's foaming mouth, in a tub erupted with soft bubbles. I didn't notice this vague resemblance until now, because at the time I was too busy trying to figure out how... how walking through life so blindly, I was able to find someone as wonderful as you.

Decoding our eyes and solving the combination, we took the freedom of our sight and locked them together - fixated on one another, suffering from tunnel vision. I knew that night was a time and place I wouldn't soon forget, a memory I would always remember, sniffing that pleasant scent of freesia roaming the air while my wrinkled fingers twirled the tips of your black hair, as we conversed about us and nonsense. Every inhale, every finger rotation, every word, it all came together like clockwork, absolutely perfect. Alzheimer's could dine and devour my entire brain but will never conquer that moment. It will never claim your existence. Britney, you have to understand something - Without you that moment is nothing. Without you, that moment would just be déjà vu I'd repeatedly forget. You might not know it but know it now - You give my world colour. You give it life. You... You give everything I do purpose. And I can only hope you feel at least half the way I do, half as much as I love you.

"Love is like ripples in the water.
They stretch out as if they are questionable timelines.
Time always finding its end."

We have nothing to worry about.

Cemetery

Dying must suck. Can you imagine being trapped in a cemetery for eternity and your neighbour is a fucking dick? I can't even.

Behind a large gate mothering the dead, humans deceased, oh so still underneath epitaphs that can no longer be read, they sleep. Moonlight accents their existence of rot and skeletons, breathing trees and crumbling tombstones, unveiling exactly why such a heavy lock forces a chain to hold iron bars close together: Grave-robbers desecrate. Necrophiliacs penetrate. Widows wait. Defending a cemetery like a fortress is the only way to respect its tenants, to keep out anyone with a working pulse. At night, the gate stays closed to protect the decomposed, holding until dawn, until the arrival of a mourning hearse: a dark carriage ushering in another life gone. This is just the way things are: Life follows the death car.

Beyond the border of the living and the dead, murky owls perch themselves on twisted treetops, searching for rodents by bobbing their heads side to side, all around as wide eyes eagerly await for the chance to turn red and sharp talons impatiently extend, willing, ready to spill blood on hollow ground. Crows also have their place. They stand loyally on headstones like royal guards keeping watch for trespassers, prepared to give warning at a moment's notice, waking their masters: ghosts who kill if disturbed. A murder of crows is most faithful and is greatly rewarded with owl leftovers.

Rogue spectres wander, re-enacting what once was: human behaviour, life. If they weren't already dead, their denial would be the death of them. Stem by stem, they pick flowers. Massing a colourful bouquet, they pretend to smell sweetness and pollen, but from a heartbeat already stolen, senses fail in their midst of decay. They dance in the rain but don't get wet. Loved ones tell them they're missed but can't hear a word. Engulfed in scenic beauty, but vision is blurred. Tongues dry-out and fall to waste, permanently halting the ability to taste. When everything has been taken away even heroes can become villains. You can not trust an apparition, no matter how persuasive, how seductive they are. First opportunity of possession, I assure you they will take it. You can not trust what is dead. You can not trust the desperate.

A cemetery is a scary place with its overshadowing trees rooted so deep, you would think they came up from Hell, especially when strong winds puppeteer their branches like a witch flailing her arms when conjuring up an evil spell, but this forest is just trees and nothing else: umbrellas for corpses. Portentous graves have a certain way of sticking out, leaving an unsettling effect stronger than ominous charms, but it's just stones and dirt, garden beds for wilted flowers, homesteads for wealthy cadavers, granite statues to jog memories and grand mausoleums, death museums, mediums to honour potential zombies are abundant. They remind us of inevitability, how we are not immortal. In time, we all end up attending our own funeral.

Underneath a beaming moon, a cemetery becomes surreal like a carefully detailed model, a diorama built by an over-imaginative lunatic. Ruin by ruin, a different story is told, giving this universe multiple personalities like a schizophrenic. Solace and misery; fatality by fatality. Relatives laid all in a row, loved ones we could no longer hold, hearts we were forced to let go, rest in caskets like unborn foetuses nestled comfortably in Mother Nature's womb. No excuses; death is a disease we contract. In time, we all end up in tombs. A cemetery is our space. We are its planets and insects are our disappearing act: carnivorous meteors that crash through us. No excuses; life follows the death car.

LIIAN VARUS GRIMM

H ere we are. We've come far, you and I. Kudos for not abandoning ship. I stopped editing when we were in 2003. Figured I'd be alone by now so it didn't matter if I quit putting Vaseline on this pig. Way to keep misery company. You're outstanding. I see a Subway gift card in your future. Welcome to 2009, passenger. That year was spent spinning old fairy tales in my image like a defunct god scrambling for relevance. I made them worse. Some had promise, but like a drunk hangman - I botched their execution. Come to think about it, can I get sued for publishing them? Guess I'll find out. Not worried. I'm in the middle of bankruptcy. Can't get blood from an anaemic. Am I right? Pound it. My evolution was still unfolding like one of those metal chairs, you hit people with. I was testing new waters to see my darkness' ripple effect. What shape, what colour, what creature would breach from these depths? It's interesting how many twists and turns, interstellar dimensions your mind has stored up there. Think I even saw a Zellers up there once. Every poem written brought more out of me - words mostly. What? Thought I was going to say something prophetic? You're cute. I will say this - this was the year I began pondering the idea of publishing a book. Fast forward nine years later - *Oh, To Be Human* was born. It's like *Is Stranged.* except it comes with a voucher for a free tennis ball at your local sports store. Any colour of your choosing. As long as that colour is green. I lied. *Oh, To Be Human* is a picture book about trees in precarious sexual positions.

Jill Doesn't Come Tumbling After

Wait. Aren't Jack and Jill siblings? SCANDALOUS.

Jill, we've held hands and prevailed over steep hillsides. For what felt like centuries, we've seized slopes the size of mountains and outsmarted jagged embankments that vanished suddenly from rising tides. Our journeys, our adventures were mere fantasies extended from our imaginations. Every day we climbed even when we didn't have to. We ventured with no expectations. Perhaps it was love, a hidden secret between me and you. I was never sure, but one day a story will be written about us, about our voyages to old wells, wishing fountains where we threw gold coins to buy our dreams but left with only a wooden bucket filled with dirty water. One day the world will know of Jack and Jill. We will inspire, motivate thousands of explorers to create bigger legacies. But because of you, I will never see what fame is capable of. Jill, because of you I've expired. People will not know the truth inside the lies you will surely tell. Jill, because of you I've missed the chance to retire before age forbade me to defeat the tiniest hill. Jill, because of you I've lost everything. Most importantly, I lost out knowing if pure love was really true. And for that I hate you. Jill, I had strong aspirations for you and I, but you said goodbye. You went for the kill, pushed me into your lie, screaming, "Die! Die! Die!" as the dark swallowed me whole, deep into our last well, down the gaping throat of our final hill. Now blackness surrounds me like closed eyes. It's peaceful. Far inside somewhere in the middle of nowhere, I give my mind permission to explore. It finds, it tells me that fetching a pail of water was our symbolism of love. I slaved for an idea I thought was beautiful and it taught me a terrible lesson: Living in a perfect world like a painting, a vivid portrayal where the grass is shaded green, the sky is coloured blue, and in-between, an artist's rendition of a well on a hill with a boy and a girl merrily ascending toward it is impossible, a simplistic world where a boy and a girl skip beside one another while hand-in-hand try not to let their sides split from uncontrollable laughter is clearly impossible. This happiness can not be Elysian, because such a thing doesn't exist. I don't know why I was betrayed by you, but I do know how this ends. Diving farther, farther, too far, I am left for dead and you don't come tumbling after.

Another Android

The only thing that's going to destroy mankind is mankind. If you're looking for inspiration, then you've purchased the wrong book, my friend.

Sometimes I feel like a human being amongst people: cardboard cut-outs with no sense of morality. It's cannibal eat cannibal, every one protecting themselves, leaving others to fend against others. It is because of this mental ferocity, why there is the existence of strangers. Up in smoke like a magic trick, there goes humanity. Everything seems automatic: a world controlled by synthetic flesh gift-wrapped over robotics. Something is playing mechanic, replacing hearts with tiny motors and souls with electrical currents. This mystery is misery. If not corrected, our downfall will be imminent. My body is ripe; check my blood type. Am I human or am I machine? I fear I am becoming what I fear: another android through the assembly line.

Black Widow
(Along Came A Spider)

Women who own spiders have daddy issues.

Underneath a leafless tree, a little girl's body is sprawled out in the grass, covered in curds and whey. Lying very still beneath a darkened sky of grey, she's directing silence with her stiff limbs pointing most innocently. Strong winds seem to desperately push fallen leaves against her, almost like some unseen force is trying to wake her up and place her back on her tuffet, but this is no nursery rhyme. She's paralysed to the courtesy of time. Happy endings are for the close-minded; this little girl could not be any more dead.

There is a vicious spider bite, two tiny circles punctured on her hand where infection started to spread and has badly eaten it into submission. I can see how far the venom stormed up her arm, where it shot up like twisted roots looking for a strong foundation, a home to grow from, somewhere to wreak havoc. It sieged into her heart and made her toxic, convincing her body to turn on itself. By her swollen, burst veins brushing themselves underneath her skin like they were people buried alive, frantically trying to crawl their way out from six feet of dirt, I can tell nothing could intervene. There was no way she was going to survive.

As I drown myself into her eyes, into her massive black holes staring out into the abyss, my focus becomes discouraged by a faint rustling from beneath the foliage. Beside me, a red leaf subtly shifts, then lifts, unmasking two black legs. The culprit comes out of hiding. A black widow slowly emerges, concealing her red hourglass that is tucked away underneath. It

344

weaves in and out secretly between dead leaves, looking so cunning as if it were the Queen of Thieves. But vengeance is lurking. Without thinking my foot plunges, stomping down on the eight-legged killer. Grinding. Grinding. Smearing its guts into the ground deeper, deeper, as I grin to the crunching sound of crushed life. The arachnid is no more. A bitter-sweet ending to a terrible tragedy. A sad story that started with...

"Along came a spider, who sat down beside her..."

The Tower

Statutory rape, anyone?

One day I was wandering through the forest, looking for reasons why I was there in the first place when I heard an ethereal voice: a song capable of resurrecting hearts from corpses new and old. It was such a powerful sound, I even questioned if I dug myself out of the ground. With my interest peaked and my heart pounding, I followed the lulling serenade. I followed and I followed until the forest hollowed. And there she was, locked away in a medieval tower where the only entrance and exit was a small window high above. From it, she was combing her golden hair, singing, still in tune, romanticizing the sun and moon. She was so ravishing she could tempt gods. She could make Aphrodite jealous. If she wasn't entombed in that ruin, she could make the world burn. Like Helen of Troy, wars would be waged for her beauty. She could direct Hell on Earth, unleash misery. If she wished it to be.

Her name was Rapunzel, a girl imprisoned by an evil enchantress, Dame Gothel; put there because her father was a coward. I was fifteen years older than her, but I was so deeply in love; my vision was narrow. I didn't care about the age difference or consequences of my actions. There isn't much you can do when you're shot by Cupid's arrow. I am a prince and she was going to be my princess. I was going to be king and she was going to be my queen. If I was a god, she would have been my goddess. This is love I speak of, not infatuation. Though, I was infatuated about how I could love someone so young. It might be wrong but believe me when I say this: I would risk the guillotine for one long kiss. Unfortunately for me, the only thing stronger than love is tragedy. We tried to devise a plan to escape, except Dame Gothel's crueler version of an oubliette made freedom

346

virtually impossible. One entrance, the one exit was too high up. Jumping would definitely be a leap of faith, but I didn't want her to play roulette on a safe landing and cheating death. All that was left was for me to exile myself from the world and grow old with her in the gloomy tower. For Rapunzel, I was willing to give up freedom, my future kingdom. Throwing everything away to be with her was the easiest decision I've ever made. Nothing was going to keep us apart, not even a dark sorceress like Dame Gothel. With God as my witness, we would have our happiness.

Now, Rapunzel's hair was really long, endless it seemed. She told me to use her golden mane to scale up the steep wall and to hold tight to make sure I didn't fall. She told me not to worry, she would deal with the pain as long as I hurried, because she couldn't wait to hold me. So quickly as I could, I scurried, but every step I took, the rope got thinner and thinner, for I was ripping the hair off her head. Rapunzel's screams got louder and louder. I wanted to let go, but she urged me on. I should have let go because now she's gone. Gravity took over; it snapped her neck and scalped her. I just weighed too much.

What happened after is a blur, but now I'm in the tower, covered in blood, suffering from two broken legs, kept company by Rapunzel's corpse blankly staring at me from a dark corner. She looks like she has something to say beyond her beginning stages of decay, but nothing is said. Rapunzel is dead, and I'm not too far behind.

Glass Impersonator

PEEK-A-BOO! I C-4 YOU!

Blue eyes captivated in a bedroom mirror, waiting in anticipation for something inexplicable to unfold. Past the blur, through scarce clarity, sanity becomes harder, more unrealistic to hold. Delirium invades, calling itself *Insanity*, and etches letters of its identity in bold. I'm piercing into another dimension, waving to myself from the other end of the spectrum. A split second later I wave back. My image doesn't copy what I do; I imitate my glass impersonator. This delay of acknowledgement makes me wonder who is who. Am I anything less significant?

Sometimes I believe I'm not human, just my reality's replicate. *Obsessed* is short form for *fucking obsessed*. I am fucking obsessed with this delusion I have inflicted upon myself. I am not flesh and blood. I am possessed, a re-enactment. My entire purpose in life is to prove to my owner he exists. If I am the glass impersonator, this would make sense why I always fail to move forward: I live in a world where everything is backward. I am an actor portraying a genuine character: lunacy shaking hands with dementia praecox. I've stumbled into a labyrinth, found my way out, came back with a mind anchored by heavy rocks. Confusion is spreading rapidly from my crushed mentality. I'm tripping in and out of crazy. I'm real. I'm a hallucination, a bastardized cousin of an apparition. I'm a shadow coloured in, a figment of imagination, anything but human.

When I look at myself in the mirror, I brace myself for my duplicate to stretch his arms out and pull me through. Sometimes I'll glare for hours for an opportunity to fuse, but I'm constantly disappointed by my glass impersonator. We are Siamese twins, a separated pair split by a successful operation, but one of us got sucked into a portal. Now, we both live in a different world forever to roam, never complete. Yes, I may be thinking way too far out of the box, but that's what happens when you drown yourself in your thoughts: your mind dwindles until logic becomes obsolete. I try to tell myself I only feel this way because a few threads of sanity snapped, but that doesn't stop me from feeling trapped. I want to solve this mystery. I want to feel free.

My mirror is caked with C-4. I'm going to exterminate my glass impersonator. With one push of the button on this detonator, I'll find out who is fact by the one who stays intact. If we both die in the blast, then I will surely know every staring contest I've ever had with myself really did end in a draw. Reflection: two halves halfway from being whole. One catastrophic explosion: to go from empty to full. Soon I will see if my thesis is true. Here's to connecting parallel universes, or possible extinction. Glass impersonator, I see you are prepared to destroy me too. So, on the count of three, let's unleash our sickness on one another. Ready? *One... Two... Three!*

Three Billy Goats Snuffed

Baaaaaaaaaaa...

Starvation grows on a barren wasteland where three goats have engorged themselves. Gluttony reigned supreme with a coercive hand. Now what was a meadow is now a harvester of scarab beetles, a dry, dry desert in the midst of building an array of monumental sandhills. East of Eden is lost, but the west still flourishes. It sits there peacefully as its tall grass sways calmly from warm winds, convincing three rapacious billy goats to devour its plentiful greenery until it too lies in ruins, until it is a sea of shattered hourglasses violently pushed into waves forming mountainous dunes. The west is a tempest yearning for the chance to whirl its own sandstorms.

Eden is divided by a deep, rocky, fast-moving creek, but a small bridge allows passage; it's an extension to the other ridge. A good enough reason for three hungry goats to gallivant across a crossing poorly built. Drowning is a minuscule risk; these four-legged locusts are famished. They will have the west pressed against their palates. Their insatiable cravings won't cease 'til every piece of grass has vanished. Three billy goats. Who would have known they would be the apocalypse to shrivel Eden down into desolation? Every mouthful swallowed for digestion, colours Eden closer to the shade of an eclipse, and there's not a person to stop them because everyone is in Hell, burning; everyone is a sinner. So not wasting any time to get their tongues wrapped around the verdant pasture, they eagerly make their way across the rickety old bridge, to end what they have begun.

The smallest of three makes it across with ease, ready to finish what he started. The middle-sized one gets across with a breeze, prepared to finish what he started, but both brothers are selfish and decide not to wait. They turn away to dine without their big brother, giving themselves a great chance to hog this illustrious banquet before he bullies his way in and takes over. As soon as they take their first bite, they hear splashing and thrashing; their brother has fallen in. Frantic; he's drowning, drowning. His brothers looking, looking on. Sickening groans and blood gushing, gushing from smashing against sharp rocks. His brothers are frightened and aren't rushing to help him to shore. They sit; watch in horror as he is taken under. Not quite understanding what just happened, they walk backward very slowly, not taking their eyes off the suddenly calm water. They look at each other like humans sharing sadness. They look at each other like humans feeling what it's like to be one less while using their peripherals from their odd-shaped eyes to keep a constant view of where their brother was lost, where he submerged into his watery grave, where Nature took its course.

Just when all seems hopeless, the creek regains life and forms a series of widening ripples. To their surprise, their brother emerges out of these resurrecting circles, but he looks lifeless. His eyes are down. All four legs are broken, but still, he is able to walk. Limping closer, closer; they call out to him, but he doesn't talk. He is maimed beyond maimed, cut, sliced, gashed. Wool around his stomach is bloody. Their brother's body is badly bashed from the creek's puncturing rocks, but his pace is steady. As he gets only a leg-length away, they call out to him again. No answer. Drool is occupying his tongue. Sensing something is very wrong, they call out to him hastily. That's when they see it: a spiked club pushed out their brother's guts, held by a slimy brown hand. Before they have time to react, a grotesque troll bursts out their brother's skin and bludgeons both of them on the head. Barbarically he crushes their skulls with his large wooden object, past the point of being dead. He then grabs their hind legs with his giant minotaur-like mitt and drags their battered corpses toward the biblical tree where Adam and Eve are buried. There he will sink his carnivorous teeth into his kills, reward himself with freshly plucked apples after their meaty bones are cleaned, then go back to hiding, back to playing guardian. Proving even the most gruesome of creatures are not always the evil ones.

Ringmasters' Sewer Circuses

Step right up! Step right up! Oops, you're dead.

Circuses are travelling insane asylums harbouring the lunacy of clowns, minimum security prisons disguised to lure in unsuspecting patrons. Circuses are rogues; they aren't affiliated with any crime syndicate, only diabolical ringmasters. Ringmasters direct traffic for thieves, rapists and murderers: face-painted criminals in rainbow jumpsuits, clowns. Beware of backflips, jumping jacks and other wacky antics; they are synchronized distractions, open invitations for your eyes. Be careful of colourful acrobats; they are kaleidoscope illusionists. It is not fun and games, but a bright sign of danger. Stand aware. Pay attention, or there will be missing wallets, untamed perverted acts and knives wedged in backs. Do yourself a favour - skip the popcorn; it's laced with tranquilizer. One bite and you'll find yourself lucky to be alive. Do not eat this buttery appetizer. You'll wake up numbering fingers on your hand, crying you couldn't count to five because of a stolen wedding ring. Clowns are fiendish jokers; don't be provokers. Stay away from the circus; under the big tent, there is no justice. Forget the bears in tutus, dancing elephants, tightrope walkers and trapeze death-defiers. Buying a golden ticket is not a pass to see the show. It's a voucher for your newly purchased casket. You have to believe me when I tell you this. Circuses multiply clowns like parasites spread disease: swallowing the innocence of small towns with ease, without any amount of remorse. Once ringmasters figure out how to take control of cities, circuses will form into corrupt corporations. The good will be flushed into sewers where circuses first hatched, where they took in our unwanted abortions, put them back into fresh abdomens, giving birth to a carnival army of clown henchmen, turning our children against us. We have to burn them!

Burn everyone! Before we are all victims of the circus!

Red

She died for a basket of blueberry muffins. Remember that.

Down goes the sun sheepishly to another part of the world, surrendering time to an emphatic dusk with paintbrush in-hand, darkening the sky a glossy black. The forest quiets with a sudden hush, as the moon is recaptured with the stroke of a brush. Horror scenery complete. Little Red Riding Hood needs to move her feet. Nocturnal beasts are awake and savage. She doesn't have much time to reach her grandmother's cottage. Maniacal creatures are already in the midst of stalking her, tracking her down. The scent of her young essence has alerted every monster of her presence. A horde of biting mouths give chase; salivating tongues lead the way. In this spooky forest, bloodshed is a constant shadow - drool bitten into flesh.

Playfully skipping, Little Red Riding Hood hears sticks breaking and leaves rustling. Throughout the wood, she hears the orchestrated sounds of predators howling. Scared almost lifeless, she drops her basket filled with sugary sweets; tries to outrun sharp claws and pointy teeth. Hundreds of eyes orbit around her like hostile planets closing her in, turning a winding dirt trail into a feeding gauntlet, but she keeps running, hoping to escape the meat grinder. In the distance, she sees a light. Her grandmother's cottage is in sight; salvation sits on the horizon. Little Red Riding Hood might have a chance. If her feet don't break she just might make it.

Running faster than she ever has; she's close, but the arch of a soiled-breached root seemingly mischievously put holds her foot like a bear trap, throwing her cruelly to the ground. Powdered with dirt, bloody knees, shaken up, she recovers quickly and continues to run to where it is safe and sound. She makes it and wastes no time banging on her grandmother's door. She sees her grandmother staring at her fearfully through a window beside her. Tearfully, she begs her to let her in. But she won't. She yells at Little Red Riding Hood, "You're a wolf! You're a wolf! You're a wolf! My dream told me so! You're a wolf!" Little Red Riding Hood tries to convince her it's safe, but her grandmother is stuck in her delusion; she won't risk an intrusion. Desperate, Little Red Riding Hood grabs a rock to smash a window, make an exit. Winding her arm back, she stops mid-throw as her tiny heart sporadically skips, because of a frightening reflection licking his lips: a werewolf standing poised behind her, twitching to murder. She has one direction to go, to live but her grandmother won't let her in.

Trapped in a moment where everything is still, except the danger that proudly announces itself - the werewolf; Little Red Riding Hood is left for the kill, helplessly forced to watch the inevitable. With her terror-expanded eyes, they seem to inhale the werewolf as he lunges towards her like two cosmically-charged black holes swallowing anything in their path. From the gravitational pull, he knocks her down and sinks in his claws and teeth, mauling her. Little Red Riding Hood cries in agony as her clothes tatter and blood splatters. She reaches out towards her crazy grandmother, but she doesn't bother. Her insanity insists her granddaughter is a wolf in disguise. Little Red Riding Hood screams out one last time. Her hand drops to the dirt. Then silence. Betrayed by a paranoia-deranged grandmother who watches on and a hunter who must have left with the sun, Little Red Riding Hood didn't have a chance. Her young corpse says it all: Having a red cape does not always mean you're a superhero. Sometimes it makes you a target for a raging bull.

The werewolf picks up the remains of Little Red Riding Hood and tosses her over his shoulder with ease, fleeing quickly into the Hundred Acre Wood as he speaks softly to himself in a sinister voice, "Innocence is better complimented with violence."

SeweRat

I'll gnaw on your dick if you say you love me.

I chewed through my heart, gnawing off any lasting remnants of you, and yet, I had the nerve to crawl back into you like a wounded pet. What I did was criminal, but this selfish act seems stable, or will at least have to do.

Your love is surprisingly potent toward a rodent, a rat like me. Allowing my plague and I to return says a lot about your vulnerability: You'll do anything to be infested with vermin.

You are a sewer I call home: Eden locked away underneath a manhole. I don't know why I wanted to roam, to scurry distance between us, but I've explored and found the outside world ruthless. I found out life without you is cruel. Explanation for my disappearance? I have none. I only know when I am with you I need no sun. There isn't a sun in this entire universe that can warm me like you can.

We are meant for each other: you, me, your tunnels to forgotten destinations and rivers of human excrement. Together, we thrive: you, me, your crocodile smiles and missing person files. Alive above subway stations, below other populations, we will live the love story between a rat and a sewer.

Let's Kiss

When I wrote this, I was struggling with figuring out if I wanted to be single or really wanted a cigarette. Turned out, I just wanted a cigarette. What? Separating love and addiction is practically impossible.

Cracked lips pressed down on a lit cigarette. Inhaling, dragging a burning amber closer to touch, hoping the smoke from exhaling lungs carries away the past, and I'll finally be able to forget that love died way too fast and destroyed so much. Smoking does do its part of acting as an anaesthetic, but the cancerous film wedged between my fingers reminds me of the painful memories of us which still lingers. Our love should be glowing red, but failure to keep things bright has caused my cigarette's amber to burn redder. You feel utterly dead; I sympathize. My heart is a zombie eating my brain, so by looking into your eyes I can see I'm far deader.

You did your best to rip a dream from an idea and make it come true. I succeeded in its destruction by pretending I could live such a life without you. Now staring at this empty prescription, I can see what I did was wrong. Substituting my pills with ignorance was not worth the price I paid: the loneliness between us my selfish decision made. Maybe our half hearts don't quite match, but you know how to stitch. If we re-enact our last kiss and make it anew, together we can figure out how to make them fit, because I can't picture living a life without you. I have refilled my prescription to prove the things I say are true. So, let's kiss with an eternal passion to make it impossible for us to unglue. Erase the past with me and let's push forward as one.

You might not ever really forgive me; I understand this. And I know not everything can be healed from a kiss; I understand that. It's no big secret I am far from perfect but believe me when I say I have changed. Lies have not tainted these lips, so believe me when I say I'm dying knowing what it's like to be estranged from someone I cannot exist without. Be my sun and murder this eclipse. Let's kiss. Cut this noose loneliness hangs me by or be my executioner and leave me lifeless. Choose. You have your doubts, but I feel the love you have for me when we see eye-to-eye. Give me another chance, our first second dance. Let's waltz past my faults and create a real epic love story. I'll flick my last unlit cigarette; kick my bad habit. If you believe I am truly sorry, if you choose to love me, let's kiss and bind. Let's fuck like wild lovers; if you don't mind. Let's rekindle what was lost, what I took away: love I had no right to feel in the first place.

I'll replace my looming cancer in exchange for forever: you and I side by side. If you want to checkmate the past and reset our love in the present, let's kiss. If you wish the worst for me, then light this cigarette in my mouth and leave me hanging in agony; desert me in loneliness' noose. If things can't be different I want to self-destruct. A life without you? I would rather die. If I am not to be forgiven, kiss me goodbye. No matter your decision, let's kiss. It's all I ask.

So, will you?
Will you have me once more?
Shall we kiss?

The Relocation Of Necropolis

The Walking Dead was inspired by this poem. No. You can't convince me otherwise. Rick Grimes is my real dad.

Piles of dirt breach from the soil like pregnant mothers about to burst; damp wombs saturated with moisture will ease the birthing process. Decayed fingers wiggle out Mother Earth like worms with a vague sense of awareness, vulnerable to hungry birds who are dying to digest. Green fingers stretch out into blue forearms. Blue forearms flail into black shoulders. Black shoulders push up rotting heads and rotting heads direct to finish resurrection. One by one like daisies all in a row, the living dead population starts to grow. Hell must be full because it's spitting up decomposition.

Zombies trudge with flesh-starved palates moaning in Mother Earth's vast nursery, searching for her copious amounts of milk. In threatening waves, they pour out from their shallow graves, rise from autumn-bleached cemetery grounds, and hunt for their kill like rabid bloodhounds. The cemetery is quiet, vacant; Necropolis is a ghost town. Abandoned tombs and disturbed bouquets are all that remain. It's an invasion; the dead are coming. It's a death parade marching in the 21st-century apocalypse, black paint putting on the final coat to humanity's eclipse, a pandemic that's hungrier than anything else, the relocation of Necropolis.

Outnumbering life itself and wedged so tightly together as they march out into the city, maggots are able to squirm into different hosts without the risk of falling. Swimming like parasitical sea serpents, they burrow and chew through dead matter. With so much decay, maggots can be gluttonous until the dead scatter. Darting like famished projectiles, they stick and dine on rot like empty leeches. With such a long food source, maggots can eat for miles and miles, until the dead find their victuals. Easily these tenacious larvae damage. Similar to their dead counterparts, they are just as savage. Infinite zombies imitate half-eaten apples with their destructors still sporadically slithering in multiples. If it weren't for murders of crows weakening the maggots' bodily transitions, the dead would have surely succumbed to their own physical conditions. So, with pecking beaks acting as guardian angels, the dead press on.

With the first humans coming into sight, zombies quickly break formation and chase after. Like ravenous vultures in flight, they circle and swoop in for the kill. People are caught in carnage and confusion, as they're picked off one by one with ferocious precision. Like any spreading of a superior virus, the relocation of Necropolis will happen within the day. Initial bites from deceased strangers have got family members devouring family members. The city is disoriented, infected, overrun with unimaginable dangers. City streets are stained red from death chewing on live flesh. With only a few stragglers left of the human race, humanity is on the verge of annihilation. With these creatures still hunting in maniacal droves, it's just a matter of time before complete extinction. By the time the morning sun comes up rolling up past the horizon, all that will be left are reanimated corpses and severed body parts. The relocation of Necropolis is cannibalism. The relocation of Necropolis is Armageddon. The relocation of Necropolis is only the beginning. Cemeteries around the world are vengeful mothers that won't stop birthing until all their young are eating. The relocation of Necropolis is a mother's scorn. The relocation of Necropolis is the end of the world.

LIIAN VARUS SURE DOES LOVE HIS REMIXES

It's so nice to see you! I was worried you wouldn't make it past my insulting renditions of old children's stories. You look exhausted. You deserve a break. Wait. Don't get up yet. There are a few more of them in this chapter, too. You don't seem happy. Would this be a bad time to mention the incest poem? You're right. One thing at a time. Not sure if it will erase your obvious buyer's remorse, but 2010 was a promising year. I swear. My abilities as a poet glimmer through. If only slightly. There are many examples of hope throughout. No. I can't give you a goddamn refund. Please stop asking. You made the conscious decision to buy this. Live with it like everybody else. I'm laughing because there is nobody else. You're the only one who bought it. You're suffering alone. Sorry. But my growth... so less shitty than before, right? You're angry. I see that. Need a moment? Come on. Don't stop now. You've come so far. Um... you going to share that cigarette? Okay. Okay. I've crossed a line. My apologies. Listen. You don't have to do this. It's fine. Quit. I won't tell anyone. No one would believe me that someone bought this book anyway. It's your word against mine. I have less influence than a dead mime. I appreciate you, you know. Thanks for being with me through this endeavour. No. I didn't fart. I told you. It's just the book. It's shitty.

Medusa
(A Gorgon's Last
Chance For Love)

So fucking hard right now.

Medusa, you are lonely and I want you to admit it. You might have these fucking snakes and their sinister smiles, but what is the worth of their scales and venom? Is love starvation worth this ophidian tandem? You might be coldblooded but I have kissed colder reptiles. Medusa, I am not Poseidon. I have not come to force myself underneath your gown. I am not a messenger of Athena. I am not here to add to your monstrosity. Medusa, I am not Perseus, so stand down. I do not want your head for a trophy. You are a Gorgon, but if the stories are true and Pegasus lies within you, then there must be a part of you that's still human. There has to be something inside that makes you pure. Please Medusa, slay the hydra slithering and coiling from your head, make them all acephalous, tongues without a hiss, fangs less than dangerous. Leave the Gorgon; remember what it was to be human. Surely, you don't want to be alone forever. Do you, Medusa?

I know what you're thinking; stop it. I know the severity of your stare: a gaze upon you is an ageless nightmare. I am aware of the curse that's scabbed over your eyes. I see your cave is decorated with hundreds of stone statues: untrustworthy onlookers who got too close to you. I am not invincible. I am mortal, easy to vanquish. Your stare can harden my flesh. I can be added to your collection of remembrance: another victim to remind you of your sculpture-trance. You don't need to know who I am, or how I came to know of your existence. Just know if you'll have me I will remove my eyes. Medusa, oh Medusa, for you I am willing to go sightless, so you can stop from living loveless. Take my hand; surrender your addiction to manipulate sand. Kiss me; together we can alter mythology, if only slightly. But if you want to stay this way... If you want your asps and to turn everyone grey, then I will look at you. I will be another piece of memorabilia to your damnation because it's either me or no one. So, what do you want, Medusa? Think about it hard, because I could be your last chance for love.

Organism

Oh yeah, baby, dissect me harder.

I am a hideous person. There is some innocence left in me but it's mostly filth. I'm a monster, an abortion resurrected inside a dumpster. I can stretch a smile but not without guilt. I have no right to display such an expression. Pulling the corners of my mouth ear to ear might seem flawless but it can take a lifetime, a long while. Everything is strange when you're adored by depression. Yes, by eye it takes less than seconds but to grin that far, it be faster for me to walk a mile. I could step out of the fog if I forgive myself for everything I've done but I can't make amends. Darkness won't remove itself from my pupils; I can't see the promise of a burning sun. This eclipse bestowed to me keeps my judgement cloudy, my understanding of myself dark and murky. Depression tells me it's a friend, but it's a shade of the spectrum I cannot bend. I can't tell if it's lying. I only hear it's propaganda: the satisfaction one gets when dying. I try not to listen but it's the only thing that glistens.

They say love comes in all forms; mine is a sickness that squirms. It has built a niche inside my brain and a tunnel to my heart. I am its playground; it moves about freely without discretion. Depression is a living organism. I have felt it spawn. With what? I don't know, but I can hear eggs cracking. I can hear its young hatching; new life is crawling around inside. Logic is anchored down by the extra weight; my sanity is about to capsize. My flesh is ripe. There's oxygen in my windpipe, but my soul has died. I am vulnerable, under arrest, and maybe it's for the best. Suicide: A future I kept at bay with _hellos_. Now, it's a lifestyle welcomed with one goodbye. A noose can sway me loose; it can separate years and years of agony. Asphyxiation will be the hero to set me free. I am sorry to everyone I have failed, but you will forgive me once I have sailed. You will come to understand what I had to endure and why I decided I no longer wanted to be here.

Crows Of Goldilocks

Fuck this porridge. Fuck this chair. Fuck. This. Bed.

Once upon a time, a young village girl named Goldilocks went for a skip, a frolic during a warm summer day. She gallivanted as her arms kept sway while her little legs coaxed her far away; into the forest's gaping mouth she danced. She spun and spun until green was a blurry circle and she lost the way to where her adventure began. With the sun burning the horizon and waking stars taking notice, Goldilocks realized she had forgotten what direction home was. Tears bloomed from her ducts; they rolled and stuck like a flash flood suddenly stopped. Doing her best to stay focused, she called out for help. Staying very relaxed, staying just as calm, she shouted and listened. No voice journeyed to her ear extended by a palm; wind was the only response in motion. By the way, her hand circled her ear, she swore she could hear the waves of the ocean, but it was just teetering trees and misguided foliage caught up in a breeze. Hyperventilating, Goldilocks fell to her knees and pressed her face into her trembling hands. Tears did not recede this time; they poured like blood gushing from a severed artery. She knew she was hopelessly lost. She knew most definitely. Scared and alone, all Goldilocks wanted was to go home.

She wept and wept, but her focus to cry could not be kept. Steady on rocking treetops, an assembly of black crows appeared mysteriously like phantoms and their sudden excessive cawing was so deafening, blood trickled from her ears and ran down her jawline. Decibels from their nightmare sirens were threatening. Sending eerie shivers down her little girl spine was more than fair warning. It was time to get her feet moving; time to find her way out of the forest of tall pine.

From the way they perched, their bodies lurched, you could tell these scavengers were starving. As she started to stand, crows began diving in unison. Spinning in a vertical spiral, they stretched their talons and pointed their beaks. Wave after wave, crows attacked, clawing and pecking at Goldilocks. She swatted with her left, with her right, doing the best she could to defend herself. Valiant effort, but she failed to protect all of her flesh. Crows tore chunks off like ripping worms from morning soil. Goldilocks looked a lot like leprosy's prisoner, but she was able to escape the murder. Hidden inside an abandoned mine, feeling safe, she stood up to straighten her spine. Cautiously she looked around. Where she was she didn't know, but it did not harbour a single crow and that was good enough for now.

It wasn't long until she realized something was wrong about that place. Something did not feel right. Struggling from the human flaw of sight at night, she was still able to tell something was awry. As she wondered why the situation still felt scary, why the crows flew sporadically like bats but wouldn't dare follow her into the cave, why the cawing was louder than before but everything seemed perfectly quiet, she knew something wasn't right. Goldilocks was beginning to feel she fled inside her own grave. And that's when she heard a menacing grunt. She turned around and saw three spectres. Cautiously waving her hand through them and realizing they were cold breaths, sent shock. They disappeared, and there emerged three angry bears. Paralysed with fear, she was locked in their instinctive stares. Knowing this was the end, she closed her eyes, held her breath, and waited for the bears to strike.

Next morning, Goldilocks was found scattered on the ground. Crows were devouring everything they could when searchers arrived. Half-eaten with limbs littered about finalized their doubt. Her golden locks were tarred with blood and her sky-blue dress was blackened with mud. No one could keep eyes locked with hers, because it looked like she was reliving the horrors, almost as if her soul was still trapped inside. The suspects were obvious. Bear tracks are distinctive and everyone knows they're capable, they're dangerous, but no set traps could ever portray as clocks; no killed bear would bring back Goldilocks. The next morning there was a funeral, the burial of a little village girl, an eight-year-old corpse by the name of Goldilocks.

Burial
(Proper Funeral Etiquette)

And they called it puppy love.

Your lips are iced blue from confessions about how much you love me. Hypothermia has that effect when my responses have been so cold, despite how many times I've been told. Permafrost on your lips should prove that I don't love you. Hasn't anyone ever explained to you why clay hearts don't beat? Shape it to any form you like; you will never hear me say *I love you*. My heart is a dud grenade; it's in remission. There will be no big explosion, no fire to rekindle our dead passion. This love you want to resuscitate is impossible because I am fond of its permanence. I will not crack open its coffin and escort it away from its own deserving burial. It's not proper funeral etiquette. We are not a love story; you're delusional. No sweet kiss will make me emotional. My lips are quicksand. I will drown you. I will swallow you until nothing is left. I will destroy you and I will not apologize for such vindictive theft. You might believe in fables, but I'm not stable. I'm busted. I simply can't be trusted. What else is there to say? Leave... me... alone. Leave me with my Medusa - unrelenting depression. I want to stay as stone. Take your pathetic "reuniting love" proposal and tell someone who doesn't prefer a burial. I'm sticking with formalities. I won't break proper funeral etiquette. That's it. I'm done with this. Listen to me carefully - I don't love you, so fuck off!

Sirens

This was an ad I wrote for PlentyOfFish.com.

S irens, they are the Grim Reapers of the sea. Sweet wing maidens, like vultures they perch themselves on high cliff-sides, patiently waiting for passing ships. Their alluring songs persuade sailors to their death. Mellisonant witchcraft entices even the largest of vessels into low tides. Huge constructs smash into rocks and sink. Entire crews drown into the bottomless drink, and emotionless Sirens watch on like stone gargoyles. Saccharine arias play as coercive whirlpools, as if their mouths were black holes pulling in anything in range of sound. When beguiling songs act as compelling gravitational pulls, no ear is deaf enough to fend off such enchanting evocations. These oceanic harpies have been here for centuries; the graveyard underneath them is their testament to time. Keen observation and loose lips is a hex, a spell that men eagerly follow into the vortex where jagged rocks bite like monstrous pointy teeth, and devour mindless slaves where mesmerized men willingly capsize themselves into their own watery grave. Not much is known about these water-bound banshees, but this carousel of temptation and destruction is infinite. It will always be, as long as there's a sailing ship. Sirens will continue to sing their death songs until a way is found to shut down their lungs and silence them for the rest of time. Many have tried and many have died; you can tell by numerous bodies floating like scattered buoys and shipwrecked corpses washed ashore that have dried. When their death toll challenges populations of stars, hope from the closest point of view can seem too far. Sometimes things are best left alone even if it means a great loss of life.

Belle And The Beast

Bestiality done right.

I am a beast once a man. I love you only like an animal can: truly and fiercely. You're a woman who rose above, saw past my curse and fell in love. When your pale skin presses against my black fur, I can see why people say you're a prisoner, not a lover. And that could have been true if you weren't able to transform my dungeon back into a castle. You're the white angel who extinguished my Hell. Damnation had me by the heart, had me at will, force-fed my hunger to kill, and oddly enough that brought me to you. I could have devoured you that night in the forest, but your innocence overcame my violence. I was entranced. Your beauty reversed the decomposition of my humanity. I came alive from what felt like decades of death because I felt the warmth of your mortal breath. My appearance still ignites folklore, but my love for you is no myth. You are my pulse, my queen, my amour. My existence still resembles the outer reaches of Hell, but torment no longer boils my blood. I am tame, obedient, almost human. I don't know what would ever become of me without you, Belle. I love you more than you could dare imagine, more than our hearts can compensate. It might be on the borderline of sin, but it's irreversibly too late. What is done is done.

My bite can't change you, but that doesn't stop us from fucking like raging animals. People can't see past my animality. They falsely accuse you of bestiality, but I'm more human than I've ever been. In a world where all eyes are closed, you can't expect anyone to understand. Hard to believe I am royalty with the way angry mobs hold their fires and shake their pitchforks at me, but it's my fault. I'm in this state to begin with because of my cruelty and I made matters worse by preying on mankind. Now you're caught up in this mess. Although I'm constantly hunted, our love will never be defeated, but since you're in love with a monster, you're forced to share the same danger. People think you're possessed by the Devil. They want to burn you for witchcraft. Because they don't understand why you love me, they want to scorch your flesh into ash. It's unfair for us. I'm finally at peace, but I'm still at war. I'm sorry you love me, but I'm glad you do. We will get through this. If I have to kill to keep you, then my claws and teeth will stay vigilant but for now, how about a kiss?

How I envy werewolves. Full moons are the cause of their metamorphosis; being alive is the cause of mine. I want to be able to turn back to my human form. It's hard to wish for that when I know I deserve this. Thankfully, I have you, Belle. Without you, the forest would be nothing but trees and corpses. I would be searching for other kingdoms to feed upon. My blood lust would be unquenchable. I just hate how you're involved in threats that can't be resolved. We should run away. Let's leave this castle, my servants who were turned into inanimate objects and vengeful warlords that once were my faithful subjects. There is nothing left for us here. Tomorrow, we will make our escape through the morning fog, sneak outside the kingdom and trudge across the forbidden bog. Past miles of forest, through days of desert sand and a gruelling ascension up the mountains, we will find a farther away land. Nothing can reverse my curse; I'll never be human. To truly live happily ever after, we can't be worrying about avoiding capture. When we're capable of catching clouds, then we know we will be safe. Let's walk into the great unknown and leave behind everything, everyone. Belle, our life is waiting for us just beyond, so kiss me, hold my paw and let's head towards the direction of home.

No Diagnosis

Funny story - turned out just to be gas.

Pills stick to my tongue; the taste leads to no diagnosis. The long swallow of each pill fails to result; my bitter prescriptions are an endless insult. Promise to correct is courtesy to dissect. I am so young. Role as a pharmacy has me ageing horribly. I'm an old man a wrinkle away from rot. Every solution is sanity-dilution. Sacrificing brain cells for blood cells, is there really any logic to this? Do I shatter my jaw to keep my mouth open even if I know it will lead to no diagnosis? Do I digest until my cerebrum swells? Pills have my thought generator circling counter-clockwise; I am beginning to meltdown from its winding. It doesn't feel right; maybe I am supposed to spin backward. If I were to suddenly overdose and my frail body dies, will I still find white labels in my red cabinet blinding? What shall become of my brain? Will it be a specimen pickling in a jar of formaldehyde? Am I to stay this course of a steady downward slide? Is my existence at all relevant? Does my significance have a name? Am I to live my entire life with no diagnosis?

Controlled by black and white swirls of this entity's hypnosis; this spiral is viral and I am its tamed victory. The professionally dressed can't find what makes me possessed. A few more suicidal episodes and I am history. Physical form is true; mental state unidentified. Analysis: Takes these pills, and these pills, and these pills. Heavily medicated, but no diagnosis. Tablet pollution, you are waste and I am your toxic dump. Poison, stay in the shape of a pill and I'll always be your faithful landfill. What choice do I have?

One thing for certain is that I am sick. My brain is a wound I wish I could lick. I am having trouble deciphering doctors from scientists. Operations have magnified, but I can't see the difference. No hope. No diagnosis. Health has fluxed its last outburst. Needles enter the fold and proceed as new experiments. I am biological matter claimed in the name of science; yet, I wait patiently for a cure in unwavering silence. White coats, my angels, my heroes, you are cutthroats, devils, foes. I am your lab rat and suffering for a cure is my cage. Mannequin status uprising; I feel nothing. Being fixed has lost my interest. You have failed miserably, but I knew that was a probability. Whatever is drowning me must have its reasons. If it refuses to heal, then it must be ideal. This worm inside me is bigger than all of us. This is why there is no diagnosis: Because it's the first of its kind. I have been chosen. I am its host. Whether this thing is or isn't for the best, I will accept what is happening to me and let it infest. And we will know its intentions by the colour of my flesh, or by the pale translucency of my ghost.

Hello, Bordello

This poem makes me feel like a dirty, old man now. Before it would give me boners, but now it's just copious amounts of shame. AND... PUBLISH.

Hello, bordello. Give me your lust, slavery, every extent of your debauchery. Your dolled-up girls: I want their sex, the leather, lace and latex. Money is no object, so flow the wine; stand your ladies in line. I'm a gentleman stuck in a broken marriage, but tonight I am a beast without a leash. I am thirsty for moist lips. I am horny, savage. I am starving for the company of a soft face, so let's powder our noses with cocaine and fuck like the world ends tomorrow. The life I live is a mistake I can't erase, but these white timelines will ease the pain. From this point on we live in the present; we forget the past and the future. Tonight, we nosedive and forget wasted time we've spent.

Hello, bordello. Is there more burlesque for this lonely fellow? Your Cyprian women are beautiful. Their luxuria is more than fruitful. They give me passion I've lost; my heart beats again. I do not care for risk, nor cost. Bottles are empty; replenish the alcohol. Forget them; I don't need rubbers. It's au naturel or nothing. I want everything to do with this place of sin. Bring me scented oils and lit cigars. I want to fuck and smoke like stars. Some call this place a cesspool, but this is a kingdom I wish to rule. Tonight, I am king of sin. Crown me. Be my subjects and subdue me. Cuff me. Dominate me. Humiliate me. Hurt me. Penetrate me. I might be king, but I'm your prisoner. Let's hold champagne high; try to reignite that sparkle in my eye. This is paradise: your corsets and thigh highs. This is Heaven: your angels of bondage and whips of sexual rage. You have me on my hands and knees. I am yours. Punish me to any degree you please.

Hello, bordello. I need more grapes for my dominatrix and another pillow. It's true. Cunts and cocks are a perfect mix. Your orgies are sublime, a perfect passing of time. There are so many room numbers: addresses to different mistresses. Every open door is a new ecstasy. Dignified women might call you a house of whores, but it's a warm place that every man adores. These women are just jealous because you have what they don't: Class. You are a dream come true and I love how your chatelaines come too. You are my escape. You are my favourite infidelity. You are my Victorian castle, my Eden of midnight activity, my crumbling sex life's trestle. I know your girls are young enough to be my daughters, that's why fucking them strangely feels like incest, but that is the exact amount of perversity I'm after. I never said I was a good man. Adultery is a bad habit of mine. My wife deserves better. Too bad she's not aware. I know I shouldn't be here, but there's nowhere else I'd rather be. You are the only thing that makes me happy. Enough talk. Give me your lust, slavery, every extent of your debauchery.

Love The Monster

If you're looking for couples counselling, you've come to the wrong place.

She grows over me like a debilitating mould. She's a reoccurring death-fungus far too cold. By her, I am severely frostbitten. I am iced blue because I am smitten. I love her but monsters don't know how to respond to such a thing. They claw and bite. They attack. Her split personalities are buzzards dining on my innards. She empties me every chance she gets. I'm frail. I'm human but she always forgets. Creatures of her calibre shouldn't exist; explain that to the putrid green corroding my heart. Decomposition is her kiss and it's breaking me apart. This love needs to be tranquilized, but her ferocity can't be neutralized. She kills me with words in the cruellest of ways and selfish actions that affect me for days and days. She makes me hard, stiff; rigour mortis makes me that way. She is my vampire and I am her blood. Sharp teeth pierce and I bleed: This is our relationship. Love, you are my damnation. Please, tear into my jugular; for once be my salvation.

I am a dying patient and she's my nurse driving the hearse. She races with sirens wailing but passes the hospital. Into a tiny graveyard in her heart, she skids to a halt. She laughs maniacally and slightly goes methodically in reverse. She wheels me out in a stretcher and pushes me into a grave. Falling into what seems like a permanent gravitational pull, I count the number of kisses she blows towards me and saliva she spits down at me as I descend and tumble. This darkness is her madness, the annihilation of our romance, space I find myself drowning in sadness. With her, there is no ascension. She's a hole; with her, it's down and nowhere else. There is no equilibrium, only vast delirium. I'd place decades between us, but love... love keeps me near. I would loosen my grip, but she's a monster I hold dear.

Tormented as sanity can be before it becomes demented, I am balancing on this line and my wobbly ankles are dented. I was always destined to fail. She is Miss Universe and I am her planetary corpse. How could I ever expect her to be mine when there are so many stars that shine? I'm a dead planet, and I can't wait for this all to be over.

No promises for potential truths; this monster only tells lies. I was handed Heaven, but somehow I'm burning in Hell. I'd like to think she loved me once, but I shouldn't dwell on what was. We've held hands, kissed and love was exchanged. Now I'm beaten, fed on and suddenly estranged. I just don't understand why she's still in my bed. Futures were planned. Our road was made. Brick by brick it began to fade. All that is left is my devotion to love and the sick mutation it gives off. She has control of me because my heart has a disturbing fetish for cancer. I tried to let her go, but her spells are strong for a young necromancer. I obey, obey, obey. No matter how many times I try to stray. I'm prey. The big picture here is that I am prey. Yesterday, today and definitely tomorrow, her teeth are embedded in my bone marrow. I'm a carcass covered in gangrene and pus, but my heart is still beating, because she's not done feeding. Monsters do exist. I'm sorry I ever believed.

She says I will always be hers. I poise myself and yell, "Never!" She grabs me by the throat, lifts me up against the wall, stares at me with a malevolent grin and whispers into my ear, "This is forever."

Infant

Me: "This isn't half bad." *writes the last sentence* "What a piece of shit."

At the top of a twisted tree, an infant sleeps. Contorted branches are slithered around him like protective pythons. Tightly coiled by layers upon layers he is safely cradled, guarded so vigilantly as if he was the source of life itself. For years he has slept peacefully past many moons and many suns. God only knows what dreams the infant keeps. He is unaware of the outside world because his eyes have never opened. He just sleeps in his nest of branches and leaves, avoiding nightmares that dare him to believe there is more to life than remission. He is not phased. He knows such a thought deceives. What is wrong with chasing and counting sheep? It's the perfect way to spend an eternity. There is nothing wrong with tranquility. The age of the infant is unknown, but if his interior was anything like his Mother Tree, we would see rings around his bones. Alas, he is nestled away and out of reach. From that height, danger is hushed and by the wind the infant continues to rock gently. Severe weather has tried to destroy, to break, force apart the loyal pythons and have the cradle fall with sleeping infant and all, but devotion to keep his eyes closed thwarted any plan that dare opposed. Until the end of time he will dream and never know of the darkness that surrounds him. Safe and sound above the ground, his tiny red heart will softly pound. He will capture our imaginations because we can not capture his. And maybe one day when the entire world forgets about him, we'll be able to focus on our own dreams and conquer them.

Troll Of All Whores

Yes. HER. Again.

Your skin is soft because you bathe in milk. The stench burns the senses because the milk is sour. Your auburn hair is tied by a long stem from a flower, but the wild rose that blooms is wilted. Beauty tears away at you. You are the walking dead. I've swam in your sea of red: all the drama from past lovers still buoyant. Come down from your pedestal. You're just flesh that's expired and stagnant. Stun gods? Hardly. You're alive. Barely. Eclipsed by the shadow of your former self, you can't see truth past your own outline. Arrogance draws a fine line to ignorance; you're wedged in this vise and you're smiling. You are standing straight with a crooked spine. On the outside you're stunning, but I see through your cunning. You're a fucking disaster. I know because I fell victim to this. Your heart is black and oily. No operation needed. Remember? You're dead. A heart like that is expected and there would be no recovery after the surgery, because underneath the scalpel you're an autopsy. Can't you see you're the troll of all whores?

I've tried to reminisce about you, but it only reopens old wounds. I've ached to extend my fingers to touch your essence, but vomit always interrupts when I think of your presence. You are a troll. The troll of all whores. I feel sorry for you. I'm sorry you've never known love, only warts and sores. Carnivorous little man-eater, your demons will one day turn on you. A predator lurks and I hope his attack hurts, it fucking kills. You have mastered the taboo language of sex and you've devoured many under this complex. How you still walk on two fucking legs is a fucking miracle. If you shake the wasps' nest long enough you're bound to get stung, but you're a clever troll that knows how to keep men following along. Should I be your slayer?

Seems only fitting since I am the only one who has ever bitten back. Should I put you out of your misery, or allow you to spread your legs and unleash disease? There is plenty of animosity between us. We are bitter exes swinging battleaxes. One of us is destined to perish. I have been known to be a snake; my venom could draw us even. I can make you fall in love with me, then one bite and you're dying. A troll versus a snake; let's see how this plays out.

Your move, you fucking whore.

Atom And Eve

If you like pina coladas...

Nuclear war looms, so bring out your brooms and prepare to sweep up the dead. Inevitable death is not a theory; we are on the verge of being history. A push of a button. A push of a button and we're forgotten. When insanity dictates there are consequences and their actions will birth billions of corpses. A bomb named Atom will destroy in waves, and as I give warning this could be the eve, the last day we stand before falling in mass graves. The apocalypse is the extension of an index finger. To stop obliteration requires the same act. How else do you stop madmen? Their agility to escape assassination is fact. It's as if they are invisible, invincible. They are like ghosts, ghosts who are capable of unleashing Hell. The launch of an atom bomb is not war. It's the beginning of the end. What goes up must descend. I fear this is the eve of goodbye; tomorrow we are all going to die. Fireballs of great enormity will engulf us. Our skeletons will vaporize underneath a blacked-out sun and any memory of what civilizations lived here will be gone. An atom bomb promise. The eve of no life as we know it. The thought of being a lamb surrounded by wolves is frightening. The longer I wait the sooner I want to be devoured. Dreaming of a Utopian existence has soured. Paranoia inside me is rabid and has overpowered. I want to be a terrorist's sacrifice. I don't but do I really have a choice? Someone tear out my eyes; I don't want to see the death in front of me. One atom will multiply into thousands of fiery meteors. Today could be the eve of any last and remaining survivors. Tomorrow the sun will rise up past the horizon and that's when you reach for a loaded gun, because I fear suicide is the only way out of this. Tomorrow just might be our last day on Earth.

Wooden Son

Ah... The sound of a living puppet screaming while burning alive makes me so wet.

Liar, liar, pants on fire; your self-combustion burns down forests. Your carefully carved tongue never rests. Tell truths or close your mouth. There is a reason why your father insists. How do you ever expect to be loved? It's bad enough you're made out of wood. Nobody wants to hold you; you aren't worth the splinters you create. Be more admirable. Be honest. Be thankful you don't need strings to be animate. Justify your worth with truth, or your existence dies with your lies. What a fairy does is never permanent. You're almost a boy on the verge of being a puppet. There is a reason why your only friend is a cricket. Change your ways, or risk being firewood. Your father loves you more than you know. Deceit accomplishes nothing, only on how far your little nose will grow. Pinocchio, join the human race. Be the son your father always wanted. Do you want every expression on your face drawn on? Do you want to be lifeless and clothed in rags? Do you want your pulse to be nothing more than strings? If you ever want to be real, if you want to be flesh and bone, if you want a heart, if you want to be loved, then start choosing your words wisely and be a good son. It's up to you what you want to do. Better make a decision fast, because your father is running out of wood and he needs to replenish the fireplace. Cold nights can make men do desperate things and having you as a son might not outweigh the heat you will bring. Do you want to be a bed of coals? Because ashes are in your future. Pinocchio, it's up to you. Keep your nose small or live not at all.

The Insanity Of John Doe

Hi. My name is Liian Varus. Nice to meet you.

I am nobody's son. I am a creation of an unknown creator. I am a bastard. What is love? You're looking at a pure hater. Home doesn't exist. I am searching for a graveyard. What is sleep? I tuck myself into bed inside my wrist; insomnia convinces eyes to peek through the slit. Veins and arteries coil around me soundly. In this crowsnest's of life supply, strangulation is the best way to die. Severing ties is also alluring. A machete is an angel of excruciating amputations and I want to stand between it and botched separations. I have two hands. I can spare another. Mutilation is a perfect reason to suffer. It is clockwork with forced asphyxiation. And what kind of person would want to be maimed? The exact same person who wishes not to be named. An abomination doesn't need to be known. Identities don't reveal themselves when altered by disfigurements. I am a future corpse found hidden facedown in deadfall. I am a life always short of breath and I'm at a slow crawl. Worthless; I am John Doe.

Whispers of humanity are too soft to hear. This joyous unification will never occur because I am a fucking monster. Gangrene surfaces as if I were Frankenstein. Ownership of my soul can be questioned, but this body... this body is undoubtedly mine. Zombies do walk above ground, but I can't help feeling buried alive. This sums up everything: Confusion is a starting gun; insanity is the finish line and I'm about to dance on a landmine. Does this mean I have won? Two legs propel me like mankind intended. This is not how I balance on the food chain. Logic devolves into prehistoric instincts when ruined by deformities. I prefer hunting on hands and knees. Killing on fours is how the foam in my mouth stays red. I am a fucking beast of monstrosities! Does it fucking matter how badly I'm marred?! Does it fucking matter how badly I'm scarred?! I am John Doe! None of you mother fuckers even know who I am! John Doe is not my name. A toe tag will tell you otherwise. My death will be an ending without goodbyes and if there is any hope for this writhen organism, if all my personalities reunite and break from their schism, maybe my funeral won't be so inhumane. Not fucking likely.

One day someone will find me facedown amongst deadfall and no coroner will be able to confirm my existence with a name. And when no human living thing comes to claim, they will finish their report by dotting puzzling question marks. I will be declared as 'John Doe,' a life and death no one will ever know.

Madness must never have a face.

Ghost In My Room

Don't mix your meds, kids.

A pulse is meant for living; bloodletting is for more than giving. Surgically cloning arteries isn't multiplicity; it's the cause of your ghost in my room. Scarification had a deeper vendetta. Behind blue eyes was a desperate simplicity: death in response to a loveless heart. How could you question my obedience? Your shallow sense of truth is now bottomless in your shallow grave. You are proof, death lets no one rest. Midnight-moans keep me up late at night; I've forgotten the sound of utter silence. Every night you haunt me by re-enacting a last moment on Earth. With your dead fingers shoved into my eyes, you've convinced me to be your audience. I see my lover's tragedy displayed. I see the aftermath of a woman decayed. I see a ghost in my room, a lady I once passionately knew. Love is everything I have for you; blood loss is what you gave me. Heartache reigns because of suicide reminders. For every red droplet spilled, my skin turns another shade of pale. And I know you won't stop until my sanity surrenders. But I am resilient. I am having trouble differentiating between what's real and what's not. Are you really a ghost in my room, or am I the apparition who is a descendant from a body of rot? I can't concentrate over screams echoed by your white noise. Sorrow and anguish vibrate my skeleton into specks of dust. Weakened by a woman's scorn, I harden as my heart materializes into a frail block of rust. She's killing me for a betrayal I never committed. I won't bow to her. I won't crucify my wrists for her satisfaction. I won't! But I would be lying if I said I wasn't tempted. Our fairy tale romance was a most beautiful obsession; your jealousy has damned it into a demonic possession. Felicity, ghost in my room, please stop this nightmare. Her, you, she, you, Felicity, ghost in my room, do you love me? You don't have to enslave me because I am already your prisoner. I love you. This felo-de-se theatre you star in has to end. The carousel of your demise is something I can't comprehend. Stop this! Please, settle your hand into mine. I promise things will turn out fine. You, her, you, she, ghost in my room, Felicity, if your hatred can't be tamed I must be really the one to blame. If you can't forgive me, then I beg you to have your vengeance. Finish your descent into madness and show me fear without mercy, because if my spirit will calm your soul I will happily join you in the afterlife. With you eternally, I will be the other ghost in the room.

Suffer, Kate Ing

Wordplay is so suffocating to literature.

My fingers tiptoe up and down the sides of your neck. Like a ballet interlude before a murder, they slide and twist as they form to respective hands. As our eyes struggle for supremacy, anger grasps your throat harder and harder. Cruelty does not accept one's submission; it demands. Ambidextrous weapons are coiling pythons. Suffer, Kate Ing! Suffer! Suffer, Kate Ing! Suffer! Bulging eyes flow rivers of fear. Drowning in sadness, there is no air to rise for. Is this how you want me to hold you, dear? Illuminating through soft texture, bruising spreads like a necklace. This jewellery may have no worth, but it complements your pretty face. Choking, choking; past your lips, your tongue is poking. Screams try to call for a hero. Villainy counts heroic attempts: zero. Suffer, Kate Ing! Suffer! Suffer, Kate Ing! Suffer! No one is coming to save you. Chivalry exempts whores.

A music box performs the perfect score. You can almost hear children laughing at the blood gurgling from the back of your throat. Are you listening? This is your opera. Crushing your trachea, this is me combating your aorta. How does betrayal feel? Suffer, Kate Ing! Suffer! Suffer, Kate Ing! Suffer! With the chameleon appeal of your face, with alternating colours from blue to black, you are my mood ring and I'm feeling a little jealous. You are my mood ring and I'm feeling a little zealous. Suffer, Kate Ing! Suffer! Suffer, Kate Ing! Suffer! Do you regret everything? I might. Premature breaths have no extension; they are oxygen illusions under heavy tension. Asphyxiation drags circulation to a halt. Your death could be considered my fault, but acid melts fingerprints. You'll be dead; I'll be a ghost. There will be no suspects, just you very quiet in your white dress. So, as you can see, you'll be dead, I'll be a ghost.

How fitting: bruises on your neck match the bruises on your thighs. Elevation of damage unveils your true self: a piece of fruit rotting. Suffer, Kate Ing! Suffer! Suffer, Kate Ing! Suffer! Love is supposed to be a full circle; you u-turned from guy to guy. Half hearts don't play well with others, so tonight you are going to die. Siphoning out your breaths with this cold embrace, two ex-lovers say goodbye underneath satin covers. An eyelid collapses over one eye. Suffer, Kate Ing! Suffer! Suffer, Kate Ing! Suffer! Volcanic eruptions of desperation calming into blood pooling in your mouth tells me death has vacated your pulse. Don't matter; you can't escape my perversion. You will be my one-night-attraction and I'll be sodomy disguised as a bachelor. I am going to fuck your corpse. I will fuck you like the dirty whore that you are. Latex protects the ghost. Latex secures the final insult. Kate Ing, to me, you can never suffer enough. Be thankful you're dead.

Bloodlines

You're about to read a poem about incest. Not any kind of incest, but conjoined twins incest. What? This book wouldn't be complete without a little brother/sister action... I'm so thrilled you're almost done reading this book. Sick of explaining shit all the time.

Ageing has caught up with us. We might be confined to a wheelchair, but my heart races like adrenalin. My pulse goes electric when we hold hands. Love doesn't fade with terminable lifespans; love is forever. However, time entraps everyone. On the verge of dying, it's just us because nobody else cares. Abandonment brought us too close together; it makes sense to die as unwanted orphans. Nothing is tighter than how our hearts are tethered. Nothing is redder than these red, red organs. We have always been outcasts and exiled; we've repaired the damage that had compiled. White tourniquets applied froze the bleeding of loneliness. Plastic tubes wove our hearts to a disapproving closeness. Love transfusions bounce back and forth; our romance is a continuous cycle of rebirth. That is our immortality.

Unacceptable behaviour has been endlessly repeated and preached. We understand between right and wrong; we were prepared for the disadvantages of our relationship. No one understands the explanation I've exited past my lips: Separation would be a pale horse licking our hearts until they've bleached. Untying a tandem is death unravelling. Don't flatten knots; we're not ready to come crashing down. Thick stitches are not a solution for what's torn; it will cause blood clots. Complications from surgery are unpredictable. Anything can happen, especially when both patients are physically worn. Many beg for a curtain call of this freak show. Opinions dull as theirs are ignored. Who are they? And what the fuck do they know? Their minds are slammed closed. Doors can't hide what is already exposed. If God loves everyone, then why do they try to drag us underneath his feet? Are you not his daughter? Am I surely not his son? Is it true? Are his demands really something we can't meet? Are we to be crushed?

We are conjoined twins. We are brother and sister; love is our criminal offence. Bloodlines are thicker than water. Sharing the same blood supply means this can't be disputed and sweat pouring from our arousal has undoubtedly contributed. The junction of our spines allows us to kiss. Both blessed with two sets of hands lets fingers wander and touch. When we sleep we're comforted by complementing heartbeats. Genetic flaws gave the opportunity but they, all of them birthed this monstrosity. And they dare judge their own creation? We're not irascible, nor vengeful. We thank them for the seventy years of incest. What we have is something beautiful. No grudges are held. Decades of insulting our lineage are nearing an end. Only a few days obstruct us from awaiting our deathbed's glow. Death is a travelling salesman; we will buy what he's selling. At last, their souls will be consoled when our fingers and toes have lost all feeling. Our body is reaching its expiry date, but love has made us ageless. Incest is permanence. We won't be forgotten because they spent all this time remembering to hate us. We know courting your sibling comes with no acceptance. Sometimes that's all there is. A mutation left us limits and we're happy we crossed them.

Bleacher

She's the Mr. Clean Magic Eraser of everyone's self-esteem.

Red blush powdered on porcelain masks beautifies dangerous creatures. White dresses fashion-hide scales and other failed ostentatious features. Disguises won't protect you anymore. I see right through, whore. The cave you dwell in is a crystal dollhouse. Cracks spreading from thrown rocks prove you haven't changed. Victims can't handle the sensation of fading pigmentation: that is why my shadow sways around like an innocent man hanged. Lurking around your fragile castle, I'm waiting for the moment you supersede your reputation. Blending in with ghosts is a lifestyle I can't reconcile. Prepare me for a makeshift funeral. This leeching given to me is terminal.

Bleacher, I'm pale.
Impale.
Stake me.
Be my Van Helsing.
Bleacher, I'm pale.
Impale.
Stake me.

I'm your vampire embracing. Your black eyes are holes I fell in. I'm still falling. Further, I fall the more I'm winter. Your love has an allure like no other. Acidic qualities you drip corroded colours; theatre-white is a scab I once called skin. We held hands and pulled ourselves close. We crossed fingers and I held my tongue. Words couldn't describe what I was feeling. Eyes bulged when I saw myself decompose. A carnivorous pale engorged itself and expanded, as beige extremities submitted to peeling.

Representation as Cinderella can't be matched; your facade reveals when interaction is scratched. Fairytale promises you spoke of were submersible; I drowned in your lies of what I thought was ideal. So here I am at your tempered door pleading for a mercy kill.

Bleacher, impale.
I'm pale.
Stake me.
Bleacher, impale.
I'm pale.
Stake me.
Stake me.
Bury me.
I'm begging you to end this.

I was a tall, tall figure. Because of you, I'm of small stature. Arc of shame has me replicating a tombstone. Accessorize me with a hand-dug grave. Broken fingernails stuck in the soil will remind me there's no escape. Vanishing in a casket will prove to me you've won. As I look up I am greeted by your Halloween face, your sinister grin. I see my humanity wedged between your teeth. Was I worth those morsels, cannibal? Is it gratifying that I am struggling to breathe? On my hands and knees, I am Death's pale horse. Another decrease in hue, I will become your corpse. All I wanted to do was be with you. Now I'm shaded as purgatory. I should have known your mask was self-explanatory. Yet, for some reason I let you bewitch me. So here I am, a snowman forlorn at your feet. There you are, sadistic with no sign of retreat. Lesson learned: Some witches can't be burned. It's time for you to end this. We are not dearly departed, so finish what you started. Bleacher, I'm pale. Impale. Bathe me in red tidal waves. Bury severed limbs in different graves. I don't fucking care. Just end this peroxide nightmare.

Bleacher, stake me!

Stake me!
Stake me!!
STAKE ME!!!

LIIAN VARUS TAKES ADVANTAGE OF EVOLUTION

At this point in my poetic career, depression and creativity had a great working relationship. Was a lot like that movie *Pretty Woman*, or was it *I Spit On Your Grave*? Not sure. I constantly get those two mixed up. Hold on. None of those are *The Shawshank Redemption*. I'm too drunk to be typing this out right now. Carrying on. I never had writer's block. There was always a story, an extension of vocabulary as if a box of Alpha-Bits cereal was shoved inside a cock pump - oh, grow up. Wordplay and metaphors came out of me... I'll let your imagination run with that one. My mental illness and I were in unison. A lot of 2011 made it into *Oh, To Be Human* so unfortunately all that amazing shit about teamwork I've been talking about, you don't get any of that. You get the aftermath of what happens when synergy is propelled by heavy drinking and unattended sexual frustration - so essentially most of my 20's. As the year went on, I felt if I stayed the path, it would be only a matter of time before my poetry got noticed, and maybe, depression would finally give up its plans of taking me out altogether. Nope. That fucking asshole still rolls its eyes at me, pretending to slit its throat like it's the goddamn Undertaker. It's not as threatening as it used to be, but I can't let my guard down. Never again.

Home (Lost Horizon)

Remember that book - Are You My Mother? It plays out like that, but there's no happy ending. Why? Because life isn't yogurt rainbows and sponge cake unicorns. It's shit. Just absolute shit. Kidding. It's so fucking great. Was that sarcasm? You bet your ass it was.

Cold palms supporting broken fingers. Incessantly-chewed nails pointing in every direction. Eyes spinning out of control; calculating. Which way do I go? Must I butcher myself into an irreparable dissection? Split personalities of flesh can journey their own route. I'll chase the blood flow. Expansion to accommodate my compass of growing confusion is how I'll hope to find my way back home. 360º rotation. Which path should blistered feet roam? I've travelled endlessly. Is there no horizon to this odyssey? Sunshine must rise somewhere. Losing faith to venture forward drags tornado-eyes downward. Holding a shovel speared into earth defines *desperation*. The tip of its spade is my arrow home. Secretly, me trenching is a death plot: disorientation whispering to me where to roam. Open sky flares curiosity. Wingless attempts to soar means I can't fly. Confined by the laws of gravity, I can never venture upward. Accepting this fact says I'm letting myself die. I'm going to occupy my private graveyard and forget any chance of finding home. This could be realistic. Maybe I don't really have a place to go. Maybe there's no need why I should roam. Tunnelling a passage into darkness, you will forgive my response to distress. You will forgive me because I am your son. I am your sun searching for the lost horizon.

Lust Hunts Me Down Like Feral Dogs

I am not a rapist.

Lust hunts me down like feral dogs. Female prospects surround me with bare knees on the ground. Composure often than not eludes, it fogs. Thinking blurs straight across; my dick makes a curious sound. Sadistic instincts are aroused by hormones; caveman ancestry quickly boils from pheromones. Back to human basics, I struggle to stay evolved; women stalk closer when friendly traits are dissolved. Lust hunts me down like feral dogs. Parasitical persuasion dines on the brain and parasitical brains devour tender hearts. Every day I battle to stop such organ cannibalism. Every day I'm killed in action and look for chances to orgasm. My mercy's sorcery is warlock-powerful, but lust hunts me down like feral dogs. Sometimes I must touch something beautiful. Promiscuity sodomizes monogamy, that's why I feel bent over all the time. This vertigo puppeteers my anatomy. This Pinocchio wants to fuck other puppets, other wooden dolls posable as cheap sluts. Sex conflicts and comforts me. Illicit decisions make me horny and flaccid simultaneously. People spend their entire lives searching for love; I've found it so many fucking times I've had enough. I now spit on Cupid's face and lick between his mother's thighs. Lust hunts me down like feral dogs. Who am I to run away from such a formidable foe? Matrimony is a fairy tale. I don't live lies. I'll never be behind the prison bars of wedlock, not while my cock craves an unchaste lip-lock. Lust hunts me down like feral dogs; I lead the pack and fuck everyone, anyone, everything. I'm just a barbaric sex fiend underneath gentleman's clothes. I do what I can to hide the testosterone-fuelled deviant, but lust hunts me down like feral dogs. I am a weak, weak man holding on to very little constraint. The head of my cock shadows my heart. Love can't penetrate past pornographic intentions. Intimacy with libidinous strangers directs my erections because seduction is savage and wild. Lust hunts me down like feral dogs and tears me apart as so. True love stands no chance against animalistic behaviour. When human relations turn raw and bestiality feels familiar, then why bother convincing myself I'm more than primal? I can't follow 21st-century human expectancies because I walk on all fours. Don't you see? I am an animal. Perverted encounters and ecstasies are tendencies; they are ejaculation promises I hold in high regard. As long as my throbbing cock hardens, I will always be lust's feral dog. Love will never lift depraved visions from a woman's cunt to her heart. It is how it is, for I am a rapist.

Burrower

There's no harm in hoping you come across buried treasure when digging yourself a hole to die in.

Fingernails clawed and situated themselves into my back, and there you are gripping my spine; there you are wrecking my vertical basis. Whirling vertebrae in the air to a rare degree of madness, I ask myself when will she draw the line. Crawling without a backbone, shifting like a severed torso attempting to stand, slithering as a dying snake would, it seems I'm yours for the taking. Confidence isn't where it should be. Exposed capillaries flourish; blood loss will tap my heart until it's breaking. Will you take a quick moment and fix? The gaping canyon on my back could use a few licks. Stitches would be a thoughtful gesture. Please sew me up; suture. Repair this wound so I can squirm how a worm is meant to. Writhing in dirt I can see you're not my lover. You are a poor man's conqueror. Squashed butterflies don't flutter; dead love leaves no traces of sympathy. Blinded by witchcraft facades, I've become the mole you've wanted me to be. Posing with one foot on my back, you're over. Taunting with one foot on my back, I'm under. Face-first in mud, I am a burrower. Kick me. Kick me down farther. Encourage me to tunnel and I will leave you. Humiliate me with another boot to my ribs and I'll dig to see how far agony goes. Yell at me like you do and I will rest. Deep into the earth I will submit and decompose. For you, the world. For you, the universe. You lick my spinal cord and say, "I've got everything I need."

Deface My Identity
(Romance-Scissors)

Deface my identity with your romance-scissors. Carve, mutilate, cut me down to size; gouge flesh to make me acceptable in your eyes. Ageing traumatic events stand vigilant like loyal scars should. Without hesitation, I would surrender you my skin. Impossible. However, deface my identity and I'll be your loyal identical twin. Disfigure me until I'm unknown, until blemishes need to be sewn. Maim and magnify, until we see eye-to-eye. Love works in mysterious ways, so let me be your mirror image before our youth grows and decays.

We are both half of one pure heart. Do not insult what we have; tear my face apart. Mar, scar, go too far. Stab with purpose. Clone your misfortunes with haste. Time is precious, something you don't waste. Peel muscle off my skull; release the monster you know so well. Do whatever it takes to make certain, we will eternally share the same burden. I am yours; do you hear? As long as our reflections complement one another, you will always be mine. Do you hear me, my dear? Nothing can stop this freak show. As dismembered as we are, we will always both be half of one pure heart.

Honour me with this act of uncensored love. Take this scalpel and reduce vanity to a despicable degree; kill the handsome me and birth light on my new monstrosity. Deface my identity. Let's live as things forgotten. Knife-sculpted faces mask any probability; no one will recognize us. While you deepen amorous incisions, kiss me where it hurts. Lick your lips and comfort bleeding lesions. Deface my identity, until we've both vanished like ghosts.

Thrust romance-scissors in sporadic spurts; hide me where you swore you've died. Bold scarification denies facial reconstruction, so widen my smile a mile longer. Surgical prowess performed with emotions raw, you've proven love can conquer. Celebratory exclamation begins by adding another flaw. Deface my identity. Let's leave this place. I am your chameleon. You are my surroundings; camouflage me as you see things. Love me harder than you ruin and let's live like we are the last two people alive, the last two people in this world. Let's live how we intended: together and blissfully.

The world is a hateful place; let's abandon it all behind our faces. As monsters-developed, let's walk into distant shadows and leave behind the human race.

Creatures devoted is humanity evolved.
We truly are people amongst a planet of apes.

Rabbit Holes

Curiouser and curiouser.

In pursuit of Wonderland, I've poked my head down hundreds of rabbit holes. Scar tissue marks my face and hands from countless times bitten. Don't laugh. You don't seem to understand. Wonderland is not folklore; I've been there once before. But alas, it's elusive as a clear thought lost in a hallucination. Could I be endangering myself with my own imagination? No. Wonderland is not folklore; I've been there once before.

Productivity flashing an unorthodox style; locating the White Rabbit is taking awhile. Wearing a tuxedo of furs from rabbits I've skinned is a fashionable outcome from frail sanity thinned. Gallons of blood with no pocket watch to show for: What a waste of bloody time. Another candidate, another slit throat: no white rabbit in a waistcoat. Dementia in season; irrationality is reason. Proof emanates from blood loss staining the moss beneath me. Bite after bite, more saliva seeps in. Rabies fits just right but rudely interferes again and again. Intruding into rabbit holes worsens my condition, but there is no other way. Wonderland or death? Eroding internally won't hinder me from searching. Until I huff out my last breath I will always choose Wonderland.

Eat this; drink that. I've perfected swallowing, not like it matters. Not like I see Mad Hatters, March Hares, or Dormice. Just an unattended party without hot tea, that is what I see. In relation to mercury poisoning, rabies makes the Hatter and I in relation. Madness strikes at will. Consequently, we've fallen from our lost heads; permanently we're crawling into our deathbeds. Or at least I am. Difference is, he's hosting six o'clock tea parties in Wonderland and I'm reaching into a rabbit hole with a skeleton hand.

Yet, I stay optimistic. With so many rabbit holes I'm bound to tumble down one. I swear I'm not crazy; my logic is just lazy.

A smile first and a purple cat after; in-between transitions I want to hear his laughter. Dear Cheshire, I miss your sporadic salutations and impossible riddle invitations. Will we ever converse again? Restricted speech trapped behind a foaming mouth makes it unlikely. Paralysis mummifying me adds to complications. However, I may find you upside down in the next of endless rabbit holes. If not, then I'll send you a letter via sign language. Oh! And dear Cheshire, if I expire, please tell the Red Queen I still think she's a bitch. Thanks. Yours fondly, a friend dying to see you.

Kicked at the knees, I trip; paralysis saddles me and rides me nowhere. Motionless. No rabbit holes. Bleeding unmercifully in one spot means Caterpillar cannot lose me in broken thought. Coiled on an arcing mushroom, we blew smoke at boredom and into billowing conversations. Colours we puffed flew up into inexplicable constellations, where he inspired me with his wisdom and excerpts from literature known only to him. Why I ever left Wonderland, that is something I will never understand.

Farewell to all my mad friends. To the unmentionables and unthinkables, I'll miss you just as much except the Red Queen, because she truly is a bitch.

Death sailing in my mouth of foam emerges promptly on my heart's shores. I'm too deteriorated to return home. Affliction inhabits every one of my pores. Curled up. Staring at unexplored rabbit holes. Left eye following the right eye as it rolls. Dying, I see why I never escaped. Madness is a gift, a gift I've not yet earned, but I am defiant because I know, I swear Wonderland is not folklore. I've been there once before. Sanity may say otherwise, but sanity never stepped through the looking glass. Besides me, there was Alice, my mother. Rabies killed her too as she tried to find her way back: Like schizophrenic mother like schizophrenic son. How many more of us have to die before the madness is gone?

LIIAN VARUS TRANSCENDS

Congratulations! You've made it. This is the last stop. No need to adjust those pretty eyes of yours - the year is 2014. Everything I had written in 2012 and 2013 was way too good for this trash heap. There's two chapters you won't have to suffer through. You're welcome. Must be your lucky day. Breathe. Breathe a sigh of relief. Pat yourself on the back. Well done. You did amazing. You slayed the beast. Regrettably, it's the end of our adventure together, my friend. I'm sorry I never got the chance to know you. I talk too much. Maybe in another life, another book, you can tell me everything about you. I know my sense of humour hides deeper fragments of me. I hope you were able to capture me as a familiar face amongst the chaos. I see us as friends. Friends stick together. If you can stick out this Hell with me, then we are truly friends. Alas, I must keep going. This is only a prequel to a much greater problem. Darker roads lay ahead. *Oh, To Be Human* - such tragedy, we weave. So - *Good Night, Titan Arum, And Farewell*, by the time you reach me, I'll be basking in the light at the end of the tunnel or submerged in another pitfall that I just might not be able to write myself out of. But life is crazy. No matter what happens to me, we will see each other again... one day... Bring beer.

Debate

Excuse me while I ruin the book with politics.

Serpentine tongue in libertine cheek; I've crossed the morality line again. I don't give a fuck. Oops, looks like I struck another nerve. Stunned in disbelief, you mutter something about taking a stand. But no one steals a point of view like me, not this cynical thief.

You threaten me on how my ignorance makes me blind. But I'm ignorant, so in actuality, I see just fine. Parliaments can burn as I believe was always their true purpose. Marshmallows in the hot gallows; I've got my roasting stick.

Urgently pleading to me about the importance of voting, you beg to inspire me from your knees. I'm sorry. My opinion does not waver. Re-elects and candidates never do anything worth noting. Besides, my dick isn't even hard, so I don't know why you're down there anyway.

I want dead politicians and the thickening of morticians' wallets. I want corruption sealed in body bags: building blocks for a fantastical mausoleum. Pandora's Box constructed from which I can only describe as fucked up LEGO: Sometimes I get lost in that beautiful dream. Up for a game of Jenga, mister? Come on, before the tower eats the sun. Let's overthrow this empire of fixed cards. Kings, queens on the bottom; jokers on top. With our revolutionary swords drawn, we can watch the sun pass through and marvel at a sky never so blue. Oh, wait. I forgot. You're trying to convert me to your view of things. I apologize.

Well, it looks like we're at a stalemate. However, if you fuck off you can have the checkmate. Come on, mister. This debate is dry; my brain is chapped. And for whatever reason, you're still on your knees. Listen, mister. You have your opinions and I have mine. Don't get me wrong, I do appreciate your oral fixation, but I think I'll stick with masturbation.

As We Watch Blood Cascade Into Our Glass Hearts

I wrote this poem for my wife while we were dating. I don't dare make fun of it. I'm crazy, not stupid.

Holding hands as we watch blood cascade into our glass hearts. From the back of our soft-spoken tongues, behind words we use to describe admiration confessed, we stare at love spilling, filling, making us whole, making us one. As we watch blood cascade into our glass hearts, we see the strength of our future in these ramparts, these structures where lovers stand tall with lips pressed. Fragility may concern, but with blood so thick, our steadfast adoration lies encased in brick. Permanence could not be any more secure. And from time to time, yes, life's obstacles with their tiny hammers may attempt, may force them to exercise their right to be unjustly righteous. They may take sledgehammer-swings. They may tap but it will be to no avail because there's no one quite like us. We are simply meant to be.

Red falling to the whims of our hearts' calling; there's no place I'd rather be than right here. Red gushing to the whims of our hearts' blushing; there's no place than right next to you, my dear. Red flowing to the whims of our hearts' glowing. Red crashing to the whims of our hearts' splashing. Red storming to the whims of our hearts' warming. This is exactly how love should be expressed, and it's ours, all ours.

As we watch blood cascade into our glass hearts, we stare in awe at a romance people would kill for. As we watch blood cascade into our glass hearts, we ready to dive headfirst into a purity not seen in an eternity.

Locking eyes, whispering sweet promises, laughing politely, holding so tightly, we coil the vice of this embrace. Kissing slow to the streams of blood flow, we dive headfirst into our glass hearts.

Underneath the blood cascade, we don't swim like smitten strangers; we drown as Shakespearean-written lovers because that's love: all or nothing.

I can't believe you fucking read this book.

DRAW A PICTURE...
HOW DID THIS BOOK MAKE YOU FEEL?

Send your drawing to

www.facebook.com/LiianVarusPoetry

to be featured.

Made in the USA
Middletown, DE
03 February 2022

60405090R00246